# Matrimonial Finance Handbook

Other titles available from Law Society Publishing:

**Open Justice and Privacy in Family Proceedings**
David Burrows

**Matrimonial Finance Toolkit**
Mena Ruparel

**Family Law Agreements and Consent Orders**
Stephen Parker

**Family Law Arbitration, 2nd edition**
Dennis Sheridan and Suzanne Kingston

**Unbundling Family Legal Services Toolkit**
Ursula Rice and Mena Ruparel

**Family Law Protocol, 4th edition**
The Law Society

Titles from Law Society Publishing can be ordered from all good bookshops or direct (telephone 0370 850 1422, or visit our online shop at **www.lawsociety.org.uk/bookshop**).

# MATRIMONIAL FINANCE HANDBOOK

Mena Ruparel MCIArb

All rights reserved. No part of this publication may be reproduced in any material form, whether by photocopying, scanning, downloading onto computer or otherwise without the written permission of the Law Society except in accordance with the provisions of the Copyright, Designs and Patents Act 1988. Applications should be addressed in the first instance, in writing, to Law Society Publishing. Any unauthorised or restricted act in relation to this publication may result in civil proceedings and/or criminal prosecution.

The author has asserted the right under the Copyright, Designs and Patents Act 1988 to be identified as author of this work.

Whilst all reasonable care has been taken in the preparation of this publication, neither the publisher nor the author can accept any responsibility for any loss occasioned to any person acting or refraining from action as a result of relying upon its contents.

The views expressed in this publication should be taken as those of the author only unless it is specifically indicated that the Law Society has given its endorsement.

© The Law Society 2020

Crown copyright material is reproduced with the permission of the Controller of Her Majesty's Stationery Office

ISBN-13: 978-1-78446-142-3

Published in 2020 by the Law Society
113 Chancery Lane, London WC2A 1PL

Typeset by Columns Design XML Ltd, Reading
Printed by Hobbs the Printers Ltd, Totton, Hants

The paper used for the text pages of this book is FSC® certified. FSC (the Forest Stewardship Council®) is an international network to promote responsible management of the world's forests.

# Contents

*Preface* ix
*Table of cases* xi
*Table of statutes* xiii
*Table of statutory instruments* xv
*Table of international legislation* xix
*Abbreviations* xxi

**1　Pre-instruction** **1**

   1.1　The client's journey – meeting your client for the first time　1
   1.2　Freelance and unregulated services　2
   1.3　Regulatory matters in brief　3
   1.4　Matters to consider　5
   1.5　Different charging models　6
   1.6　How clients pay for solicitors' time　8
   1.7　Non-court dispute resolution options　18
   1.8　At the end of the first meeting　18

**2　Non-court dispute resolution** **20**

   2.1　Introduction　20
   2.2　List of non-court dispute resolution processes　21
   2.3　Mediation information and assessment meeting　21
   2.4　Mediation　25
   2.5　Collaborative family practice　29
   2.6　Arbitration　31
   2.7　Early neutral evaluation/private financial dispute resolution　34
   2.8　Solicitors' negotiation　36
   2.9　Summary　39

**3　Disclosure** **40**

   3.1　Introduction　40
   3.2　The principle of disclosure　40
   3.3　Disclosure in practice　42

|   |      |                                                              |     |
|---|------|--------------------------------------------------------------|-----|
|   | 3.4  | What if a client helps themselves to their spouse's documents? | 46  |
|   | 3.5  | The remedy for non-disclosure                                | 50  |
|   | 3.6  | Penal notice – is an application needed?                     | 52  |
|   | 3.7  | Committal applications                                       | 53  |
|   | 3.8  | Adverse inferences                                           | 54  |
|   | 3.9  | Obtaining evidence from third parties                        | 55  |
|   | 3.10 | Joining parties                                              | 56  |
| **4** | **Financial remedy procedure**                           |                                                              | **58** |
|   | 4.1  | Introduction                                                 | 58  |
|   | 4.2  | The standard procedure for financial remedy applications     | 59  |
|   | 4.3  | Applications in the High Court and Family Court, and cross applications | 59  |
|   | 4.4  | The Form E                                                   | 64  |
|   | 4.5  | First appointment hearing                                    | 68  |
|   | 4.6  | The financial dispute resolution appointment                 | 77  |
|   | 4.7  | Final hearing                                                | 83  |
|   | 4.8  | Costs rules                                                  | 85  |
|   | 4.9  | Judgment/order                                               | 85  |
|   | 4.10 | The fast-track procedure                                     | 86  |
|   | 4.11 | Costs orders in financial remedy proceedings                 | 89  |
| **5** | **Available orders**                                    |                                                              | **91** |
|   | 5.1  | Introduction                                                 | 91  |
|   | 5.2  | Clean break                                                  | 93  |
|   | 5.3  | The remarriage/civil partnership trap                        | 95  |
|   | 5.4  | Income claims                                                | 97  |
|   | 5.5  | Lump sum orders                                              | 107 |
|   | 5.6  | Property adjustment orders                                   | 111 |
|   | 5.7  | Pension orders                                               | 117 |
|   | 5.8  | MCA 1973, s.25 and CPA 2004, Sched.5, Part 5                 | 120 |
| **6** | **Financial remedy for children**                       |                                                              | **126** |
|   | 6.1  | Introduction                                                 | 126 |
|   | 6.2  | The Child Maintenance Service                                | 127 |
|   | 6.3  | Applications for financial orders for children following divorce and dissolution proceedings | 137 |
|   | 6.4  | Applications for financial orders for children under the Children Act 1989, s.15 and Sched.1 | 140 |
|   | 6.5  | Conclusion                                                   | 145 |

| 7 | **Experts in final remedy proceedings** | | **146** |
|---|---|---|---|
| | 7.1 | Introduction | 146 |
| | 7.2 | Choosing and instructing the expert | 148 |
| | 7.3 | The court's consideration | 150 |
| | 7.4 | The letter of instruction | 151 |
| | 7.5 | Duties of the expert | 152 |
| | 7.6 | Experts' costs | 153 |
| | 7.7 | After the final hearing | 153 |
| 8 | **Negotiations and consent orders** | | **154** |
| | 8.1 | Introduction | 154 |
| | 8.2 | Negotiations – open/without prejudice/without prejudice save as to costs | 155 |
| | 8.3 | Consent orders | 159 |
| | 8.4 | Enforcement proceedings | 162 |

**APPENDICES**

| A | **Disclosure** | | **165** |
|---|---|---|---|
| | A1 | Pre-application protocol | 167 |
| | A2 | What to do when your client gives you a document belonging to a third party | 170 |
| B | **Available orders** | | **171** |
| | B1 | Table of spousal/civil partnership orders available | 173 |
| | B2 | Remarriage trap flowchart | 177 |
| C | **Financial remedies for children** | | **179** |
| | C1 | Income options for children flowchart | 181 |
| | C2 | Orders for children that can be made in divorce or dissolution proceedings | 182 |
| D | **Negotiotions and consent orders** | | **183** |
| | D1 | Negotiations and consent orders checklist | 185 |

*Index* 187

# Preface

When I was first approached to write this book, it was my intention that it would sit as a companion to the *Matrimonial Finance Toolkit* published by the Law Society in 2017. I hope that this book succeeds in doing so. I anticipate that this handbook will be used by family law practitioners, by those who hope to become family lawyers and maybe even by those self-representing in financial remedy proceedings. Financial remedy is a complicated area of work, full of traps for the unwary – I have tried to highlight as many of the practical problems that may arise as possible, so that they can be considered and avoided. I have immensely enjoyed my career as a financial remedy practitioner and feel privileged to be able to share my experiences through writing this book.

Readers should note that where they would like to see checklists, precedents and tips about filling forms, these may all be found in the toolkit. There is only one exception, which is the inclusion in this book of a link to new precedent to instruct a pension on divorce expert (PODE). Since the publication of the report of the Pension Advisory Group, *A Guide to the Treatment of Pensions on Divorce* in July 2019, their precedent is much more useful than the one I included in the toolkit. In the interests of full transparency, I am a committee member on the Pension Advisory Group.

When I started writing this book, the Family Court service was chugging along as it had done for years and suddenly in early 2020 coronavirus landed and turned the court system upside down. I have not made any mention to this and to the emergency measures that were introduced as a result of the pandemic. When this book is published, it may be that there are many more options available to deal with directions appointments remotely or by agreement. This is currently what is expected, but not what the normal rules set out – the new measures and emergency interim provisions may not survive when normal service is resumed after the crisis is over. We can only wait and see what happens next.

I would like to thank a number of extremely knowledgeable practitioners and friends who have corrected my mistakes, suggested new ideas and helped me to get this book over the finish line; any errors that still exist are mine alone. Karen Dovaston of Dovaston Law for her support and superb knowledge of child support and financial remedy practice; Jo O'Sullivan of O'Sullivan Family Law for her invaluable input and corrections regarding the non-court dispute resolution chapter; Camini Kumar of Fourteen Chambers for her excellent knowledge of financial

## PREFACE

remedy procedure and practical tips through the eyes of a barrister; Roopa Ahluwalia, partner at BDB Pitmans for all-round knowledge and assistance; Sarah Newens, consultant solicitor and higher rights advocate, for her feedback; and Lewis Hulatt, consultant solicitor, of Major Family Law who has always been a great help reading my book drafts. Calvin Walker of Major Family Law, and Rene Panayiotou and Peter Vassila of Chapman Pieri solicitors, were all extremely helpful readers of my first drafts, sharing with me their perspectives as young solicitors looking to build on their already extensive knowledge. I am very grateful to Joanne Major, managing director at Major Family Law, and Karen Chapman and Christina Pieri, directors at Chapman Pieri Solicitors, for letting me test out the book on their juniors and supporting me as a consultant solicitor working for them. It isn't always easy juggling a portfolio career, and it is only possible with the support of those who are willing to put up with me and my many battles with the Piccadilly line.

Finally, I would like to dedicate this book to my father, Mr Ishwar Ruparel, who sadly passed away while I was writing this book. Without his support and prodding I doubt I ever would have qualified as a solicitor.

The law is stated as at August 2020.

**Mena Ruparel**
August 2020

# Table of cases

ABX v. SBX [2018] EWFC 81 .................................................................. 8.2.1
AR v. ML [2019] EWFC 56 .................................................................. 4.5.5.5
BR v. VT [2015] EWHC 2727 (Fam) ..................................................... 5.6.4
CB v. KB [2019] EWFC 78 .................................................................. 6.3.1
CM v. CM [2019] EWFC 16 ................................................................. 7.4
D v. D (financial provision: periodical payments) [2004] EWHC 445 (Fam) ...... 5.4.2.1
D v. D (lump sum: adjournment of application) [2001] 1 FLR 633 ................ 5.5.3
D (minors) (conciliation: disclosure of information), Re [1993] Fam 231, CA ....... 4.6.3
Dickson v. Rennie [2014] EWHC 4306 (Fam) ......................................... 6.2.6.3
Duxbury v. Duxbury [1987] 1 FLR 7, CA ............................................. 5.2, 5.4.4.3
Goddard-Watts v. Goddard-Watts [2019] EWHC 3367 (Fam) .......................... 4.5.3
Hamilton v. Hamilton [2013] EWCA Civ 13 .......................................... 5.5.1
Livesey (formerly Jenkins) v. Jenkins [1984] UKHL 3; [1985] AC 424 ............... 3.2
McCartney v. Mills McCartney [2008] EWHC 401 (Fam) .................. 5.4.3.2, 5.4.4.3
Martin v. Martin [1977] 3 All ER 762 ............................................ 5.6.5.4, 8.2.2.1
Mesher v. Mesher and Hall [1980] 1 All ER 126, CA .............. 5.6.5.3, 5.6.5.4, 8.2.2.1
Moher v. Moher [2019] EWCA Civ 1482 ..................................... 5.5.2, 5.5.2.1
Myerson v. Myerson [2008] EWCA Civ 1376 ......................................... 4.7.1
NG v. SG (appeal: non-disclosure) [2011] EWHC 3270 (Fam) .......................... 3.8
North v. North [2007] EWCA Civ 760 .................................................. 5.4.3.1
OG v. AG [2020] EWFC 52 .................................................................. 4.6.5.2
Radmacher v. Granatino [2010] UKSC 42 ............................................... 5.6.3
RK v. RK [2011] EWHC 3910 (Fam) .................................................... 1.6.3.7
Rose v. Rose [2002] EWCA Civ 208 ............................................... 4.6.4, 4.6.4.1
Rubin v. Rubin [2014] EWHC 611 (Fam) .............................................. 1.6.3.6
S v. S [2014] EWHC 7 (Fam) .............................................................. 2.6.12
Sears Tooth v. Payne Hicks Beach [1997] 2 FLR 116 ................................ 1.6.3.7
Sorrell v. Sorrell [2005] EWHC 1717 (Fam) ............................................. 5.8
Tattersall v. Tattersall [2018] EWCA Civ 1978 ....................................... 5.4.4.3
Tchenguiz v. Imerman; Imerman v. Imerman [2010] EWCA Civ 908 ................ 3.4.2
TL v. ML (ancillary relief: claim against assets of extended family) [2005]
 EWHC 2860 (Fam) ...................................................................... 3.10
UL v. BK (freezing orders: safeguards: standard examples) [2013] EWHC 1735
 (Fam) ..................................................................................... 3.4.4
Waggott v. Waggott [2018] EWCA Civ 727 ........................................... 5.4.3.1
White v. White [2000] UKHL 54 ...................................................... 5.1, 5.8
WS v. HS [2018] EWFC 11 ................................................................ 5.6.4
Wyatt v. Vince [2015] UKSC 14 ................................................. 5.2, 5.3.1, 5.3.2
Wyatt v. Vince (terms of settlement) [2016] EWHC 1368 (Fam) ....................... 5.2
Young v. Young [2013] EWHC 34 (Fam) ............................................. 3.7, 3.8

# Table of statutes

Arbitration Act 1996
   s.42 ............................... 3.5.2
Bankers' Book Evidence Act 1897
   s.7 .................................... 3.9
Child Support Act 1991 ........ 6.2.1, 6.2.5
   s.3 .................................. 6.2.2
   s.8(6) ............................ 6.2.6.3
     (9) .............................. 6.3.1
   s.44 ................................ 6.2.3
   Sched.4B(2) ..................... 6.2.8
Children Act 1989 .................... App.C2
   s.2(2) .............................. 6.4.2
   s.15 .... 6.1, 6.4.1, 6.4.2, 6.4.7, 6.5,
                     8.2.1, App.C1
   Sched.1 .... 4.10.1, 6.1, 6.2.3, 6.4.1,
              6.4.2, 6.4.7, 6.5, 8.2.1,
              App.C1
      para.1(2) ..................... 6.4.1
      para.2(5) ..................... 6.4.3
      para.3(1) ..................... 6.4.4
      para.4(1), (2) ................ 6.4.5
Children and Families Act 2014
   s.10(1) ........................... 2.3.2
Civil Partnership Act 2004 ...... 3.3.2, 5.1,
              5.2, 6.4.1, 6.4.3, 6.4.7,
              App.B2, App.C1
   Sched.5
     Part 1
        para.2 ........ 5.4.1, App.B1,
                    App.C2
          (1)(f) ............... 6.3.1
     Part 2 .............. 5.5.1, App.C2
        para.7 ...... App.B1, App.C2
          (1) .......... 5.6.2, 6.3.1
     Part 3
        para.10 .................... 5.5.1
        para.11 ..... 5.6.5.1, App.B1
     Part 4
        paras.16, 19A ....... App.B1
     Part 5 .... 4.1, 4.4.1, 4.6.5.1, 5.8
        para.20(b) ............. 4.5.5.5

        para.21(2) ............. 8.2.2.1
          (c) .......... 4.5.5.5
          (f) .............. 5.1
        para.22 .................... 6.3.2
        para.23 .......... 5.2, App.B1
     Part 6
        para.24 ............... App.B1
     Part 7 ....................... App.B1
     Part 8
        para.38 ........ 5.4.1, App.B1
        para.38A .... 1.6.3.6, 5.4.2.1,
                         App.B1
          (10) ......... 1.6.3.6
        para.38B .... 1.6.3.6, 5.4.2.1
     Part 10
        para.47(5), (6) ....... App.B1
        para.48 ........ 5.3.1, App.B1
        para.49 .................... 6.3.2
     Part 11 ..................... 5.4.2.1
        paras.50–52 ............ 5.4.4.2
        para.51 ........ 5.5.1, App.B2
   Sched.6 ........................ 4.10.1
Computer Misuse Act 1990 ......... 3,4.5.1
Data Protection Act 2018 .......... 3.4.5.1
Domestic Proceedings and Magistrates'
   Courts Act 1978 ............... 4.10.1
Family Law Act 1996
   s.30 ................................ 5.6.4
Fraud Act 2006 ............... 3.3.2, App.A1
Inheritance (Provision for Family and
   Dependants) Act 1975 ........ 5.4.3.3,
               6.3.2, 6.4.4, App.D1
Judgments Act 1838
   s.17 ................................ 5.5.2
Legal Aid, Sentencing and Punishment of
   Offenders Act 2012 ....... 1.5, 1.6.3.8
   ss.49–54 ...................... 1.6.3.6
Matrimonial Causes Act 1973 ....... 3.3.2,
              6.4.1, 6.4.3, 6.4.7, App.C1
   Part 2
      ss.21–25 ....................... 4.1

xiii

Matrimonial Causes Act
 1973 – continued
  Part 2 – continued
   s.21A ...................... App.B1
   s.21B ...................... App.B1
   s.22 ............... 5.4.1. App.B1
   s.22ZA ... 5.4.2.1, 5.6.4.App.B1
    (10) ................ 1.6.3.6
   s.22ZB ..................... 1.6.3.6
   s.23 ...... 5.4.1, App.B1, App.C2
    (1) ................ 5.3.1, 5.5.1
     (d)–(f) ................ 6.3.2
    (2) ........................ 6.3.2
    (3) ........................ 5.5.4
    (4) ................ 6.3.1, 6.3.2
    (6) ........................ 5.5.2
   s.24 ........ 5.6.4, 6.3.2, App.B1,
          App.C2
    (1) ......... 5.3.1, 5.6.2, 6.3.1
   s.24A .......... 5.5.1, 6.3.2, 8.4,
          App.B1
    (1) ................... 5.6.5.1
   s.25 .......... 3.3.2, 3.3.3, 4.4.1,
    4.6.5.1, 5.1, 5.4.2.1, 5.4.3.1,
          5.8, 8.2.2.1

s.25(1) ... 3.2, 4.5.5.5, 5.6.3, 5.8
 (2) ................ 4.5.5.5, 5.8
  (a)–(c) ................ 6.3.2
  (e) .......... 6.3.2, App.B1
  (f), (g) .......... 5.1, 6.3.2
  (h) .................... 6.3.2
 (3) .................... 5.8, 6.3.2
s.25A ....... 5.2, 8.2.2.4, App.B1
ss.25B–25D .............. App.B1
s.28(1) .................... App.B1
 (a), (b) ............. 5.4.2.1
 (1A) ......... 5.4.2.1, 5.4.2.2,
     5.4.2.3, 8.2.2.4, App.B1
 (2) .................... App.B1
 (3) ............ 5.3.1, App.B1
s.29 ......................... 6.3.2
 (1) .................... App.C2
s.31 ..... 5.4.2.1, 5.4.2.2, 5.4.2.3,
          App.B2
 (2)(d) .................... 5.5.1
 (7A)–(7F) ............ 5.4.4.2
Trusts of Land and Appointment of
 Trustees Act 1996
  s.14 .................................. 6.5

# Table of statutory instruments

Child Support Maintenance Calculation Regulations 2012, SI 2012/2677 .......... 6.2.6.2
Civil Procedure Rules 1998, SI 1998/3132 ........................................ 4.5.5.1, 6.5
Family Proceedings Rules 1991, SI 1991/1247 ................................... 4.7.1, 8.2.1
Family Procedure Rules 2010, SI 2010/2955 ........................ 1.6.3.6, 5.3.2, 6.5, 7.1
    Part 1 ............................................. 2.3.2.1, 4.4.2, 4.5.1, 4.5.3, 4.5.5.2, 7.3
        rule 1.1 ................................................................. 2.3.2.1, 4.5.1
    Part 2
        rule 2.9 .................................................................................. 2.3.1
    Part 3 ............................................................................................. 2.3.1
        rule 3.8 .............................................................................. 2.3.2.1
    Part 4 ............................................................................................. 4.5.1
    Part 5 ............................................................................................. 4.5.2
    Part 6 .......................................................................................... 4.3.2.1
        PD 6A ............................................................................... 4.3.2.1
    Part 9 ...................................................................................... 4.1, 4.2
        rule 9.4 .................................................................................... 4.1
        rule 9.9B(4) ......................................................................... 4.10.1
        rule 9.12 .................................................................................. 4.2
        rule 9.13 ............................................................................. 4.3.2.2
        rule 9.14(2)(b)(ii) ................................................................. 4.4.1
            (3) ...................................................................................... 4.4.4
            (5) ...................................................................................... 4.4.5
                (c) ................................................................................ 4.4.5.3
                (d) ................................................................................ 4.5.4
        rule 9.15 ................................................................................ 4.5.1
        rule 9.16(1) ............................................................... 3.5.3, 4.5.5.2
        rule 9.17 ................................................................................ 4.6.1
            (2) ........................................................................................ 4.7.1
            (6), (10) .............................................................................. 4.6.3
        rules 9.18–9.21 ................................................................... 4.10.1
        rule 9.18(1) ............................................................. 4.10.1, 4.10.2
        rule 9.18A(4)(b)(i) .............................................................. 4.10.1
        rule 9.19 .............................................................................. 4.10.2
        rule 9.20(1), (4) .................................................................. 4.10.3
        rule 9.26 ................................................................................ 8.3.1
        rule 9.26B .............................................................................. 3.10
        rule 9.27 ........................................................ 4.4.5.5, 4.5.3, 4.10.2
            (3) ........................................................................................ 4.6.2
            (4) .......................................................................................... 4.8
            (7) ........................................................................................ 4.5.3
        rule 9.27A ..................................................... 4.5.3, 4.6.3, 4.6.5.2

Family Procedure Rules 2010, SI 2010/2955 – *continued*
   Part 9 – *continued*
      rule 9.28 ............................................................................... 4.7.3
      rule 9.30(1), (2) .................................................................. 4.3.2.2
      rule 9.31 .............................................................. 4.3.2.2, 4.3.3.2
      rules 9.40–9.44 ..................................................................... 8.3.1
      PD 9A ................................................................ 3.3.4, 4.4.2, 4.6.3
   Part 15
      PD 15B ..................................................................................... 7.4
   Part 17
      PD 17A .................................................................................. 3.3.2
   Part 18 ................................... 3.6, 3.9, 3.10, 4.5.5.2, 4.5.5.3, 4.6.3, 7.2
      rule 20.2(1)(c)(v) ................................................................. 5.6.4
   Part 21 ......................................................................................... 3.9
      rule 21.1(1), (2) ....................................................................... 3.2
      rule 21.2(6) ............................................................................. 3.9
      rule 21.3 .................................................................................. 3.9
   Part 24 ......................................................................................... 3.9
   Part 25 ......................................................................................... 7.1
      rule 25.4 .................................................................................. 7.2
         (3) ....................................................................................... 7.3
      rule 25.5(2) .............................................................................. 7.3
      rule 25.6 .................................................................................. 7.3
         (d) ....................................................................................... 7.2
      rule 25.7(2)(b) ......................................................................... 7.2
      rule 25.9 .................................................................................. 7.2
         (2) ....................................................................................... 7.5
      rule 25.10 ................................................................................ 7.5
      rule 25.12(2) ........................................................................... 7.4
      PD 25B ........................................................................... 7.4, 7.5
      PD 25C .................................................................................. 7.2
      PD 25D .................................................................... 7.1, 7.2, 7.4
      PD 25E ................................................................................... 7.4
   Part 27
      rule 27.3 ............................................................................... 4.7.1
      rule 27.4 ............................................................................... 4.7.1
      PD 27A .......................... 4.4.5.2, 4.5.1, 4.6.2, 4.6.5.1, 4.7.2, 4.10.2
   Part 28 ............................................................................. 3.5.3, 8.2.1
      rule 28.1 .............................................. 1.6.3.6, 3.9, 6.4.7, 8.2.1
      rule 28.3 ............................................... 1.6.3.6, 3.5.3, 6.3.4
         (5) .......................................................................... 4.11, 8.2.1
         (7) ...................................................................................... 4.11
            (a) .................................................................................. 3.5.3
      rule 28.3(8)(c)–(e) ................................................................. 4.11
      PD 28A ................................................................................. 4.11
         para.4.4 .................................................................. 4.6.5.2, 8.2.1
         para.4.5 ................................................................................ 4.11
   Part 29
      rule 29.11 ................................................................................ 4.9
      rule 29.15 ................................................................................ 4.9
      rule 29.16 ................................................................................ 4.9
   Part 33
      rule 33.3(2)(a), (b) .................................................................. 8.4

    rule 33.11 .............................................................................. 8.4
    PD 33A ................................................................................. 8.4
  Part 39 ........................................................................................ 8.4
  Part 40 ........................................................................................ 8.4
  Part 41
    PD 41B .................................................................. 4.6.4.2, 8.3.1
Pensions on Divorce etc. (Charging) Regulations 2000, SI 2000/1049 .............. 4.3.2.2
Pensions on Divorce etc. (Provision of Information) Regulations 2000, SI 2000/1048
  reg.2(2) .................................................................................. 4.3.2.2

# Table of international legislation

Convention on the International Recovery of Child Support and other forms of Family
    Maintenance (The Hague, 23 November 2007)
        Art.10 .................................................................................... 4.10.1
Council Regulation (EC) No 4/200925 (Maintenance Regulation)
        Art.56 .................................................................................... 4.10.1
European Convention on Human Rights
        Art.8 ........................................................................................ 3.9
General Data Protection Regulation (EU) ................................................ 3.4.5.1

# Abbreviations

| | |
|---|---|
| ADR | alternative dispute resolution |
| AI | artificial intelligence |
| APR | annual percentage rate |
| CA 1989 | Children Act 1989 |
| CE | cash equivalent |
| CETV | cash equivalent transfer value |
| CFA 2014 | Children and Families Act 2014 |
| CFP | collaborative family practice |
| CMS | Child Maintenance Service |
| COLP | compliance officer for legal practice |
| CPA 2004 | Civil Partnership Act 2004 |
| CPPO | child periodical payments order |
| CPR 1998 | Civil Procedure Rules 1998 SI 1998/3132 |
| CSA 1991 | Child Support Act 1991 |
| DB | defined benefit (pension) |
| DC | defined contribution (pension) |
| ENE | early neutral evaluation |
| ESA | employment and support allowance |
| EU | European Union |
| FA | first appointment |
| FC | family consultant |
| FDR | financial dispute resolution |
| FJC | Family Justice Council |
| FLA 1996 | Family Law Act 1996 |
| FLBA | Family Law Bar Association |
| FPR 1991 | Family Proceedings Rules 1991 SI 1991/1247 |
| FPR 2010 | Family Procedure Rules 2010 SI 2010/2955 |
| FRWG | Financial Remedies Working Group |
| HMCTS | HM Courts and Tribunals Service |
| IFA | independent financial adviser |
| IFLA | Institute of Family Law Arbitrators |
| JA 1838 | Judgments Act 1838 |
| JSA | jobseeker's allowance |
| KYC | know your client |

| | |
|---|---|
| LAA | Legal Aid Agency |
| LASPO 2012 | Legal Aid, Sentencing and Punishment of Offenders Act 2012 |
| MCA 1973 | Matrimonial Causes Act 1973 |
| MIAM | mediation information and assessment meeting |
| MOU | memorandum of understanding |
| MPOP | maintenance pending the outcome of proceedings |
| MPS | maintenance pending suit |
| NCA | National Crime Agency |
| NCDR | non-court dispute resolution |
| PAG | Pension Advisory Group |
| PAO | pension attachment order |
| PCAO | pension compensation attachment order |
| PCSO | pension compensation sharing order |
| PD | Practice Direction |
| PIAM | pension information and assessment meeting |
| PODE | pension on divorce expert |
| PPF | Pension Protection Fund |
| PPO | periodical payment order |
| PRPA | person responsible for the pension arrangement |
| PSO | pension sharing order |
| SJE | single joint expert |
| SOD | schedule of deficiencies |
| SRA | Solicitors Regulation Authority |
| TLATA 1996 | Trusts of Land and Appointment of Trustees Act 1996 |
| UC | universal credit |

CHAPTER 1

# Pre-instruction

## 1.1 THE CLIENT'S JOURNEY – MEETING YOUR CLIENT FOR THE FIRST TIME

Your prospective client makes their first step to contact you via your profile on your firm's website. Very rarely these days will your client come to your office for a first meeting without any idea of your background and qualifications. Sometimes, the client will be referred directly to you, and on the strength of that referral they may have made no further enquiries about you. It is, however, much more likely that they used a popular search engine to find a suitably qualified, possibly cheap, geographically compatible 'lawyer'. Specialist family solicitors (or Chartered Legal Executives) sometimes choose to accredit their specialisms by taking exams with either the Law Society, which currently offers two suitable accreditations but no general membership category; or with Resolution (formerly the Solicitors Family Law Association), which has a general membership category and offers an accreditation option. It is difficult to know to what extent clients are aware of these accreditations, or if they use the member association websites and search features to locate an accredited specialist.

If the client decides to contact your firm, you might receive a telephone call to make an appointment, in which case the call handler, often not the solicitor, will jot down sufficient details to undertake a conflict check and make the client an appointment. In my view, it is good practice for a telephone call to be taken by a family solicitor to ensure that the first point of contact is satisfactory for the client. It is ideal if the solicitor who is likely to take the meeting can book that appointment personally – this saves any confusion on the day if it transpires that the client doesn't really need a family solicitor at all!

Occasionally, some pre-meeting reading will be sent to the client, with information pertaining to the costs of the first appointment and directions to the office. Standard compliance matters – such as money laundering regulations and identification checks – are usually dealt with at this early stage, to ensure that the firm complies with the relevant Standards and Regulations of the Solicitors Regulation Authority (SRA) (which came into effect on 25 November 2019, replacing the SRA Handbook).

An alternative scenario is that the client might send an email in the middle of the night requesting information, having read and downloaded various online leaflets from your website, or those of your rivals. Likewise, the client's personal details will need to be taken so that an appointment can be made with a suitably experienced solicitor, or the first available appointment with any solicitor if the matter is deemed to be urgent. At this stage, very little information has been extracted from the client, save for those details required for the all-important conflict checks.

There is, however, another way forward in our technologically advanced world. It is becoming increasingly popular for firms to ask their prospective clients to complete more detailed information factsheets before the client makes an appointment to see a solicitor. This can either be done by way of an initial questionnaire which is emailed to the client or by using an online platform to harvest the information using a chatbot, generating a 'report', giving broadly tailored information (but not advice) to the user. True artificial intelligence (AI) options are still in their infancy, and it is difficult to predict how useful they will be for the client and solicitor.

Some professionals take the view that the chatbot options to gather client information are limited and believe that a client will prefer a personal approach, particularly in an emotionally fraught time. Others believe that by getting the basic information in advance of the appointment, a more fruitful appointment with a true opportunity to give advice follows. Every practitioner needs to find their own way to ensure that the first appointment is as productive and cost-effective as possible for the client. The answer probably lies in a mixture of harvesting important information in advance of the meeting, and following up with a meaningful personal approach.

## 1.2 FREELANCE AND UNREGULATED SERVICES

### 1.2.1 Freelance solicitors

Solicitors can now choose to practise via the freelance solicitor route, which was introduced by the SRA in November 2019. Freelance solicitors practise as regulated members of the SRA and are bound by the Code of Conduct for Solicitors, RELs and RFLs; they do not practise within an SRA-regulated firm and are therefore not bound by the SRA Code of Conduct for Firms, but are subject to regulation as individual solicitors. As practising freelance is a relatively new option at the time of writing, there is nothing further to comment on save that it could be said that these solicitors are unregulated, when in fact they are not.

### 1.2.2 McKenzie friends

The rise of the 'McKenzie friend' – as these often unqualified, unregulated and usually uninsured advisers are usually called – cannot be ignored. McKenzie friends do not need to have any formal legal qualifications in order to assist a litigant in person (i.e. a self-represented party, without legal representation from a solicitor or barrister). They cannot conduct litigation unless they have been given permission by the court to do so, and such permission is rarely granted. Conducting litigation means filing documents on behalf of the litigant in person or entering into correspondence on their behalf. Therefore, in the event that a McKenzie friend commences correspondence with a solicitor directly, unless an order has been made to allow them to do so, the solicitor should continue to correspond with the litigant in person.

The McKenzie friend can be given permission to speak on behalf of a litigant in person at court, but it is also an unusual step for the court to grant these rights. The role of the McKenzie friend at court is to help and assist by taking notes, and quietly to remind the litigant in person of matters that they might need to raise during the hearing. McKenzie friends are not regulated; they are usually uninsured, but frequently levy charges for their services. It is entirely possible that a prospective client may have taken 'advice' from such an unqualified adviser before coming to a solicitor. The general perception from a client is that a McKenzie friend offers services that are in some ways equivalent to the advice given by solicitors, but cheaper. It is worth bearing that in mind when a client contacts your firm to arrange an appointment with a solicitor, they also have non-regulated options; solicitors are sometimes competing for work with unregulated providers.

There are many reasons a client might choose to take advice from a McKenzie friend, or choose to self-represent. I advise solicitors not to assume that these reasons are always connected to the inability to afford regulated legal advice. Any solicitor dealing with a litigant in person should read the excellent paper by L. Trinder et al., 'Litigants in person in private family law cases' (Ministry of Justice, 2014) (**www.gov.uk/government/publications/litigants-in-person-in-private-family-law-cases**). This shines a much-needed light on the various reasons people choose to represent themselves and the court process from their perspective.

Solicitors should also be aware of the *Practice Guidance: McKenzie Friends (Civil and Family Courts)*, 12 July 2010 (**www.judiciary.uk/wp-content/uploads/JCO/Documents/Guidance/mckenzie-friends-practice-guidance-july-2010.pdf**).

## 1.3 REGULATORY MATTERS IN BRIEF

It is not intended that this chapter will detail all the fine requirements of practice as a solicitor, which is another book entirely. However, it is always important to consider regulatory matters to ensure that they are not overlooked.

### 1.3.1 Money laundering

The client should have been asked to bring identification documents for money-laundering purposes and 'know your client' (KYC) checks. Usually the client will be asked to bring a form of photographic identification so that the solicitor can identify the client and a form of identification to confirm their address. The government's 'Proof of identity checklist' (available at: **www.gov.uk/government/ publications/proof-of-identity-checklist/proof-of-identity-checklist**) sets out in detail which forms of identification are suitable for money laundering purposes. Money laundering is a serious issue which can involve solicitors. The National Crime Agency (NCA) reported a drop of 10 per cent in the number of money laundering reports made by solicitors in 2018 from the year before. The NCA is working closely with the SRA to identify the reasons for this and to ensure that the threat of money laundering is properly assessed by solicitors.

### 1.3.2 Payment

Before the client attends the first meeting with the solicitor, they should be informed how much the appointment will cost (including VAT) and how they will be able to pay (cash (subject to money laundering regulations); debit or credit card; or bank transfer). Firms have varying policies on whether they will accept cash, and if so, how much and how regularly. Occasionally solicitors will offer a free first appointment, or a free half-hour appointment, and will start to charge once the half-hour is complete. It is useful to ensure that this information is given in writing either by email or letter so that there is no room for misunderstanding at the appointment.

### 1.3.3 Conflict of interests

The SRA Codes of Conduct require that solicitors ensure that they have undertaken a conflict of interests check before a client is taken on. This usually happens at the pre-instruction stage, possibly by an administrator, but it is worth remembering that it is a regulatory requirement. A conflict can occur if the firm has previously given advice to the parties jointly, perhaps if they purchased a property using the firm's conveyancing department or made wills with the firm. In these instances, it is for the firm to decide whether there is a conflict or not. Occasionally the fact that previous instructions have been taken will not produce a conflict for the family solicitor. The firm may have a policy that needs to be consulted about such matters, and that should be the first port of call about such matters.

It is also important to recognise that a personal conflict can arise, and this can be much more difficult to identify objectively. For example, acting on behalf of a friend or family member can create problems that cannot always be anticipated at the outset of the case. From an ethical perspective, I find that the more blurred the lines become, the more difficult it will be to be able to act in the client's best interests. A good rule of thumb for me is, if I find myself trying to justify reasons why I should act for the client, it might be a good indicator that in fact I shouldn't act for the client. In these situations, your decision-making should be discussed with the compliance officer for legal practice (COLP) at the firm and consultation with any internal policies and any decisions documented, so that if your choice becomes contentious you can look back at your reasons for acting.

## 1.4 MATTERS TO CONSIDER

There are various issues that need to be dealt with during the first meeting with the solicitor, and many of these will be dictated by the specific circumstances of the client. They include but are not limited to the following:

- gaining the client's trust and confidence;
- letting the client tell their story;
- listening to the client, in order to be able to address their concerns during the appointment;
- reassuring the client;
- signposting services for the client to contact (e.g. financial services, child maintenance, welfare benefits);
- advice about the next steps each should take after the meeting, including referral to non-court dispute resolution (NCDR);
- ensuring that the client understands any advice you have given;
- ensuring that the client has realistic expectations of the process, costs and outcomes (where possible, given the early stage);
- advice about divorce or civil partnership dissolution;
- advice about separation;
- advice about children/child maintenance;
- advice about emergency protective injunctions;
- advice about financial matters including any emergency financial applications;
- other urgent business.

It is important for the practitioner to be able to prioritise the needs of the client when giving advice about these matters. It is very difficult to create a template that will accommodate all eventualities – any template used must be employed with great sensitivity and empathy for the client's situation. It is inevitable that the needs of the client and those of the practitioner will be different. The client will have emotional issues that spurred them on to make an appointment, and the practitioner will need to collect information to give advice. It is important to be patient at the first meeting, as the client may be apprehensive and worried about the advice.

Not every client in a difficult relationship has the intention permanently to end the relationship when they meet with a solicitor for advice. As a newly qualified solicitor, I made the mistake of assuming that everybody who walked through my door wanted a divorce (civil partnership had not been introduced at that time). I thought it was a fairly good bet that divorce was the reason the client had come to see me. One client commented that I was a bit pushy when I chased them after a first meeting for their marriage certificate so that I could prepare the divorce petition. It was then that I realised that the client had not yet decided that the marriage had irretrievably broken down. Since then, I try to be more careful to listen more and assume less about the advice and action the client needs.

The list above can easily be split into (a) listening to the client and reacting appropriately; and (b) giving advice and information which requires the client to listen. It can be difficult to get the balance between talking and listening right at the first meeting. An initial meeting can last from one hour to three hours, depending on the client's situation, the advice that needs to be given and the client's ability to absorb the advice. Anyone who has ever attended an important hospital appointment will know the feeling of walking out of a consultation and all the information and advice you have been given suddenly disappearing. The client should feel free and be encouraged to take notes, ask questions and bring an appropriate person to help them remember and understand advice. You will probably follow up after the first appointment with written advice, and this can be reassuring to the client. If the client has come to see you on a limited retainer or under an unbundled services retainer, then it is possible that there will be no follow-up contact from you, in which case the client needs to have taken detailed notes or should leave with a copy of the solicitor's notes and advice on next steps.

A word of warning: it is increasingly popular for the client to make an audio-recording of the first meeting without asking for permission first. Where permission is sought, you may be perfectly happy for the meeting to be recorded, but be aware that any advice you give could be shared with their spouse or third parties. This is no different to a client sharing written advice, but often hearing a solicitor give advice can be more difficult for a third party to absorb but easier for the client to understand. If the client asks me for permission to record the meeting, I need to understand their reasons for doing so and what use they will make of the recording. I tend to err on the side of caution and refuse to allow recordings, but each situation is different. Be aware of mobile phones on display and try to ascertain sensitively whether a recording is being made at the start of the meeting.

## 1.5  DIFFERENT CHARGING MODELS

It is vital to discuss the issue of funding both before the first meeting and during it. Often solicitors will charge separately for the first meeting so that the client has the opportunity to meet the solicitor and decide whether or not they want to progress the matter forward.

The first meeting can be charged as a fixed-fee; pro bono; hourly rate; or a mixture of pro bono and hourly rate. For example, the first 30 minutes might be free and any time spent after that will be charged at the solicitor's hourly rate. Whichever way the charging structure is set up, it must be clear for the client to understand. The SRA is keen to ensure that solicitors are as transparent as possible about their charging structure. As such, price transparency rules were introduced by the SRA in 2018 (see **www.sra.org.uk/solicitors/resources/transparency/**) which require solicitors to be transparent about costs in a number of specified specialisms – although family law doesn't fall within these categories, the rules could be expanded to include family law in the near future.

Solicitors have historically charged on a retainer basis – this involves the client signing terms and conditions of business and agreeing that the solicitor will represent them with regards to agreed legal matters. In a full hourly retainer agreement, the solicitor will file a notice of acting with the court (if court proceedings have commenced). The expectation is that the court and the solicitor representing their client's spouse will communicate directly with the solicitor on record. If no solicitor has been appointed, then the solicitor on record will communicate with the client's spouse directly. With this type of agreement, money is usually paid by the client on account of future costs; the client may be billed on a regular basis, usually monthly.

I have met solicitors who bill weekly to ensure that there are few unpaid debts to the firm – this is less usual, but I am told it works just as well as or better than monthly billing. The client should be given sufficient information to explain the costs incurred – often this will mean that they receive a printout of all fee earners' time spent on the case. This is easy enough to do with the right case management system, but if no case management system is in place a written indication of how time has been spent on the case is sufficient. Sadly, the hourly rate method of charging is expensive and sometimes does not suit the client's purse or purpose.

In recent years, solicitors have been urged to work more flexibly to enable greater access to justice, particularly as legal aid is not generally available in family matters as it was before the introduction of the Legal Aid, Sentencing and Punishment of Offenders Act (LASPO) 2012. Instead of offering only the full retainer service, it is possible to offer the client:

(a) fixed-fee services;
(b) unbundled services; or
(c) a limited retainer.

A *fixed-fee service* is an agreement to undertake specified work for an agreed sum. I think of it as using a minicab charging a fixed agreed price, rather than getting into a black taxi charging per mile or per minute – anyone who has sat in the back of a black taxi in London will know the heart wrenching palpitations while sitting in traffic watching the meter as you remain in the same spot. Any sensible user of legal services may think of a full retainer service in the same way. The advantages of a fixed-fee should be obvious to a user of legal services: it is better to know how much you will be charged in advance rather than risk the uncertainty of being charged for the time used. Arguably, charging hourly rates encourages inefficiency on the part of the solicitor. Also, less experienced solicitors may inevitably charge more overall for fairly straightforward work as compared to a senior solicitor. This is because the junior solicitor on a lower hourly rate may take more time to complete the same task, whereas a more expensive senior solicitor may be able to complete the task more quickly albeit at a higher hourly rate; the lower rate doesn't balance out the additional time it takes for the junior solicitor to do the job.

*Unbundled services* have arisen recently – they offer the client a 'pay as you go' option, so the client seeks advice from the solicitor only when they need it or when they can afford to pay for it. The client is charged only for the advice given; they are expected to complete any agreed actions without any assistance from the solicitor.

For further detail see; U. Rice and M. Ruparel, *Unbundling Family Legal Services Toolkit* (Law Society Publishing, 2016).

A *limited retainer* is a retainer limited to a specific cost (e.g. no more than £1,000) or time (e.g. no more than 10 hours).

## 1.6 HOW CLIENTS PAY FOR SOLICITORS' TIME

### 1.6.1 Overview

Irrespective of how the solicitor charges for their work, the client needs to find a way to pay for such services. The following choices are available (explained below):

(a) paying from the client's own:
  (i) income; or
  (ii) capital or investments;
(b) gaining access to joint capital or investments;
(c) incurring debt by:
  (i) using credit cards;
  (ii) securing loans from high street lenders;
(d) securing loans from friends or family members;
(e) securing loans from specialist litigation loan lenders;
(f) making an application for the other party to pay for their legal services;
(g) agreeing a Sears Tooth arrangement with the firm (if available); and
(h) legal aid (if available).

### 1.6.2 Good practice guidance

It should be noted that any distrust injected into proceedings would be contrary to both the Resolution Code of Practice (Resolution is a community of family justice professionals who work with families and individuals to resolve issues in a constructive way); and the *Family Law Protocol* (4th edn, Law Society Publishing, 2015). Both organisations encourage lawyers who subscribe to their ethos to do everything they can to encourage co-operation and minimise inflammatory behaviour. Amicable divorces cost less and are over more quickly, and the more aggressive the steps that are taken, the more expensive proceedings tend to be – it is better to reflect and consider steps and their fall-out, rather than to lurch from threatening letter to court application. It is therefore important to recognise and challenge any action that a client proposes which may be interpreted as aggressive. The client should be advised of the consequences of their proposed actions. As funding is one of the first issues to be dealt with, it needs be discussed sensitively and with an eye on the consequences.

It is important to remember that solicitors must not give financial advice, as they are not authorised to do so. It may be difficult when dealing with financial remedy work to draw a line between advising on settlements and giving financial advice. Practitioners should always be cautious about this and ensure they do not give financial advice.

### 1.6.3 Client payment methods

#### 1.6.3.1 Using the client's own income, capital or investments

In most cases, the client will not be able to fund the entirety of their legal advice from income, capital or investments unless the client is extremely wealthy or they take legal advice only when they can afford to pay for it, using the unbundling model (see above). It may be that a first meeting and initial advice can be paid for by a combination of utilising income and capital/investments, but for the majority of people even this may not be possible.

It is always advisable for the client to take financial advice at the outset of the case, as this will assist them to understand their finances and funding options. In financial cases with complex assets, where capital gains tax is likely to be a consideration, early financial advice can help save thousands of pounds in the payment of tax. Financial advisers who are able to work with solicitors and add value to the case are very valuable, and the solicitor should seek out professional advisers to work with in some cases.

#### 1.6.3.2 Using joint savings or investments

It can sometimes be tricky for the client to draw down joint savings or investments without causing undue alarm to the other party. Joint savings accounts are often easy to access online or with a debit card or chequebook, but doing so can distress the joint account holder if this is not dealt with sensitively and transparently. The parties can agree to withdraw equal sums from those accounts, although it would be unusual if both parties had equally contributed to those savings. Either party could potentially withdraw the entire savings pot. Although this could be raised as a 'misconduct' issue within the proceedings, if those monies were spent on legal representation (and sufficient evidence exists to support that), it is unlikely that the court will make any findings of misconduct.

Where joint investments are concerned, solicitors should check whether their client has signed an authority for one spouse to deal with those investments unilaterally, which may be lodged with a wealth manager. This would allow the wealth manager to act on the direction of one party alone, and if this is the case such authority should be withdrawn.

If the client wants to draw down from joint investments where one party alone is not permitted to deal with the investments, the co-operation of their spouse will be needed so that investments can be sold or transferred to release funds. Sometimes, this is a matter that is easily agreed between the parties who will both need to fund legal costs. At other times, a wealthier party may not need access to those funds, and they may resolutely refuse to release funds, which may cause the other spouse financial difficulties.

There is no power for a court to order a spouse to sign any paperwork to release joint investments during proceedings – only a final order can achieve that result. On an interim basis, another way to fund legal costs will need to be sought.

If a spouse controls the parties' joint finances with the intention of preventing a spouse from obtaining legal advice, they are unlikely to get a better result from proceedings. In fact, it may be more cost-effective to ensure that the spouse has proper legal advice to enable a settlement to be reached sooner rather than later. In my experience, I would much rather deal with a specialist family lawyer than a litigant in person (or a McKenzie friend), as disputes are likely to settle quicker in these cases. Allowing the other party to be able to take legal advice is sensible in the overall scheme of things. Naturally, limitations can be placed on the funds available if it is feared that the other party will spend wantonly on legal advisers; or it can be stipulated that any capital advanced for the purpose of paying their legal costs will form part of their overall settlement, which should encourage them to spend carefully. However, these options are not likely to be available in low-asset cases as there may not be any savings or investments to speak of.

### 1.6.3.3 Getting credit cards or loans

If the client can obtain credit from credit card providers or high street lenders, it will go some way to help them pay for their legal costs. Most firms will accept credit and debit card payments these days – if this is not possible, it should be made clear to the client early on. The client must be made aware that there is no power for the court to redistribute debt within matrimonial finance proceedings – each party is expected to be responsible for the payment of their own legal costs. Although the court can make a costs order in limited circumstances, it would be highly unusual to make such an order in the majority of matrimonial finance cases as it goes against the general costs rule (see **4.11**).

As with any other debt, it is for the client to decide how to manage their financial affairs (preferably with the assistance of competent financial adviser) and understand whether they can repay any debt. They should not incur debt believing that their spouse will be responsible for the repayment of the debt at the end of proceedings. Solicitors must to be careful not to give financial advice, and there is a fine line between giving sufficient information for the client to make a decision and giving financial advice.

### 1.6.3.4 *Getting a loan from a friend or family member*

Sometimes clients prefer to borrow money from friends or family, as they usually offer more flexible credit facilities than a bank or a building society. Often these loans are unwritten, informal with terms that are only very loosely agreed between the parties. For this reason, these loans are viewed by the court as 'soft debt'. Effectively this means that the terms of the loan agreement are fluid, and repayment is not demanded weekly or monthly as it would be if borrowing from a high street lender. No repayment may be expected until the end of the case.

This can be problematic if the client intends to repay the loan from the proceeds of the settlement, particularly if they hope to get a larger settlement to reflect the sum owed under the terms of the loan, as only 'hard debt' is considered in the recovery of monies in the context of the dispute.

In order for the loan to be viewed as a 'hard debt', the terms would have to mirror those of a high street institution, and the agreement would need to be in writing and signed by the parties. The agreement should be contemporaneous with the loan, therefore backdating an agreement or entering into an agreement weeks or months after the loan has been made will not be sufficient. The agreement should set out the terms of repayment and any interest levied where applicable. Only then will the court consider such a debt to be on a par with a commercial lender.

A client should be made aware of the difference between 'hard debt' and 'soft debt' and how this may impact the recovery of monies in the context of the dispute. The friend or family member who is willing to loan money in the circumstances should be independently advised about any loan agreement entered into, and encouraged to enter into a written agreement where possible.

### 1.6.3.5 *Getting a specialist litigation loan*

There are currently a number of specialist litigation loan providers in the matrimonial finance market. Essentially, these providers will lend money to the client if there is sufficient security to justify the loan; and some providers offer unsecured loans at higher interest rates. Each provider has its own lending criteria, but most charge higher than usual rates of interest on the loan. Some require the solicitor to give undertakings to the lender before lending money to their client. As with any undertaking, a solicitor must be careful to consider whether to give an undertaking and comply with the firm's policies in respect of the same.

**Table 1.1** Commercial litigation lenders and interest rates

| Lender | Interest | Paid monthly or one payment | Simple or compounding Interest | Security | Fees |
| --- | --- | --- | --- | --- | --- |
| Novitas Loans | 1.5% per month, 18% annual interest rate | Minimum payments per month | Simple interest | The client signs deed of assignment and possibly pays an insurance premium | £500 setup fee or 1% of the facility if the loan is above £50,000 (this can be rolled into the loan or paid upfront) |
| | | | | | Fee to take independent legal advice on the terms of the agreement, estimated at £300 |
| Iceberg Client Credit LLP | 1.5% per month, 18% per annum (variable) | Minimum payments per month plus drawdown fee | Not known | Not known | No application fee, but there are drawdown fees |
| Schneider Financial Solutions | Standard unsecured rate: 2% per month or 24% per year fixed rate (24.8% APR representative) | No monthly payments – single payment taken from settlement | Simple interest | Various options offered from fully secured to unsecured | £500 arrangement fee or 1% of loan amount |
| | Partly secured rate: 1.5% per month or 18% per year fixed rate (18.9% APR representative) | | | | Fees to take independent legal advice in respect of the credit agreement, estimated at £250 |

PRE-INSTRUCTION

| Lender | Interest | Paid monthly or one payment | Simple or compounding Interest | Security | Fees |
|---|---|---|---|---|---|
| RateSetter | Fully secured rate: 1.25% per month or 15% per year fixed rate (15.9% APR representative) 14.9% per annum variable | No monthly payments – single payment taken from settlement | Not known | The client signs a deed of assignment | Fees to take independent legal advice in respect of the credit agreement |

**Note:** Information correct at time of writing.

The client must always take separate legal advice regarding the loan agreement paperwork – the matrimonial solicitor cannot give such advice as they would be in conflict. A solicitor cannot give financial advice, and the solicitor should bear this in mind.

In my experience, it is not terribly difficult to secure such loans if there are assets in England and Wales, but it can be more difficult if the assets are located overseas. If there is not sufficient security, then the loan provider may insist that the client takes out insurance with them, which attracts an additional fee.

One of the interesting issues that can arise as a result of this type of lending is that the client may lose their sense of proportionality in respect of the monies which are utilised for litigation funding. When I was a legal aid practitioner, I found that sometimes a client would not seriously commit to reaching an agreement if they knew that their case would be funded to include a 'day in court'. The same can be said for a client in receipt of a litigation loan – the fact that the loan needs to be repaid in the future can be lost to the immediacy of the litigation process. This means that the client doesn't feel focused on settling the dispute at an early stage as they know that they can afford to litigate the matter to the final hearing. The rates of interest may be uncomfortably high, but these loans are a viable option for many people whose money is tied up in inaccessible investments or real property.

Table 1.1 summarises some of the current specialist litigation lenders and the interest rates they charge. These are likely to be subject to change, and therefore should be checked by the solicitor in the event that this option is being explored for the client.

### 1.6.3.6 An application to fund legal services

BACKGROUND AND OVERVIEW

One party can apply to the court to fund their legal services following the issue of a divorce or civil partnership dissolution. The application is made under Matrimonial Causes Act (MCA) 1973, s.22ZA or Civil Partnership Act (CPA) 2004, Sched.5, paras.38A–38B. Such an order is known as a 'legal services order' and was introduced by LASPO 2012, ss.49–54.

Legal services are defined in both MCA 1973, s.22ZA(10) and CPA 2004, Sched.5, Part 8, para.38A(10) as follows:

(a) providing advice as to how the law applies in the particular circumstances;
(b) providing advice and assistance in relation to the proceedings;
(c) providing other advice and assistance in relation to the settlement or other resolution of the dispute that is the subject of the proceedings; and
(d) providing advice and assistance in relation to the enforcement of decisions in the proceedings or as part of the settlement or resolution of the dispute,

and they include, in particular, advice and assistance in the form of representation and any form of dispute resolution, including mediation. This is very useful, as money can be secured to pay for one of the NCDR processes and not just for litigation.

When weighing up the pros and cons of making this application, the applicant should consider the statutory factors – the court will not make an order unless it is satisfied that without the order the applicant would not reasonably be able to obtain appropriate legal services. The applicant therefore needs to set out in their statement what efforts they have made to secure funding for applying to the court. If there is any other affordable way to fund the case, then this application should not be made as it is unlikely to succeed.

Sometimes people refer to these orders as 'Rubin' orders. In the case of *Rubin* v. *Rubin* [2014] EWHC 611 (Fam), Mr Justice Mostyn set out those matters that the applicant must address when making such an application. Specifically, with reference to litigation loans charged at a higher rate of interest, he noted that it would be unlikely to be reasonable to expect the applicant to take out such a loan unless the respondent offered an undertaking to meet the interest, if the court later considers it just so to order. This is an important point to note regarding the issue of whether or not to take a specialist litigation loan. It could be cheaper and quicker to secure a litigation loan than to incur the legal cost of making an application for the other party to fund the case. The solicitor should spend time weighing the potential cost of a legal services order application against the interest that may accrue on a litigation loan. Additionally, a court application will take some time to resolve due to delays at court, but the litigation loan could be secured within seven days. These are all options for the solicitor to consider carefully with the client.

If an order is granted, the court should make it clear which legal services the payment is for and how it is paid to the recipient. The guidance states that the court should not agree to fund the matter beyond the financial dispute resolution (FDR) appointment. This ensures that the parties will (hopefully) use their best efforts to negotiate before and at the FDR appointment, rather than wait for a day or more in contested court proceedings. It is better for the payment of costs to be made monthly rather than as a single lump sum payment. This resembles the way in which legal aid was authorised to be paid before the introduction of the legal services order (albeit at a much lower cost). A legal aid certificate, if granted, is limited to costs incurred up to the FDR hearing with the costs limit capped. It is much easier to control the expenditure of legal costs if managed on a regular monthly basis rather a one-off payment.

APPLICATION PROCEDURE

An application is made under Family Procedure Rules (FPR) 2010 SI 2010/2955, Part 18 (**www.justice.gov.uk/courts/procedure-rules/family/rules_pd_menu**). The correct form to use is the D11. The application form must be supported by written evidence – this is usually the applicant's evidence regarding efforts to secure alternative forms of funding and other matters. The application form, statement and fee should be sent to the divorce centre where the petition was issued or to the court dealing with the financial matter.

The statement of the applicant should address the following matters;

(a)  the statutory factors set out in MCA 1973, s.22ZB/CPA 2004 equivalent;
(b)  those matters highlighted by the case of *Rubin* v. *Rubin*;
(c)  a breakdown of the anticipated legal costs to be incurred by the applicant;
(d)  where costs have already been incurred then they should be detailed.

With regards to the payment of historic costs (legal costs already incurred in respect of the same matter), the court must take into account whether or not the applicant would have been able to secure future legal services without the payment of the historic costs. It is important that all costs figures are as accurate as possible, otherwise adequate funds will not be made available for the payment of legal services.

A costs order may well be made in respect of this application, by reference to the relevant rule at FPR 2010, rule 28.1, which says that 'the court may at any time make such order as to costs as it thinks just'. However, there should be no duplication in respect of the historic costs to be paid and any costs order made. The general rule in financial remedy cases at FPR 2010, rule 28.3 regarding costs does not apply in respect of interim applications.

The fact that a costs order could be made should be factored into the advice given to a client about the proportionality of making or defending such an application.

### 1.6.3.7 A Sears Tooth agreement

A Sears Tooth agreement is a way of funding a financial remedy case between the client and the firm. The firm agrees with the client to defer collection of its fees until the end of the case. The firm agrees its terms and conditions of engagement with the client at the outset, the hourly rate etc. – however, no payment is expected until the settlement of the financial remedy case. Given that a financial remedy case can take 12–24 months to settle depending on the complexity, this is a big commitment from the firm.

The agreement is drafted as a deed of assignment, considered in *Sears Tooth* v. *Payne Hicks Beach* [1997] 2 FLR 116. If the client intends to sign a deed of assignment, they need to take independent legal advice on the terms of the agreement. The deed of assignment can only validly assign the proceeds of a lump sum order, although not a lump sum order payable in instalments which could be subject to variation or discharge.

It is possible to assign rights in relation to financial provision generally, which includes an entitlement to periodical payments. Mr Justice Moylan in the case of *RK* v. *RK* [2011] EWHC 3910 (Fam), expressed concern about this provision. With reference to the enforcement of such a provision he said (at para.94): 'I would be surprised if the purported assignment of any periodical payments order was enforceable in this case.' There seems to be no issue with the enforcement of an assignment of capital orders or property orders, but it is likely that the assignment of income orders or pension orders would be problematic.

Any solicitor agreeing to accept payment by way of a Sears Tooth agreement needs to wait for payment until the end of the case when the settlement money is available. Given the current delays in the court system, this could be a lengthy wait. No success fee can be levied, as this would be seen to be a conditional fee agreement, the use of which is unlawful in family proceedings. The solicitor also needs to calculate carefully the likely settlement funds available to the client at the end of the case; and to cross-check proportionality and the likelihood of enforcing the deed of assignment against the settlement assets. If the solicitor–client relationship breaks down, it will impact on the payment of costs due to the solicitor.

The SRA has addressed the issue of regulated consumer credit agreements and the use of Sears Tooth agreements by solicitors (see **www.sra.org.uk/solicitors/code-of-conduct/financial-services-rules/questions-answers.page**). They say that the rules allow firms to enter into this type of agreement to pay disbursements or professional fees. The agreement must comply with restrictions, such as the fact that credit must not be secured on land by a legal or equitable mortgage. The agreement is therefore an unsecured agreement with the client, which can only be enforced against assets as ordered by the court at the end of proceedings.

The Sears Tooth agreement was developed at a time when specialist litigation loans were not available and when legal aid had been reduced, making it commercially unattractive to larger firms dealing with high net-worth cases. The Sears Tooth agreement was a way of helping spouses, often the wives of rich men, to fund their financial remedy case when few other options were available. It is unlikely that this option is as popular now that specialist lenders are willing to lend in these cases. The Sears Tooth agreement is unattractive from a firm's business perspective, as there is no prospect for any payment to the firm until the conclusion of proceedings. Given the current court delays, it could be 12–24 months before any payment is made to the firm.

### 1.6.3.8 The availability of legal aid

It is incumbent upon every solicitor to consider whether a client could be eligible for legal aid at the start of their instructions. Even if the solicitor does not work for a firm that has a legal aid contract, such considerations must be taken into account. The availability of legal aid was restricted by the introduction of LASPO 2012. There are still limited instances when legal aid is available for financial remedy work, and these should be explored where appropriate. In the event that a solicitor does not explore these options with the client, they may not be able to recover any private fees incurred for that client if it becomes apparent that they could have been eligible for legal aid.

In respect of matrimonial finance work, legal aid is likely to be relevant when dealing with the requirement to attend the mediation information and assessment meeting (MIAM) or the attendance by the parties at mediation. Where one party is eligible to receive legal aid, the MIAM for both will be paid for by the Legal Aid Agency (LAA). From 3 November 2014, the LAA will fund one single mediation session for both parties, if one of the parties is eligible for legal aid. The party entitled to legal aid will continue to be in receipt of funding for the duration of mediation, whereas the other party will need to fund further mediation sessions themselves. Although there are means criteria that need to be fulfilled to be eligible for legal aid, there are no merits criteria with regard to attendance at MIAM or mediation. This ensures that the pool of people who can receive legal aid to attend a MIAM and receive funding for mediation is larger than the pool of people who would be able to receive legal aid for a litigated process.

A small number of people will still be eligible for legal aid to be represented in matrimonial finance litigation if they meet the eligibility criteria, both on means (gross and net income and capital) and merits. To meet the merits test an applicant needs to be able to demonstrate that they are at risk of domestic abuse – this includes financially abusive behaviour in addition to more traditional definitions of domestic abuse. The client also needs to get through the legal aid gateway by producing evidence of domestic abuse.

If legal aid is granted, the client needs to be made aware that the statutory charge will apply. This means that the client will need to repay the cost of their legal services (usually at legal aid rates) from the money they recover or protect during the proceedings. In the event that there is not sufficient liquid capital to repay the LAA, a charge will be taken on any property protected or recovered as a result of the proceedings. The monies owed to the LAA will be subject to the payment of interest until those costs have been discharged. Currently the LAA charges interest at 8 per cent, and interest is calculated daily.

Where legal aid is still available to a client, the client should be informed of their eligibility and encouraged to apply, even if that means sending the client to a firm that has a legal aid franchise. The Ministry of Justice has a Civil Legal Aid Eligibility Calculator online that can help practitioners give clients the right advice (see **http://civil-eligibility-calculator.justice.gov.uk**). The client would benefit from being eligible for legal aid even though it needs to be repaid at the end of the case, as the solicitor is not permitted to charge their private hourly rate but is subject to the rates of remuneration set by the LAA which are substantially lower than private rates. Where a client is eligible for legal aid, they should be encouraged to pursue this option rather than pay private rates.

It should be noted that as costs orders are very rarely made in financial remedy cases, they are only made exceptionally against a legally aided party which is an additional benefit to the legally aided party.

## 1.7 NON-COURT DISPUTE RESOLUTION OPTIONS

In all likelihood, you will spend some time talking to the client about NCDR options. These are dealt with in more detail in **Chapter 2**. At these early stages, the client might decide to refer themselves to a MIAM, and this would keep any acrimony to a minimum as the parties can discuss matters in front of the mediator if that is what is agreed. I am more than happy to give my clients details of the mediation services that I refer to so that they can explore the mediation option themselves.

It is also worth noting that the client may not have decided that the marriage has come to an end, if they are not the one initiating the relationship breakdown. If this is the case, it is worth referring the client to local marriage guidance counselling services. For example, Relate (**www.relate.org.uk**) have a good network of counsellors who could help the couple resolve any issues that have arisen to enable them to strengthen their relationship; another potential directory is the British Association for Counselling and Psychotherapy (**www.bacp.co.uk**).

## 1.8 AT THE END OF THE FIRST MEETING

At the end of the first meeting, the client should understand their options going forward. You will have discussed funding, and hopefully the different ways in which they can engage the services of you and your firm.

The client might decide to engage your services immediately, signing your terms and conditions of business and placing sufficient funds on account if signing a traditional retainer agreement. Or, they may wish to go away and absorb the information you have given them to decide whether to 'wait and see'. If they are unsure whether to instruct you, they may see other solicitors and then decide at a later stage.

It is good practice to follow up a meeting with a detailed letter setting out the instructions (if any) and information you have given. This helps in the event that there are later conflict or regulatory issues that need to be considered in more detail.

Obviously, if it has been agreed in advance that no follow-up correspondence will be sent, then such a letter is unnecessary and indeed could be unwelcome. You may have agreed not to write a letter because the appointment was a free appointment, or because the client does not want you to write to them if there are domestic abuse or coercive control issues. This should always be checked with the client in advance of sending a letter or email to the client. Family practitioners should always be wary of leaving voicemail messages with a client unless permission has been given to do so, just in case their spouse has access to them. At the early stages, the solicitor should always check what forms of communication are safe and expected by the client.

Whether an initial letter is written to the client or not, it is sensible to keep any notes from the first appointment and to ensure that these are legible for future reference. This may involve having the notes typed up if they were jotted down hastily during the meeting. It looks terribly disorganised if the client returns to instruct you six months after the first meeting and you have no recollection of the information or advice from the first meeting. It can also be useful if a client returns to give you instructions on a relationship breakdown more than a year after an initial meeting – they often expect you to remember them and what they told you! Your notes will be invaluable in such a situation.

CHAPTER 2
# Non-court dispute resolution

## 2.1 INTRODUCTION

These days it is usual for solicitors to contemplate all forms of non-court dispute resolution (NCDR) (also known as alternative dispute resolution (ADR)) both at the stage of a first instruction (**Chapter 1**) and during the course of the matter. Each practitioner will have their own preferred method of referral to NCDR processes, which will be informed by their own experience and availability of processes in the area. See the incredibly useful research paper, A. Barlow et al., 'Mapping paths to family justice' (University of Exeter, 2014), which compares people's experiences using different forms of NCDR available at the time – mainly solicitors' negotiation, mediation and collaborative practice (available at: **www.familylaw.co.uk/news_and_comment/mapping-paths-to-family-justice**).

It is generally accepted by lawyers that an agreement reached by parties between themselves is much easier to accept and enforce than an order that the parties have imposed upon them by a judge. Parties who are able to reach an agreement are often able to reduce conflict between them and reduce the impact of the relationship breakdown on any children involved. Agreements are sometimes quicker to finalise and almost always cheaper than litigation for the parties. Giving the parties an opportunity to reach a settlement between themselves is desirable, but different NCDR processes will suit different couples. It is important to understand how each process operates so that you can discuss them with your client at the first meeting and as the matter progresses.

It is not unusual for parties who rejected NCDR processes at the start of the matter to become more open to them after months of high conflict litigation. The current delays in the court process will inevitably impact on the parties' desire to use NCDR processes as a viable alternative. It is undeniable that the current government and a series of governments before it dating back to at least 2012, have emphasised that people should use NCDR processes rather than the courts.

This chapter gives a broad outline of the different NCDR processes, as well as the mediation information and assessment meeting (MIAM). The *Family Law Protocol* (4th edn, Law Society Publishing, 2015) has a much more detailed explanation of how each of these processes works. It is useful to meet with NCDR practitioners in your area to discuss the different processes they offer so that you can explain them fully to your client – this will allow the client to make an informed choice. (It is difficult to explain processes to the client that you don't offer – for example, mediation when the solicitor isn't a mediator.)

## 2.2 LIST OF NON-COURT DISPUTE RESOLUTION PROCESSES

There are now many NCDR processes used in family finance matter matters, which are:

- mediation:
    - various options are available, such as co-mediation, shuttle mediation, commercial style or even solicitor inclusive mediation;
    - child inclusive mediation – where a specially trained mediator speaks with the children; this can be a very powerful when the mediator reports back;
- collaborative family practice (CFP);
- arbitration;
- private early neutral evaluation (ENE)/private financial dispute resolution (FDR) processes; and
- solicitors' negotiation (in writing and oral round-table negotiations), which will need to be principled and ethics-based.

These processes are explained below, but first we discuss the MIAM.

## 2.3 MEDIATION INFORMATION AND ASSESSMENT MEETING

### 2.3.1 What is it?

Strictly speaking the mediation information and assessment meeting (MIAM) isn't an NCDR process, but an initial meeting used to explain the different NCDR processes to the client, and to assess the suitability of each process (listed above) for the individual attending and their issues.

This meeting is also used to assess legal aid eligibility (FPR 2010, rule 2.9).

The meeting will also have a safeguarding role to protect relevant individuals.

Although this sounds as though it could be conducted by a solicitor at the first meeting, this is a separate meeting conducted by an accredited mediator. The MIAM was introduced as a result of changes to FPR 2010. FPR 2010, Part 3 currently requires that the applicant to a prospective financial (or children) application to court must attend a MIAM before being permitted to issue any such application.

### 2.3.2 Is it mandatory?

The introduction of Children and Families Act (CFA) 2014, s.10(1) makes the applicant's attendance at the MIAM appointment compulsory, subject to a number of exemptions. Prior to the introduction of CFA 2014, the applicant's attendance at a MIAM had been strongly encouraged, but not mandatory.

There are available exemptions (see below) which mean that the applicant doesn't need to attend if they can validly claim an exemption. In these cases, the applicant can apply to the court for a financial remedy application without attending the meeting and the court must issue the application. Even in cases where the applicant could be exempt from attending a MIAM, I would consider referring them to one so that they are able to discuss NCDR options with the accredited mediator.

#### 2.3.2.1 Applicant's exemption to attend MIAM

It is possible for an applicant to claim an exemption from the general requirement to attend the MIAM. The relevant information about the applicant's exemption can be found at FPR 2010, rule 3.8. The exemptions are specific and require the applicant to have evidence to support the exemption claimed. It is not necessary to send the evidence to the court with the application form – this can of course lead to unrepresented parties ticking a box to claim an exemption without any requirement to evidence the exemption claimed.

The applicant is required to take the exemption evidence to the first hearing; in reality no judge ever asks to see the evidence. In the event that the exemption is wrongly claimed, it is unlikely that any penalty will be imposed on the applicant (or solicitor) by the court, particularly if the applicant is a litigant in person.

Broadly, the categories of exemption are:

- domestic violence;
- child protection concerns;
- urgency (which is unusual in financial remedy cases);
- previous MIAM attendance or MIAM exemption;
- other reason – for example, in financial proceedings if the prospective applicant is bankrupt, they do not need to attend a MIAM as they do not have the capacity to deal with their own financial affairs.

FPR 2010, rule 3.10 states that if a MIAM exemption is not validly claimed and the court becomes aware of this at the first hearing, then the court has the power to:

- direct the applicant or both parties to attend a MIAM;
- adjourn the proceedings to enable a MIAM to take place.

Due to the general listing delays in the family court, it is highly unlikely that the judge will adjourn a financial remedy application to allow a MIAM to take place. This would cause further unnecessary delay which contravenes the 'overriding objective' (FPR 2010, Part 1). However, attending a MIAM could assist the parties to avoid costly and complex litigated proceedings altogether by informing them of their non-court options. The overriding objective is as follows (FPR 2010, rule 1.1):

(1) These rules are a new procedural code with the overriding objective of enabling the court to deal with cases justly, having regard to any welfare issues involved.
(2) Dealing with a case justly includes, so far as is practicable–
   (a) ensuring that it is dealt with expeditiously and fairly;
   (b) dealing with the case in ways which are proportionate to the nature, importance and complexity of the issues;
   (c) ensuring that the parties are on an equal footing;
   (d) saving expense; and
   (e) allotting to it an appropriate share of the court's resources, while taking into account the need to allot resources to other cases.

If there is a mediation service at court, then a mediator could speak to the applicant and respondent on the day and explain the role of mediation and other NCDR processes in helping to resolve disputes. The availability of such services at court is patchy, as it usually relies on mediators volunteering to provide the service.

In the event that one party has not validly claimed an exemption, in deciding what to do the court will have regard to:

- applicable time limits;
- the reasons why the MIAM exemption was not validly claimed;
- the applicability of any other MIAM exemption; and
- the number and nature of issues that remain to be resolved in the proceedings.

Judges generally do not impose any type of sanction on an applicant for claiming an invalid exemption. With the overriding objective in mind (FPR 2010, Part 1), they endeavour to ensure that parties have the opportunity to attend a MIAM if this is thought to be in their best interests. This is balanced against the need to timetable matters forward and reduce delay. People often believe that their partner will not attend a MIAM or that any hope of resolving matters amicably is impossible by the very fact of the parties' relationship breakdown. Many couples are able to resolve matters by using NCDR, and the first step towards choosing the right process can start with the parties' attendance at a MIAM.

### 2.3.2.2 Applicant is referred to a MIAM

Where the applicant intends to attend a MIAM, the mediator must be accredited to undertake a MIAM. Not all mediators are able to offer these appointments as the mediator must be specially accredited. The applicant should give the mediator the respondent's contact details so that they can be invited to attend a MIAM. As the saying goes, it is impossible to clap with one hand, likewise it is impossible to proceed with any NCDR process with only one consenting party.

If both parties agree to attend a MIAM, each party will likely have a separate appointment to ensure that the mediator can assess if there are any power imbalances, screen the couple for domestic abuse issues and decide if the case is suitable for mediation. Although the mediator should give information about all NCDR processes, it is most likely that the parties' attendance at a MIAM will result in a referral to mediation. Parties are entitled to see a MIAMs provider within 15 days of making contact with them.

### 2.3.2.3 Mediator's exemption

If the mediator does not believe that the case is suitable for mediation, the applicant will be given a mediator's exemption to confirm that mediation is not a suitable. This will be recorded by the mediator signing the declaration that is usually on the financial remedy application form, which will be the Form A in a typical financial remedy case. Sometimes the mediator will be asked to sign the Form FM1 if the application form does not contain the declaration for the mediator to sign. In other areas of family law, the mediator's signature will be required on a different form, but the rules are much the same. With the signature from the mediator, the court should issue an application even if the applicant has not attended the MIAM. This will often happen where the mediator has tried to engage the respondent without any success. It is good practice for the mediator to contact the other party and give them 15 days to respond.

### 2.3.3 How many people are involved?

If the respondent agrees to attend a MIAM, the parties attend separately. They see the same mediator who is qualified to carry out a MIAM. Usually three people are involved at this stage, albeit at separate meetings.

### 2.3.4 Are solicitors involved?

The parties should take separate advice from solicitors if they wish to do so before or after the MIAM. Solicitors do not take part in the MIAM itself.

### 2.3.5 Are barristers involved?

At this stage barristers aren't usually involved, unless the mediator conducting the MIAM is a barrister accredited to offer MIAMs.

### 2.3.6 How long does it take?

The MIAM is a single meeting which can take an hour or so. Each mediator will conduct the meeting differently.

### 2.3.7 What will it cost?

The cost of attending a MIAM is between £75 and £150 per person, if neither party qualifies for legal aid.

### 2.3.8 Is legal aid available?

Yes, legal aid is available to parties if they satisfy the means testing criteria. Currently, if one party is able to qualify for legal aid, the other party will not need to pay their own fee for attendance at the MIAM. If both parties agree to commence the mediation process, the eligible party will receive legal aid for the entirety of the mediation process. The other spouse will receive funding for the first mediation meeting by the Legal Aid Agency (LAA) and then they will need to meet their own costs for mediation or other NCDR processes.

### 2.3.9 Is there a guaranteed outcome?

No. The purpose of the MIAM is to ensure the parties understand the alternative options to the litigation process. The outcome of a MIAM is likely to be a referral to another NCDR process.

### 2.3.10 Can either party walk away?

Yes. The only requirement is that the applicant attends the meeting. There is no obligation for the applicant to commit to NCDR. The respondent isn't usually required to attend the meeting, unless ordered by the court to do so. Even then, the respondent can walk away after the meeting without committing to NCDR.

## 2.4 MEDIATION

Mediation is often the first port of call for NCDR processes as it is the process that most clients and family practitioners are comfortable with. This process has been actively promoted by successive governments since the 1990s. In practice, I always encourage people to go to mediation, as it is cost-effective in most cases. Parties can be sceptical about attending, but most will find it useful.

### 2.4.1 What is it?

Mediation is a process whereby the mediator helps the parties to negotiate a settlement between them. It can be used in financial and children matters. The mediator will firstly assess the parties to ensure that the dispute is appropriate for a mediated settlement – this process is known as 'screening'. Once the mediator is satisfied that the parties can safely participate in the mediation process, the mediation will begin. The mediator acts as a neutral party and can provide information but not advice to help the parties to facilitate settlement. There are many different models for mediation – the *Family Law Protocol* sets out the different models in more detail.

The family mediation model is such that meditation takes place over a series of meetings between the parties and the mediator. These meetings could take between three to six sessions, depending on the issues that the parties need to resolve.

### 2.4.2  Is it mandatory?

No. Although an applicant is required to attend a MIAM appointment if they intend to commence court proceedings, mediation is an entirely voluntary process.

### 2.4.3  How many people are involved?

The parties and the mediator will be involved. There are therefore a minimum of three people; occasionally there are two mediators involved in the process and so four people will be in the room.

### 2.4.4  Are solicitors involved?

Solicitors are encouraged to advise clients between mediation meetings. Solicitors are rarely invited to join the parties in mediation – if they attend, their role will be to support their client rather than to advocate on behalf of the client.

There is now a 'hybrid mediation' model which is more akin to the civil mediation model. In this process, solicitor participation (either in person or on the phone) is encouraged. This works well where there is one person with legal representation and the other is a litigant in person. In this instance, the meditator will be an important source of legal information and will assist with any power imbalances (or domination by the legal adviser!).

### 2.4.5  Are barristers involved?

A barrister could be the mediator and would therefore be involved in that capacity. It is not usual for barristers to be involved in family mediation. However, there are other models of mediation that could be utilised in a family case that could involve barristers. A mediation model allowing barristers to attend as advocates is more similar to a civil or commercial mediation model, in which a day or more is dedicated to the process. In this type of mediation process, disclosure usually takes place before the mediation starts.

Mediators may refer for an early neutral evaluation to a barrister when there are complex legal issues or even when there aren't.

### 2.4.6 How long does it take?

Depending on the issues to be discussed, three to six meetings will usually be needed. These are arranged for the mutual convenience of the parties and the mediator, and so could take six weeks or six months depending on how quickly the parties want to resolve matters and how quickly the parties can get their financial disclosure together. Issues of disclosure are discussed more fully at **Chapter 3**.

### 2.4.7 How much does it cost?

It is difficult to predict the overall costs of mediation, as it will depend on the mediator's hourly charge. The costs per person could be in the region of £500 to £3,000. More experienced mediators will charge more for their time, but overall this will save the couple money as litigation will always be more expensive than a mediator-led settlement.

### 2.4.8 Is legal aid available?

Yes, legal aid is available for those people who meet the means criteria set by the LAA. The mediator will calculate whether the client is eligible for legal aid. A person entitled to legal aid for mediation may also get legal help with mediation to support them with legal advice alongside mediation services.

### 2.4.9 Is there a guaranteed outcome?

No – although the success rates of people attending mediation is quite good. There is never a guaranteed successful outcome.

### 2.4.10 Can either party walk away?

Yes, either party can walk away during the process. They are not bound to the process once they start it.

### 2.4.11 If it fails, what next?

If mediation does not result in an outcome, then the parties can try a different NCDR process or proceed to litigate.

It may soon be possible to encourage mediation clients to go on to arbitration – the arbitrator being a different person to the mediator. This could help where, say, the clients are only disagreeing on one or two discreet issues. This will be outlined in the agreement to mediate.

### 2.4.12 If it succeeds, what next?

If the parties reach an agreement the mediator will prepare a document called the memorandum of understanding (MOU). This document is marked 'without prejudice' as the settlement proposals are not binding between the parties at this stage. It is extremely important that the parties take legal advice on the proposals and if those proposals are accepted to be final after taking advice, solicitors will confirm that the proposals are binding in open correspondence. Once this is done, solicitors need to draft a consent order to send to the court, or if the applicant is represented it is now mandatory to use the digitised consent order system. In the absence of a consent order, the parties are likely to have continuing financial obligations to each other; a consent order usually contains dismissal clauses to ensure that future obligations are set out and dismissed where appropriate.

Mediators are now permitted to draft consent orders. This is a new development and further guidance for mediators can be found in the Law Society's 'Guidance for mediators in incorporating standard consent order precedents' (2019), available at: **www.lawsociety.org.uk/support-services/advice/articles/consent-order-guidance/**. Mediators won't be able to give any legal advice as they will continue to act in a neutral capacity; solicitors may still be needed to give advice on the proposals agreed at mediation if instructed to do so.

Practitioners should note that the court will not simply approve the consent order just because the parties have reached an agreement in mediation. The judge must look at the financial and other information sent to the court and decide whether the proposed settlement is fair to both parties. Sometimes, the judge may ask questions by letter to check that the parties have understood its implications or because the judge is concerned about the overall fairness of the division of assets and income. Responses to these queries should result in a court order being sealed, but occasionally the terms may need to be re-negotiated if the judge doesn't feel the proposed settlement is fair. It is unusual but possible that a judge may list a short hearing to ensure that the parties understand the nature of their agreement and the terms of the consent order. Where one party is ostensibly without legal representation, the judge may want to ensure that the agreement is understood by all parties. The parties should be made aware of the possibility that the judge will not approve the settlement or may require drafting amendments to the consent order.

### 2.4.13 What financial input is needed?

Solicitors are not authorised to give financial advice, and as such should be careful to ensure that financial advice is taken by the client before a final settlement is reached. The input of an experienced financial adviser is invaluable during this process. Often, matters of tax efficiency and financial planning will save the couple money when in the process of negotiating a divorce or civil partnership settlement.

It may be that a single joint expert (SJE) is needed to value an asset or to provide a report about the complexities of the parties' pension situation. This can be arranged during the mediation process with an understanding between the parties that they will use the expert's report in litigation, if the mediation does not result in a final settlement. The issue of the appointment of an expert in court proceedings is dealt with further in **Chapter 7**.

## 2.5 COLLABORATIVE FAMILY PRACTICE

### 2.5.1 What is it?

A client will approach or be referred to a practitioner who is trained in the collaborative process. The solicitor and client will agree to try to reach a settlement without initiating any court processes, save for starting the divorce and to submit a consent order.

The couple and their respective collaboratively trained solicitors work together to find a solution to the problems caused by the relationship breakdown. This can involve both financial and children matters.

Even though I am not collaboratively trained, if I come across a couple who would benefit from CFP, I am happy to refer them to a collaboratively trained practitioner.

### 2.5.2 Is it mandatory?

No, as with all NCDR processes this is a voluntary option.

### 2.5.3 How many people are involved?

The couple and their respective solicitors will be involved. Often it is known as a four-way process as meetings are held between the parties and solicitors which leads to settlement.

Many practitioners work with family consultants (FC) who assist the couple (and the solicitors) with the emotional side of the ending of the relationship and help to keep the process on track. In these circumstances, the couple will often work extensively with the FC, between sessions, to help with healing and practising new ways of communicating. The FC is usually at the meetings with the lawyers in five-way meetings. The use of FCs usually decreases the number of meetings the couple need with their lawyers.

Additionally, a financial neutral may be appointed to attend meetings to assist the parties by explaining the consequence of proposals from a tax-planning or affordability perspective. The neutral gives impartial advice to the parties.

### 2.5.4 Are solicitors involved?

Yes, the solicitors are usually the collaboratively trained practitioners.

### 2.5.5 Are barristers involved?

Barristers may also be collaboratively trained and can conduct the four-way meetings in place of the solicitor; they will often be asked to give an early evaluation. They may also be asked to draft complex consent orders emanating from the process. That said, they aren't usually involved in addition to a solicitor.

### 2.5.6 How long does it take?

This will depend on the issues the parties need to resolve. Much like mediation, the settlement discussions take place to suit the parties and their solicitors. The process could take six weeks or six months.

### 2.5.7 How much does it cost?

The total cost of CFP is usually comparable to the cost of the litigation up to the FDR stage. The actual costs will therefore vary from practitioner to practitioner, depending on their hourly charges. The advantage of collaborative practice is that it is likely to be much quicker than litigation and will reduce conflict within the family.

### 2.5.8 Is legal aid available?

No.

### 2.5.9 Is there a guaranteed outcome?

There is no guaranteed outcome. The parties sign a 'participation agreement' at the outset of proceedings which commits the couple and solicitors to finding a solution outside the court litigation process. This means that the parties are committed to the process, and such commitment helps to secure the trust of the parties and increases the chances of the parties reaching a settlement. There is no data available that records how successful the CFP has been over the years, although solicitors anecdotally report high levels of success which are comparable to mediation.

### 2.5.10 Can either party walk away?

Yes, either party can decide to walk away from the process. However, once they walk away from the process they also walk away from their solicitor. This is a central tenet of CFP and of the participation agreement the parties sign – that the solicitors can only represent a client outside the litigation process. If the client decides to depart from the process, they will need to find a new solicitor to represent them.

## 2.5.11 If it fails, what next?

If the parties are unable to reach a final agreement using the CFP, they will need to find an alternative route to settlement. This might be through the litigation process or an alternative NCDR process. It may soon be possible for collaborative practitioners to move forward and help their clients in arbitration.

## 2.5.12 If it succeeds, what next?

If the parties are able to reach a final settlement through the CFP process, then the solicitors will need to draft a consent order to submit to the court or, where the applicant is represented, via the digitised consent order system.

## 2.5.13 What financial input is needed?

During the CFP four-way meetings, it is possible to involve a 'financial neutral'. This will be an independent financial adviser (IFA) or financial planner who can act in a neutral capacity to give financial input to help both parties. They can, with consent of the parties, also implement the proposals.

It may be that an SJE is needed to provide independent expert opinion regarding, for example, the valuation of an asset, or even to report on the complexities of pensions. This matter can be agreed between the parties and their representatives.

## 2.6 ARBITRATION

### 2.6.1 What is it?

Arbitration is unlike other forms of NCDR because the arbitrator is a decision-maker rather than a facilitator. The arbitrator must be a member of the Chartered Institute of Arbitrators and will have passed a course about the financial arbitration scheme. The parties instruct the arbitrator to resolve a specific dispute between them – this could be as broad as a general financial remedy dispute following a divorce or civil partnership, or as narrow as deciding what happens regarding the parties' pensions. More information on the financial arbitration process can be found on the Institute of Family Law Arbitrators (IFLA) website: **www.ifla.org.uk**. There is also a group called FamilyArbitrator, run by a number of prominent family arbitrators, whose website provides useful blogs and resources: **www.family arbitrator.com**.

There are many reasons to use the financial arbitration scheme. One of the most pressing reasons in recent months is the unreliable state of the Family Court. Those matters that have been issued are often delayed in the Family Court by the lack of money to secure the services of judges to hear matters, or a lack of suitable court rooms. This means that couples who would like a structured process, which ultimately leads to a judge making a decision, are let down by substantial delays.

Those couples would very much benefit from using arbitration, which is a structured process involving a third party decision-maker. Often, parties who have prepared for a final three-day hearing will discover at the eleventh hour that their case has been adjourned. It is entirely possible to secure the services of an arbitrator at the last minute, to stand in as the decision-maker. The parties benefit by not having to prepare for another contested hearing six months down the line. Neither will they lose any counsels' fees that will inevitably be deemed to be paid by the time the court adjourns the hearing. This can run to thousands of pounds for each party.

The third party decision-maker is the arbitrator who can be chosen by the parties or their solicitors. There is a wide choice of qualified arbitrators from solicitors (like me!), to junior barristers, senior barristers, QCs, part-time members of the judiciary (whichever branch of the profession they come from) and retired members of the judiciary. As a practitioner, it is enormously satisfying to secure the services of a competent arbitrator, who is guaranteed to have read the papers and who has the expertise to deal with financial remedy work. This cannot always be said for sitting members of the judiciary, who in practice may not have any experience of family finance work and certainly do not have the time to read the case papers and expert reports in the way that an arbitrator would.

The arbitration procedure is agreed by the parties and the arbitrator. This might mirror the court procedure (without an FDR appointment) or the parties may decide that live evidence is not needed and the arbitrator can decide the issue(s) on the papers only. The flexibility of the process is one of the strengths of using arbitration

### 2.6.2 Is it mandatory?

No. Like all NCDR processes, arbitration is a voluntary process. If the parties proceed with financial arbitration, they will need to sign a Form ARB1FS and lodge it with IFLA.

### 2.6.3 How many people are involved?

This depends on each situation. The parties could approach an arbitrator directly, and therefore a minimum of three people would be involved. If the parties instruct solicitors, then five people will be involved; and it is possible that barristers could also be instructed, in which case seven people would be involved.

If the dispute involves a third party, then arbitration can only proceed if the third party agrees to be bound by the arbitration process. This obviously increases the number of people involved.

### 2.6.4 Are solicitors involved?

They can be, but this is not mandatory as the parties can instruct an arbitrator without using a solicitor.

### 2.6.5 Are barristers involved?

This depends on whether solicitors wish to instruct a barrister to attend a hearing in front of the arbitrator.

The arbitrator could be a qualified barrister and be involved in that capacity.

### 2.6.6 How long does it take?

The parties will decide how long they think is necessary for the resolution of matters. One of the big advantages of entering into NCDR is that the parties are broadly in charge of the timetable. Additionally, the parties can choose to ask the arbitrator to adjudicate the dispute using papers only, thereby reducing the cost of the process.

### 2.6.7 How much does it cost?

The arbitrator's charges need to be agreed in advance of their appointment. These costs could range from £1,500 plus VAT and disbursements for a single issue dispute, to £10,000 for a complex issue. The fees of the arbitrator will increase the more experienced they are, and if they have been appointed, the fees of retired High Court judges are likely to be the highest. These fees are often in addition to any legal advisers' fees and any experts' costs.

### 2.6.8 Is legal aid available?

No.

### 2.6.9 Is there a guaranteed outcome?

Yes. Of all the NCDR processes, arbitration is the only one that guarantees an outcome. Once an arbitrator is instructed, the parties will receive an award document which sets out the arbitrator's decision.

### 2.6.10 Can either party walk away?

If one of the parties decides to walk away from arbitration after the agreement is signed, the other party can decide to continue with arbitration in their absence. Therefore, the arbitrator can go ahead in the absence of one of the parties. However, if one party walks away and the other feels that the arbitration process would not produce a fair result, they too can withdraw from the process, in which case the parties are likely to approach the court.

### 2.6.11 If it fails, what next?

If one party walks away from arbitration, it does not automatically end the process. However, the other party could decide to withdraw from the arbitration process and to pursue litigation instead – this is the only situation in which arbitration can be said to 'fail'. The decision is ultimately in the hands of the party who is left behind to continue with the process or withdraw and litigate.

### 2.6.12 If it succeeds, what next?

Arbitration is more likely to succeed than it is to fail because the parties are tied into the process until it concludes or until both terminate the process. Therefore, it is most likely that an award will be produced by the arbitrator, and it then needs to be drafted into the terms of a consent order and sent to the court, or via the digitised consent order system where the applicant is represented as this is now mandatory, with the D81 financial statement and the award. It should be noted that a consent order based on an arbitrator's award is unlikely to be rejected by a judge. A consent order derived as a result of both mediation and CFP could be rejected if the settlement terms are deemed to be unfair.

With regards to the role of the judge in approving the consent order, in the case of *S v. S* [2014] EWHC 7 (Fam), Sir James Munby, then President of the Family Division, says (at para.21) that 'the judge will not need to play the detective unless something leaps off the page to indicate that something has gone so seriously wrong in the arbitral process as fundamentally to vitiate the arbitral award'. It is clear, however, that the judge will need to check that the order does give effect to the arbitral award, which is why the award itself should be included with the application for the consent order to be approved. Only in the rarest of cases would it be appropriate for the judge to do anything other than approve the consent order in arbitration cases.

### 2.6.13 What financial input is needed?

It is useful for the parties to have early financial planning advice if there are multiple complex investments that will need to be taken into account. In the alternative where pensions are an issue a financial planner can help to unravel any complexities. An expert might be needed to assist with a pension report where one is needed. A financial neutral could be used if the parties agree that this approach could be useful.

## 2.7 EARLY NEUTRAL EVALUATION/PRIVATE FINANCIAL DISPUTE RESOLUTION

### 2.7.1 What is it?

Once the parties have completed the disclosure process and where all relevant valuations are either agreed or experts have been appointed, the parties can place all of the evidence before a senior barrister or solicitor to assess for settlement purposes. This is often referred to as a 'private FDR', as the professional leading the process will give indications of possible settlement solutions, having heard the parties' positions. The professional acts only in a neutral capacity to assist settlement.

### 2.7.2   Is it mandatory?

No, like other NCDR processes it requires the parties' mutual consent to proceed.

### 2.7.3   How many people are involved?

Usually the parties have instructed solicitors who will in turn instruct a barrister or solicitor to give an opinion. There are therefore a minimum of five people involved, and a maximum of seven people if the parties' solicitors instruct barristers to attend the meeting. The meeting is conducted along the lines of an FDR, albeit in private.

### 2.7.4   Are solicitors involved?

Yes, usually – this would be a difficult process to navigate without solicitors involved, particularly as it is not a mainstream NCDR process and a client would probably only find out about it from a solicitor. However, this could be open to the unrepresented party.

### 2.7.5   Are barristers involved?

Barristers can be instructed to represent the parties at the meeting. Often, but not always, the person leading the ENE meeting is a barrister rather than a solicitor.

### 2.7.6   How long does it take?

Depending on the complexity of the matter, it is likely that half a day to one day is the standard for this type of meeting. Obviously a more complex case will require more time and it will cost more.

### 2.7.7   How much does it cost?

The costs of a meeting will start from £2,000 plus VAT for the fees for the person conducting the ENE/private FDR. This cost will usually be shared by the parties.

### 2.7.8   Is legal aid available?

No.

### 2.7.9 Is there a guaranteed outcome?

No – but those barristers who are involved in leading an ENE meeting anecdotally report that success rates are very high. If this is true, then the rates of success would match those for FDRs.

### 2.7.10 Can either party walk away?

Yes, the meeting is conducted on a voluntary basis and if the parties wish to walk away they can.

### 2.7.11 If it fails, what next?

This very much depends on where the parties are in the litigation process. Sometimes an ENE meeting is arranged before a court-led FDR, purely to reduce the time needed to wait for the court listing. Therefore the parties can proceed to the FDR hearing in the hope that the judicial indication for settlement might be useful. The parties could decide to follow a failed ENE meeting with a final hearing in front of an arbitrator, if it is clear that the prospects of settlement are low.

### 2.7.12 If it succeeds, what next?

The parties will need to enter into the terms of the consent order, which will be sent to the court, or filed using the digitised consent order system, with the D81 financial information. Usually heads of agreement are drafted by the parties and signed by them at the ENE meeting.

### 2.7.13 What financial input is needed?

As always, early financial adviser input is extremely useful. The parties might need to instruct experts before proceeding with an ENE meeting.

## 2.8 SOLICITORS' NEGOTIATION

### 2.8.1 What is it?

This is the most popular form of NCDR with solicitors. Solicitors will agree a way to satisfy the need for the parties to obtain disclosure of each other's financial and other circumstances – this is dealt with more in **Chapter 3**. Once the solicitors have full disclosure, and valuation and expert opinions have been sought where needed, they will proceed to attempt to negotiate a settlement either via exchange of correspondence (this can be either open or without prejudice) or via the round-table meeting and oral negotiations.

For many solicitors this is the default option when dealing with parties who have a financial remedy dispute. However, there are many practitioners in the NCDR community who believe that this is the *worst* way of resolving a dispute. Negotiations take place at arm's length, and written communications are sometimes (often!) fractious between the solicitors. Aggressive correspondence can be emotionally damaging for the parties, and does not bode well for an amicable settlement being reached.

It can also be expensive, as the exchange of correspondence between solicitors and their respective clients is copious. Personally, I am not a big supporter of this method of NCDR, as it can take much longer than anticipated at the outset and often runs into problems in the negotiation phase unless the parties commit to an ENE/private FDR if problems arise with negotiations. However, I accept that many solicitors prefer this as a method of NCDR and tell me they often resolve disputes this way.

It is possible that solicitors and their clients sometimes employ this method of NCDR in order to create delay. Although the ethics of taking this course of action would be questionable, it is possible to create lengthy delays when using this option. This should always be at the forefront of a practitioner's mind when engaged in the process.

### 2.8.2  Is it mandatory?

No – but voluntary disclosure of financial information and negotiations is encouraged by the *Family Law Protocol*.

### 2.8.3  How many people are involved?

Usually the solicitors take the lead in the negotiations, either in writing or at a roundtable meeting. The parties will be present and each can take advice from a financial adviser or instruct joint experts where agreed.

### 2.8.4  Are solicitors involved?

Yes, solicitors usually spearhead this process.

### 2.8.5  Are barristers involved?

No, unless a written opinion is sought from a barrister, these processes do not usually involve them.

### 2.8.6 How long does it take?

This type of negotiation can take a very long time to conclude. Often the disclosure process takes much longer than it would in any of the other processes, and the prospect for lengthy negotiations is very high.

### 2.8.7 How much does it cost?

This very much depends on how much time is taken in the settlement of matters. It can be as expensive as litigation. A ballpark range could be £5,000 to £50,000, depending on how expensive the solicitors are.

### 2.8.8 Is legal aid available?

Possibly. If one of the parties is entitled to legal aid, then NCDR processes can be utilised.

### 2.8.9 Is there a guaranteed outcome?

No.

### 2.8.10 Can either party walk away?

Yes. As this is a voluntary NCDR process, either party can walk away if they choose to do so.

Sometimes the parties will create intentional or unintentional delay in the settlement of these matters, which can cause anxiety to the other party. As there is no fixed timeline for the parties to follow, they can say they are in solicitors' negotiation and take their time in actually doing anything, and sometimes this is deliberate so that they can delay any litigation. This gives them time to 'restructure' their finances so that when negotiations fail, the paperwork they produce to the court shows a different picture than it would have done before the deliberate delay. Sometimes the delay is built-in to make the process unpalatable for a financially weaker party who gets more and more desperate as the delay continues.

### 2.8.11 If it fails, what next?

The *Family Law Protocol* indicates that where this type of negotiation has failed, then an application can and should be made to the court for a financial remedy order. This should not be seen as an acrimonious step, as sometimes a court timetable is needed to help matters progress to a final order. A referral to arbitration might be sensible if the parties are satisfied with disclosure.

### 2.8.12 If it succeeds, what next?

The parties will need to enter into the terms of the consent order, which will be sent to the court or filed via the digitised consent order system with the D81 financial information.

### 2.8.13 What financial input is needed?

A financial neutral can be involved in this process. The earlier a financial adviser is approached the better it will be for the parties. Experts may be approached in this process to provide reports on the basis that any such reports will be adopted (subject to the court's permission) in any litigation process.

## 2.9 SUMMARY

It can therefore be seen that there are various processes that can be used for the parties depending on their priorities. Most NCDR processes are flexible and will accommodate the parties, their legal advisers and their budgets. Serious consideration should be given to all of these processes when advising clients on settlement options.

Clients should always be made aware of their options not only at the outset of proceedings, but also as matters progress. The possibility of using NCDR processes should always be considered even after proceedings have been issued at court, particularly those proceedings that are delayed by the underfunding issues that face the Family Court. Giving the client options for settlement will be welcomed by most clients, which is likely to increase their satisfaction and possibly the referrals they send to your firm after their matter is complete.

CHAPTER 3

# Disclosure

## 3.1 INTRODUCTION

This chapter will cover an overview of the following:

- an explanation of what disclosure is;
- how disclosure works in litigation and non-court dispute resolution (NCDR) processes;
- whether a spouse can take documents from their spouse;
- penalties for non-disclosure;
- penal notices and committal applications;
- adverse inferences;
- getting disclosure from third parties; and
- joining third parties.

## 3.2 THE PRINCIPLE OF DISCLOSURE

The parties to a divorce or civil partnership dissolution are required to give each other and the court full and frank disclosure of their financial and personal circumstances and any other factors that are relevant to the division of assets between the parties. This requirement derives from the case *Livesey (formerly Jenkins)* v. *Jenkins* [1984] UKHL 3, explained below. This is a wide duty which spans the duration of proceedings.

A party *discloses* a document by stating that the document exists or has existed: FPR 2010, rule 21.1(1).

*Inspection* occurs when a party is permitted to look at or copy a document disclosed by another person: FPR 2010, rule 21.1(2).

Generally speaking, family practitioners refer to 'disclosure' as the process of both revealing that the document exists and either sending/receiving a copy of it (which is the norm) or being allowed to inspect it (which would be unusual).

Without proper disclosure:

(a) solicitors may have difficulties advising their client about the fairness of any proposed settlement; and

(b) the court is powerless to approve a consent order; or
(c) the court may consider itself unable to make an order in contested proceedings.

While most practitioners refer to the 'duty of disclosure', what is sometimes overlooked is that the duty is to give 'full, frank and clear disclosure'. Sometimes the lack of clarity or transparency in giving disclosure causes friction between the parties, and their legal representatives. Any suggestion that one party is trying to pull the wool over the other's eyes by failing to give disclosure, will lead to mistrust, which is not conducive to settlement negotiations. It is only when the parties and their legal representatives are satisfied that disclosure is full and complete that each will be able to move forward to negotiate a settlement.

The case which sets out the extent to which each party must give disclosure is *Livesey (formerly Jenkins)* v. *Jenkins* [1984] UKHL 3. The parties agreed the terms of settlement which were drafted into the terms of a consent order. After the terms were agreed, but before the consent order was sent to court, the wife became engaged to a man she had known for just over one month. She did not disclose the fact of her engagement to her solicitors, her estranged husband or his solicitors.

The consent order was sent to court in the agreed form and no update was given about the wife's change in circumstances. The court did not have possession of all the relevant circumstances at the time the consent order was approved. The fact of her engagement was a matter that the court should have taken into account by virtue of Matrimonial Causes Act (MCA) 1973, s.25(1). The wife should have made such a disclosure as soon as her circumstances changed.

The consequence of the wife's failure to give full and frank disclosure of her circumstances is that the consent order was set aside. The final words of warning from Lord Brandon of Oakbrook are notable:

> I would end with an emphatic word of warning. It is not every failure of frank and full disclosure which would justify a court in setting aside an order of the kind concerned in this appeal. On the contrary, it will only be in cases when the absence of full and frank disclosure has led to the court making, either in contested proceedings or by consent, an order which is substantially different from the order which it would have made if such disclosure had taken place that a case for setting aside can possibly be made good.

The term 'full disclosure' is expanded in this case:

> ... each party concerned in claims for financial provision and property adjustment (or other forms of ancillary relief not material in the present case) owes a duty to the court to make full and frank disclosure of all material facts to the other party and the court.

This is applicable in both contested proceedings and of course proceedings in which the parties had reached an agreement between them. The requirement extends to all forms of NCDR (**Chapter 2**) which may lead to an agreed order being sent to the court.

## 3.3 DISCLOSURE IN PRACTICE

### 3.3.1 Form D81

The way in which disclosure is dealt with in practice varies depending on which method of litigation or NCDR the parties have used; how a settlement has been reached; and what information is sent to the court. It should also be noted that when sending the consent order to the court or filing it using the digitised consent order system for approval by a judge, disclosure is condensed into the information required in Form D81. This is to ensure that the judge has sufficient information to decide whether the terms of the consent order are fair. The judge does not need to see the fully completed forms E, or any documentary evidence to support the information. This is considered more fully in **Chapter 8**.

Whether the D81 form is fit for purpose is a matter of debate within the profession. The form is unwieldy and, although only intended to give a summary of the parties' finances, is deficient when considering pension sharing or offsetting as noted by the Pension Advisory Group (PAG) 2019 report, *A Guide to the Treatment of Pensions on Divorce*, appendix V, para.V.36 (**www.nuffieldfoundation.org/wp-content/uploads/2019/11/Guide_To_The_Treatment_of_Pensions_on_Divorce-Digital_2.pdf**). I was a member of the PAG and fully endorse the content of the report. Suggestions for improvements include the requirement to list pensions separately, specify the type of pension in each case and whether it is in payment or not.

### 3.3.2 Forms C and E

When court proceedings are issued, the parties receive a timetable (Form C) from the court that directs each party to complete the Form E: 'Financial statement for a financial order under the Matrimonial Causes Act 1973/Civil Partnership Act 2004' (**www.gov.uk/government/publications/form-e-financial-statement-for-a-financial-order-matrimonial-causes-act-1973-civil-partnership-act-2004-for-financial-relief-after-an-overseas**) and file it with the court and exchange forms with the other party. This is the standard method of disclosure in financial remedy cases. It should be noted that some courts take the view that they do not need to have the bundle of documentary evidence that is appended to the Form E.

Examples of disclosure required by the Form E include:

- property;
- personal assets;
- business assets;
- pensions;
- liabilities; and
- income from employment, self-employment, partnerships, investments, state benefits.

Regional practice directions are difficult to keep track of, so it is a good idea to check with the court whether there is a generally accepted variation to the filing requirements. It would be helpful if the Form C information could be altered to allow for regional variations to be included in the directions, but alas this is not the case. These days, many courts will accept documents by e-filing, with specific limitations on the manner of filing and how large a file can be sent.

The Form E was designed to ensure that relevant MCA 1973, s.25 facts and financial information are addressed and documented. Mandatory financial documentation must be attached to the form where indicated in each section. Some practitioners believe that this means that no other documentary evidence can be attached to Form E, but this is incorrect – on the front page of Form E there is a statement which makes it clear that other documentation should be attached where it would be useful to explain any information in the form. In my view, the Form E should be as full as possible given that it is the foundation for all disclosure in the financial remedy process. As much documentary evidence as is relevant should be attached – this will hopefully minimise further questions and head off any mistrust issues between the parties. It is the only opportunity the filing party has to submit documents without further specific direction of the court or in response to specific questions.

It is noted by counsel that for tactical reasons only the mandatory filing information may be submitted in some cases with the Form E – this is not in the spirit of full frank and clear disclosure, but would fulfil the preliminary requirement to disclose information and documentation in the Form E. This shifts the onus for discovering further information and documentation to the other party to raise questions and request additional documents in the litigation process (**Chapter 4**). This approach isn't conducive to NCDR processes and is likely to be restricted to litigated proceedings.

Each party has the opportunity to dig deeper into the other party's disclosure by drafting a questionnaire document before the first appointment (FA). The judge dealing with that appointment will decide what further disclosure is required in the context of the proceedings, and the parties will be required to answer questions and produce documents as are proportionate to the assets and issues. Procedural issues are explored more fully in **Chapter 4**, dealing with the Form E, questionnaires, statements of issues and schedules of deficiencies as a method of obtaining full, frank and clear disclosure from each party.

The party completing the Form E is required to sign the statement of truth at the end of the document to confirm that the information given is 'full, frank, clear and accurate disclosure of my financial and other relevant circumstances'. In the alternative, the client may authorise their solicitor to sign the statement of truth on their behalf. If the solicitor is signing on behalf of the client, FPR 2010, Practice Direction (PD) 17A, para.3.8, requires them to explain to the client that the solicitor will be confirming the client's belief that the facts stated in the document are true. The solicitor also needs to explain the possible consequences if it subsequently transpires that the client did not have an honest belief in the truth of the facts stated.

The Form E is such an important document in the court process that it is my personal preference for the statement of truth to be signed by the client. Before the statement of truth procedure was introduced, the client needed to swear an oath and sign an affidavit. In the new Form E, the least they can do is sign the statement of truth and accept the consequences if they have not been honest in completing it.

The front of the Form E carries a number of warnings that should not be ignored by the party completing the document:

1. A failure to give full and frank disclosure may result in any order the court makes being set aside.
2. If a party is found to have been deliberately untruthful, criminal proceedings may be brought against them for fraud under the Fraud Act 2006.
3. Proceedings for contempt of court may be brought against a person who makes or causes to be made, a false statement in a document verified by a statement of truth.

There can be no doubt as to the requirement to complete the disclosure form fully, clearly, accurately and truthfully. I always highlight these three paragraphs when I send the Form E to be completed by the client and ensure they understand their obligations fully.

### 3.3.3 NCDR disclosure

In NCDR processes, the Form E is not mandatory as a method of giving disclosure. There is nothing to prevent the parties in any form of NCDR from adopting the Form E as the standard method to give disclosure, or to agree another way in which full, frank and clear disclosure can be given of all the necessary MCA 1973, s.25 facts and financial information. Whatever method is adopted, there is no different requirement to give disclosure than in litigated proceedings – the method of such disclosure is the only thing that can be flexible.

### 3.3.4 Voluntary disclosure

Where the parties have adopted the 'voluntary disclosure' method of NCDR, solicitors should refer to FPR 2010, PD 9A which sets out some detailed guidance. Although the *Family Law Protocol* (1st edn, Law Society Publishing, 2002) originally laid out the principles for voluntary disclosure, the rules were adopted and expanded by FPR 2010 when introduced in April 2011. This is now referred to as the 'pre-application protocol' and is annexed to FPR 2010, PD 9A (see **Appendix A1**below). The Law Society's protocol now simply refers to the 'FPR 2010 PD 9A'. This can sometimes be a source of confusion, as solicitors frequently refer to 'the Law Society protocol' when in fact they should be referring to FPR 2010, PD 9A.

Before embarking upon voluntary disclosure (protocol, para.2):

> ... solicitors should bear in mind the objective of controlling costs and in particular the costs of discovery and that the option of pre-application disclosure and negotiation has risks of excessive and uncontrolled expenditure and delay.

Specifically in respect of disclosure, the pre-application protocol states (at para.12) that the parties:

> ... should exchange schedules of assets, income, liabilities and other material facts, using the financial statement as a guide to the format of the disclosure.

There may be a divergence in approach depending on whether the case is a 'small money' or 'big money' case. It is very difficult to define these concepts, but broad explanations would be as follows. Small money cases are generally where the parties do not have sufficient income, assets or pensions to meet their reasonable needs and those of their children with reference to their marital standard of living. Big money (high net worth) cases are generally where the parties *do* have sufficient income, assets and pensions to meet their reasonable needs and those of their children with reference to their marital standard of living; after meeting their financial needs, the parties will in all likelihood have a surplus of income, assets or pensions to share between them if fair to do so.

The protocol does not specify that the Form E must be used in voluntary disclosure, but often solicitors are loath to depart from the trusty form even if it would be easier and more cost-effective in small money cases to adopt the exchange of schedules of disclosure. I would definitely recommend departing from Form E disclosure in small money cases where completion of the entire form is not likely to add anything and may take too much time, effort and money to complete. Commonly, parties can agree to use parts 1–3 and omit parts 4 and 5. This ensures that the parties have given financial disclosure but there is no requirement to complete the narrative sections, which can sometimes lead to unnecessarily contentious issues arising. There is also scope to disclose fewer bank statements and other potentially unnecessary documents. It is a fine balance between giving full disclosure and following the procedure of completing Form E which may not be helpful.

If parties in complex big money cases decide to use the Form E, then it is likely to be the most practical and cost-effective way forward. Although the Form E in the voluntary format should not be used in court proceedings, as it will need to be updated, the bones of it will already be ready for court if negotiations fail. The parties and solicitors should specifically confirm in the NCDR process whether they are expecting Form E to be signed with the statement of truth. Once again, some solicitors habitually ask their clients to sign the statement of truth, or are authorised to sign the statement on their behalf, and others do not sign it at all in voluntary disclosure. My preference would be that the party completing it signs the statement of truth.

The pre-application protocol makes no mention of whether the parties can raise further questions about the disclosure given by the other party. This can cause problems where one party refuses to answer questions or produce further information or documentation during the voluntary process. These issues should all be ironed out before embarking upon the voluntary disclosure process. Without completed disclosure, the parties are unlikely to ever be able to move into the negotiation phase and will be left looking for alternative NCDR processes to complete disclosure or to commence litigation. So many solicitors think that they know what 'voluntary disclosure' looks like and fail to specify what they are expecting. When they receive disclosure in a format that they do not like, problems will arise, and any time and money spent will be wasted if negotiations cannot begin.

In the 'Mapping paths to family justice' report (see **2.1**), participants expressed that any process in which disclosure could not be enforced, could be problematic. All NCDR processes (save arbitration) rely on parties voluntarily disclosing their information and documentation in order to proceed to the negotiation phase. Thus the issue of disclosure should be thought about in detail before embarking on any voluntary disclosure process.

In any case where one party feels that disclosure is not complete, settlement is unlikely. Therefore when contemplating NCDR, disclosure is a vital factor that the parties and their solicitors need to consider. Issuing court proceedings may help the parties to get to the negotiation phase, and ultimately to settle the case by ensuring that disclosure takes place in accordance with the court timetable. This is why it is important to bear in mind the availability of NCDR processes even after court proceedings have been commenced, particularly if disclosure was the issue standing in the way of settlement in the pre-application phase.

## 3.4 WHAT IF A CLIENT HELPS THEMSELVES TO THEIR SPOUSE'S DOCUMENTS?

### 3.4.1 Introduction

In some cases, one party will decide to take matters into their own hands and help themselves to their spouse's financial information. Their motivation may be that they do not believe that their spouse will give full, frank and clear disclosure of their financial situation and so they decide to help themselves to whatever documentation and information they can find, just in case disclosure isn't given.

The client may sometimes look for and photocopy (or more often these days, photograph) documents, emails, text messages and other communications. There are two ways that these documents can be obtained: lawfully or unlawfully – we will explore the difference between the two below. Solicitors should not accept any documents belonging to their client's spouse unless they first establish that those documents were lawfully obtained.

There are grey areas when it comes to the acquisition of these documents and solicitors must be as clear as possible when giving advice on this subject. I recommend that solicitors inform their clients at the earliest opportunity that they should not help themselves to documents that belong to their spouse. This information can be given in either the client care letter or the terms and conditions of business, as well as at the first client meeting (and repeated often). It is easier to emphasise the importance of this at the start than to try to rectify matters after the client has taken matters into their own hands.

### 3.4.2  *Tchenguiz* v. *Imerman; Imerman* v. *Imerman* [2010] EWCA Civ 908

This is the leading case in which the 'self-help' approach is analysed, and it changed the way practitioners deal with these situations. The wife's brothers obtained 11 files of documents from her husband. These were obtained from a joint computer server they shared with the husband at business premises they shared. They did not have permission to access his documents. The brothers feared that the husband would not give full, frank and clear disclosure during the divorce proceedings with their sister, and so they decided to take matters into their own hands. This case considers whether or not they were permitted to do this, and if the wife and her legal representatives could use any of the documents obtained by her brothers.

The financial remedy proceedings between husband and wife hadn't even got off the ground when the documents were taken. The brothers were pre-empting the husband's failure to give full financial disclosure when they took his documents. The brothers were directed to return all copies of documents to the husband – they were not entitled to have them as they had obtained them unlawfully. However, it was said that the wife *could* rely on any memory she had of the documents that she had seen, but she wasn't permitted to retain copies either. The decision may have been different if the husband had given disclosure and documents obtained unlawfully could be used to show that he had failed in his duty to disclose.

The Court of Appeal (at para.76) indicated that confidential documents are:

> Communications which are concerned with an individual's private life, including his personal finances, personal business dealings, and (possibly) his other business dealings are the stuff of personal confidentiality.

*Imerman* makes it clear that where parties are married, they have a right to expect their private documents to be kept confidential from their spouse, unless they choose to share them. Although this case did not involve civil partners, the principle will extend to rights expected when parties are in a civil partnership. The fact of marriage or civil partnership does not mean that the spouses or civil partners are entitled to access any and all documentation belonging to the other.

### 3.4.3  Lawful or unlawful accessing of documents

The type of confidential documents will vary from couple to couple and will depend on the way that the couple live. Some couples choose to jointly file their bank statements or other financial documents, either as shared files on their computers or physical files kept in a jointly accessible space in their home. If this is the case, then there is unlikely to be any accusation that by accessing these documents, one spouse has obtained them unlawfully. There is an implied consent to access these documents freely. This concept can apply to other documentation, for example private diary, business paperwork etc., as long as it can be shown that there was either express or implied consent.

However, consent can be withdrawn expressly or impliedly – for example, if one party leaves the shared home and subsequently initiates a separation, divorce or civil partnership dissolution. Estranged couples usually expect a different level of privacy after separating than when the parties were happily in a relationship. The nature of the document may not have changed, but the change in the parties' relationship status will inevitably change the expected confidentiality that attaches to documentation.

Where a couple continues to live together but a separation within the home has been established, issues with regards to joint documentation or access to the other's confidential documents may be trickier. For example, one party might lock-up or hide their confidential documentation, which is a clear indicator that they do not want to the other to access their information.

If on the odd occasion, that person accidentally leaves a bank statement lying around, this may not be an invitation to the other to look at the document. If the spouse who finds the statement knows that their spouse wouldn't consent to them looking at the document, they know that consent has not been given either expressly or impliedly.

On the other hand, a private document left in plain sight of the other spouse could be taken to be a waiver of the right to confidentiality. If they know that their spouse isn't at all concerned about them looking at the document, there could be implied consent despite their separation. These issues are never likely to be straightforward and should always be handled with care.

### 3.4.4 In practice

- Solicitors should always make it clear to the client that they must not seek out documents belonging to their spouse.
- In the event that a client produces such documentation, a solicitor should not take a copy of it, or indeed look at it, without first making enquiries as to the provenance of the document.
- If the solicitor believes that the document was obtained lawfully, they can take a look at the document but must be quick to contact the owner of the document directly or via their solicitor (if solicitors are on record) to inform them that they have a copy of it. It may also be useful to explain how their client came to have it in their possession. The original document must always be returned to the owner or their solicitor as soon as possible.

- In the event that the solicitor decides (without looking at the document) that it was obtained by their client unlawfully, the solicitor should return the document to the solicitor acting for the owner or the original owner. No copy of the document should be retained by the client or the solicitor. By doing so, the owner becomes aware that the document was taken but that the solicitor didn't look at it and no copies were retained.
- The solicitor has an ethical and regulatory obligation to be absolutely transparent about any documents they have knowledge of, those they have seen or have the original or a copy of that do not belong to their client. They must return original documents to the owner; if unlawfully obtained, they must not take or keep any copies. These documents are usually returned by one solicitor to another in the hope that if the documents are disclosable, the solicitor acting for the owner of the documents will probably disclose them.
- The solicitor receiving 'found' documents should look at the documentation and decide whether disclosure should be made. Depending on the content of the documents, unless they relate to outdated and therefore irrelevant financial information, information pertaining to another person, or personal correspondence unrelated to the proceedings, the 'found' documents are likely to be disclosable.
- In the event that the owner of the documentation is not legally represented, the documents obtained unlawfully can be kept in a sealed file unread by the solicitor. An application must be made to the court to seek directions as to whether an independent third party lawyer should be instructed to look at the documents and determine whether they are admissible. Further guidance is given in the case of *UL* v. *BK (freezing orders: safeguards: standard examples)* [2013] EWHC 1735 (Fam) para.54 onwards.
- The client who unlawfully obtains copies of their spouse's documents can rely on their knowledge of those documents even if they are not permitted to keep a copy of them. This is subject to the caveat that if the information relates to privileged matters, it might impact on the solicitor's ability to continue to act.

### 3.4.5 Risks

*3.4.5.1 Criminal and civil consequences*

There is a risk that the person who takes a document from their spouse, without their spouse's express or implied consent, could be in jeopardy of criminal penalties as well as being sued in the civil jurisdiction for breach of confidence.

Solicitors must be cautious to explain the risks very carefully at the outset of the case. It is also sensible to advise a client to change any commonly shared passwords and to de-link any shared folders or online accounts like Dropbox or cloud accounts being used to back-up several devices. It is also prudent to ensure that any implied consents that existed during the marriage are expressly revoked at the beginning of the couple's separation to avoid any misunderstanding about shared documents.

There are potentially criminal consequences of accessing information and documentation that do not belong to your client. These encompass but are not limited to breaches of the Computer Misuse Act 1990; the Data Protection Act 2018, which supplements the European Union (EU) General Data Protection Regulation (GDPR); and possibly the GDPR itself.

For example, several computers, tablets and smart phones may share the same cloud storage folders – which can be very useful during a happy, trusting relationship. However, this is not so useful if those folders continue to be shared after separation without both parties continuing to consent to the other accessing those documents. It could be argued that any person who does not change passwords or de-link cloud storage accounts is giving implied consent to their spouse to allow them to access confidential documents belonging to the other party; it could also be argued that all implied consents are withdrawn by the fact of the marriage breakdown. It is better for the parties to make decisions and access to their documents early and expressly so that there is no room for misunderstanding.

### 3.4.5.2 Regulatory issues

As soon as the solicitor is aware that they have come into the possession of documents that they should not have, they should act quickly and decisively regarding those documents, advising their client accordingly. The Bar Council's Ethics Committee issued guidance for barristers (reviewed in November 2019) which is very useful for solicitors to read: *Evidence Obtained Illegally in Civil and Family Proceedings* (available at: **www.barcouncilethics.co.uk/documents/evidence-obtained-illegally-civil-family-proceedings/**).

**Appendix A2** contains a useful flowchart to assist the practitioner with decision making regarding documents that their client has presented them with but that belong to their spouse.

## 3.5 THE REMEDY FOR NON-DISCLOSURE

### 3.5.1 NCDR non-disclosure

In NCDR processes (apart from arbitration, which has a unique perspective) if one party is not satisfied with the disclosure given by the other, the only option must be to commence litigation to obtain disclosure by court order. If all requests for pre-application disclosure are ignored by the other party, or a party believes that they have satisfied their obligation to give disclosure and the other party doesn't agree, only the court route remains viable.

### 3.5.2 Non-disclosure in arbitration

In the financial arbitration process, the parties have the option of utilising the court to enforce the arbitrator's directions regarding disclosure, if these have not been complied with.

The arbitrator decides what evidence is needed in the arbitration process and the manner in which it is presented. If the order is not complied with, the party seeking enforcement can make an application to the court under Arbitration Act 1996, s.42 for the court to enforce the peremptory order. Once the issue of disclosure has been dealt with in the court process by way of an order of the court to comply, the matter can revert back to arbitration. There is a standard order template (order 6.3) which can be used in the event that this situation arises and can be found via the link to 'Standard orders volume 1 financial and enforcement orders' at: **www.judiciary.uk/publications/practice-guidance-standard-children-and-other-orders/**.

### 3.5.3 Non-disclosure in financial remedy proceedings

If the parties have started financial remedy litigation and one party has failed to give any disclosure at all, this can be dealt with in a number of ways by the court and the other party.

If a party has failed to file Form E, the court can make an order for the non-discloser to pay all or part of the costs of the other party, for that hearing or proceedings to date. The order can be made at the first appointment. FPR 2010, Part 28 sets out the applicable rules for a court to make a costs order – the general rule is that no order for costs should be made in financial remedy proceedings (FPR 2010, rule 28.3). However, where one party's conduct is such that a costs order is justified, the court has the power to make such an order. The failure of one party to comply with an order of the court (such as the direction to file the Form E) could result in a costs order being made against the non-discloser (FPR 2010, rule 28.3(7)(a)).

However, the making of a costs order will not necessarily compel the non-discloser to co-operate and complete and file the Form E. The costs order punishes what has not been done to date but doesn't necessarily aid compliance with the order. Furthermore, waiting until the first appointment hearing to get a costs order will cause delay – which may be what the non-discloser had wanted.

One important rule regarding disclosure, which is often ignored by practitioners, is FPR 2010, rule 9.16(1), which states that: 'between the first appointment and the FDR appointment, a party is not entitled to the production of any further documents'. The exceptions to this rule set out that any directions for disclosure given at the first appointment must be complied with. This is likely to be restricted to providing answers to the questionnaire and request for documents, as approved or amended by the judge. In the event of a failure to file a Form E by the first appointment hearing, the court may allow the filing of Form E after the hearing and allow the other party to raise a questionnaire which must be answered, save as to just exceptions. This creates an element of subjective reasoning for all parties, as the questionnaire and request for production of documents are usually monitored by the court. In this situation, the parties are left to police their own further disclosure. However, it is likely to be better than waiting for the court to list another first appointment hearing at which the issue of questionnaires can be scrutinised by the court.

The only other instance in which disclosure can take place in this period is if a party applies for further disclosure and compliance with such request is ordered by the court. In practice, it is very rare for parties in small money cases to make such an application, as it would be disproportionate to the assets to do so. Often if such requests are raised, the parties can simply agree to provide additional reasonable disclosure as it is usually in keeping with the general obligation of full and frank disclosure and an application wouldn't be proportionate. Although this action is technically in breach of the rule, there is usually no sanction for the breach.

In big money cases, there is sometimes a need to make an application for such further disclosure to ensure that the court keeps a tight rein on disclosure which can occasionally threaten to swamp the process. If one party requires disclosure of facts or documents that the other doesn't believe to be relevant to the case, this can be problematic. The court will ultimately decide how to progress the matter and make an order where needed.

In any case, it is possible for one party to give too much disclosure in the hope of inundating the other spouse with documents – this will slow the process down, increase costs and possibly increase acrimony between the parties and their representatives.

## 3.6 PENAL NOTICE – IS AN APPLICATION NEEDED?

If an order for disclosure has already been made (for example, the standard directions on the Form C timetable) and ignored by one party, the applicant could make an application for a penal notice to be attached to that order. This acts as a warning to the non-discloser that if they fail to provide the information or documents, they could be committed to prison.

The standard order precedents, which have been in use since 2014 in one version or another, clearly set out the consequences of one party failing to comply with the orders of the court. The required form of penal notice (PD 37A para.1.1 FRP 2010) which should be displayed on the front page of every order states: 'WARNING: IF YOU DO NOT COMPLY WITH THIS ORDER, YOU MAY BE IN CONTEMPT OF COURT AND YOU MAY BE SENT TO PRISON, BE FINED, OR HAVE YOUR ASSETS SEIZED.'

The Financial Remedies Working Group (FRWG) Interim Report of 31 July 2014 (available from this website: **www.judiciary.uk/publications/financial-remedies-working-group-report/**) addresses the issue of the penal notice (at para.59):

In a financial remedy case the applicant is entitled to the endorsement as of right, (a point which should be wider understood by judges and court staff). We consider that it is probably wise for each order to be endorsed with a penal notice at the time it is made (often orders are seen to say 'a penal notice is attached to this paragraph' which is not enough). The full content of the penal notice should be prominently displayed on the front of the copy of the order and/or spelt out in the body of each paragraph to which it applies. All the financial orders in the suggested standard orders wardrobes follow this suggestion.

The FRWG was established by the President of the Family Division in June 2014 and chaired by Nicholas Mostyn J and Cobb J with a membership of judiciary, practitioners and HM Courts and Tribunals Service (HMCTS) officials. The interim report should be read in conjunction with the final report (15 December 2014).

It can be seen that the standard orders follow this format and therefore should be utilised in every case as freehand drafting or using old precedents is a recipe for disaster. Where there is no such penal notice endorsed on an order, then an application for a penal notice must be made, before moving to the committal application. In practice, it will now be rare for a party to need to apply for a penal notice, as most orders will have the penal notice displayed in the correct place on the order.

An application can be made to the court under FPR 2010, Part 18 to obtain a penal notice on an order for disclosure, which has been properly served and as long as the time limit for producing such disclosure has passed. Such an application should be made using Form D11, plus the fee or the help with fees form. The application should be supported by evidence – ideally this is a statement from the applicant or their solicitor, setting out the reasons why the penal notice is required. This is a simple statement which could be made within the body of the application form; the reasons can be simply stated.

This same application procedure (FRP 2010, Part 18, using Form D11, statement and fee or help with fees form) can be used if further or other disclosure is required and no order is yet in place. It is usual to attach a draft order to an application setting out the order requested from the court.

## 3.7 COMMITTAL APPLICATIONS

Where an application for a penal notice is not necessary; or if an application for a penal notice has been made, the penal notice is granted and then served on the respondent. The next step in the enforcement process is to make an application for the committal of the non-discloser. There are reported cases in which a party has either said that they have fulfilled their duty of full, frank or clear disclosure, but this is not the case, or they do not engage with the process at all which results in a committal application being made.

*Young* v. *Young* [2013] EWHC 34 (Fam) is such a case. Mrs Young made an application to commit her husband to prison for contempt of court. The burden of proof lay with the applicant to prove beyond a reasonable doubt that her husband was in breach of the relevant disclosure orders. It is important to note that in committal cases, the respondent is not required to give evidence, either written or oral.

The parties' positions were very different, the wife alleging that the husband was a very wealthy man with assets of up to £400 million, while the husband contended that he was 'penniless and bankrupt'. The wife was given permission to serve a further questionnaire on the husband, which she did but he did not respond.

As this case predates the use of standard orders, an application was first made to attach a penal notice to the order requiring Mr Young to respond to the questionnaire. Although he did provide some answers to the questionnaire, Mrs Young was not satisfied with those answers and issued a committal application. Mr Young managed to produce some remaining disclosure before the final committal hearing and the court needed to ascertain whether he had purged his contempt by doing so.

In deciding the sentence, it was found that Mr Young's contempt was so serious that a fine would not be appropriate; additionally, the judge was satisfied that he would not be able to pay it in any event. A suspended sentence was not appropriate, as he had already been subject to a suspended sentence. He was imprisoned for a period of six months; he was to serve one half of that sentence in custody. In the event that he fully complied with the orders for disclosure, his contempt would be considered to be purged and he would be released. It is worth noting that Mr Young was given multiple opportunities to comply with the disclosure orders before being imprisoned.

## 3.8 ADVERSE INFERENCES

In litigation proceedings, if it is clear that the non-discloser will not co-operate – for example, by the fact that they have not engaged in the proceedings at all – it may be necessary to proceed in their absence. Although this is an unsatisfactory outcome, it does happen in a very small number of cases every year. This places the burden of disclosure entirely upon the applicant who will only be able to go so far in gathering together the necessary disclosure required. The applicant should be able to adduce evidence regarding any joint assets and give an accurate picture of the other party's financial and other circumstances to the best of their ability.

In cases where either one party is dissatisfied with the disclosure given, for example in the *Young* case; or where one party has failed to engage, the court may be persuaded to draw adverse inferences. Any inferences drawn must be reasonable, and the court should attempt a realistic quantification of funds that have been hidden.

*NG* v. *SG (appeal: non-disclosure)* [2011] EWHC 3270 (Fam), para.16 sets out relevant matters that should be taken into account in non-disclosure cases. Mostyn J stated (at para.16): 'vague evidence of reputation or the opinions or beliefs of third parties is inadmissible in the exercise'. This is important because many applicants only have the information from third parties or a perception of the other party's lifestyle without any evidence. The court requires more than that to draw adverse inferences as to the extent of the other party's wealth.

It is very unattractive for a case to proceed on the basis that the court will be left to draw adverse inferences, because this means that the matter needs to progress to a final hearing, which is expensive and in many cases is not cost proportionate. The burden of proof throughout is on the applicant and there is a very real risk that the non-discloser will try to appeal against any order if improper inferences are drawn, as in *NG* v. *SG*. It is therefore prudent to obtain evidence, where possible, of the other party's financial position from legitimate sources rather than to rely on the court drawing adverse inferences.

## 3.9 OBTAINING EVIDENCE FROM THIRD PARTIES

Where evidence is sought from a person or organisation not joined to the proceedings as a party, an application can be made for disclosure – but should be done with great care. FPR 2010, Part 21 sets out the applicable rules regarding the disclosure and inspection of documents but only where the application is made under an Act for disclosure.

Procedurally, the application can be made without notice, although this would in practice be rare; where possible application should be made on notice. Any application of this kind would need to be supported by evidence to inform the court why the application should be granted against a third party and why the information cannot be provided by a party to the proceedings. The court will only make an order where disclosure is necessary to dispose fairly of the proceedings or to save costs.

In financial remedy proceedings, such an application would usually be made using Form D11 with a statement in support and an issuing fee or help with fees form.

The person against whom an order is made may apply (FPR 2010, rule 21.3) for an order to withhold the disclosure if it would damage the public interest.

An application for third party disclosure is unusual, as the usual route is to try to obtain evidence from a party rather than a third person who is not a party to proceedings. In deciding whether to order disclosure and inspection, the court will consider Article 8 of the European Convention on Human Rights (ECHR) – right to respect for one's private life, family life, home and correspondence. Any request made against a third party should be limited to disclosure and inspection of specific documents to ensure that the request goes no further than is necessary to obtain documents needed within the proceedings. FPR 2010, rule 21.2(6) specifically states that an order 'must not compel a person to produce any document which that person could not be compelled to produce at the final hearing'. If the court believes that the applicant is on a 'fishing expedition', the applicant is not likely to succeed.

If the third party is required to attend court with the order documents, they are entitled to be represented and the issue of costs is likely to be relevant. Such a hearing is usually referred to as 'an inspection appointment' or formerly a production appointment. The case law in respect of these types of appointments will likely be helpful although will refer to the previous family proceedings rules 1991 and not FPR 2010 The third party can ask for their costs to be paid by the applicant, rule 28.1 FPR 2010 applies, and the applicant risks a costs order being made against them for the other party's costs as well as the costs of the third party. Part 24 FPR 2010 is commonly used to order the attendance of a person at a hearing with their documents with the same risk of cost orders being made. The application is made using Form FP25 plus the fee or help with fees form.

The Bankers' Book Evidence Act 1879, s.7 allows the court to make an order against a party for disclosure and inspection and take copies of any entries of the bankers' book. An application can be made under FPR 2010, Part 18 and should be served on the bank three clear days before the hearing.

## 3.10 JOINING PARTIES

It is possible to make an application to join a third party to proceedings which means that obtaining disclosure from them will be easier. FPR 2010, rule 9.26B governs the addition or removal of a party in financial remedy proceedings. The court may add or remove a party if it is desirable to do so. This will be likely if there is a dispute in the proceedings concerning the third party and adding the party will resolve the issue. Although this may be achieved by making an application under FPR 2010, Part 18, the court has the power to do so using its own initiative. A third party who believes they should be added may also make an application asking to be added to proceedings; any third party added has the right to be represented.

The issue of joinder may arise in any case where a third party's assets are in question in respect of the divorce or dissolution proceedings. This may happen where there are trust assets and trustees need to be joined, or where there are complex business assets and other parties need to be joined for their interest to be investigated. More commonly, where a third party has an interest in assets of the marriage or civil partnership their joinder is likely to be directed. This is likely to be the most frequently encountered scenario and can arise in small money cases, often where an asset is said to be beneficially owned by a family member who may have contributed toward the purchase price. The issue of third party interests should be identified as early as possible, as it is important for the joinder to take place as early as possible in the proceedings.

The management of cases involving third parties is not straightforward, and guidance is found in the case of *TL* v. *ML and others (ancillary relief: claim against assets of extended family)* [2005] EWHC 2860 (Fam). The third party should be given the opportunity to plead their case by filing points of claim and points of defence in respect of the assets in question. Separate witness statements should be directed to be filed and the dispute should ideally be heard separately and as a preliminary issue. There is still a tendency in small money cases to list third party issues for determination at the final hearing; although it may seem more cost-effective to do so, it does waste the opportunity to settle matters at the FDR if the dispute concerning the third party is still live.

# CHAPTER 4
# Financial remedy procedure

## 4.1 INTRODUCTION

In both divorce and civil partnership dissolution proceedings, FPR 2010, Part 9 governs the procedure controlling the progress of a financial remedy application. An application, usually using the Form A, can only be made if proceedings for a divorce or civil partnership dissolution have been issued in respect of the same relationship (FPR 2010, rule 9.4).

Usually the application for financial remedy is made sometime after issue of the application for divorce or civil partnership dissolution (sometimes referred to as the 'main suit'), but it is possible (albeit unusual) to issue both at the same time. Parties will generally engage in some form of non-court dispute resolution (NCDR; see **Chapter 2**) which results in issuing the financial remedy application after the issue of the divorce or dissolution application. The financial application will be sent either to the divorce centre that is processing the divorce or dissolution proceedings or to a Family Court hearing centre if the divorce file has been transferred there. An issue fee will be payable or the applicant will need to make an application for help with fees using Form EX160.

At the time of writing, specialist financial remedy courts are being set up with the intention of de-linking the processes of divorce and financial remedy. In the future it is expected that divorce proceedings will remain at a divorce centre, or the online divorce portal, and the financial remedy application will be issued and proceed at a specialist centre.

The financial remedy application allows the applicant to pursue all available remedies under Matrimonial Causes Act (MCA) 1973 (ss.21–25) or Civil Partnership Act (CPA) 2004 (Sched.5, Part 5) for periodical payments, property adjustment, capital and pensions orders. Usually, interim orders such as maintenance pending suit (divorce cases) or maintenance pending the outcome of proceedings (civil partnership cases), are not applied for at the same time as other financial remedies unless an order is needed at this stage. We will look further at the procedure for interim remedy applications below. It is therefore standard practice to tick all other boxes on Form A for financial remedy, where such remedies are applicable. The financial applications that can be made in respect of children are explained in more detail in **Chapter 6**.

This chapter will cover an overview of the following:

- the standard procedure in financial remedy proceedings:
  - applications (in the Family Court and High Court) and cross applications;
  - Form E;
  - first appointment (FA) hearings;
  - financial dispute resolution (FDR) appointments;
  - final hearings;
  - costs rules;
  - judgment orders;
- the fast-track procedure in financial remedy proceedings; and
- costs orders in financial remedy proceedings.

## 4.2 THE STANDARD PROCEDURE FOR FINANCIAL REMEDY APPLICATIONS

Once the application is processed by the court, the 'standard procedure' (FPR 2010, Part 9, Chapter IV) will be adopted for timetabling the matter forward. It is essential that every application has a timetable to ensure that each party knows when to file:

1. disclosure (Form E);
2. statement of issues;
3. questionnaire; and
4. request for documents.

Most importantly, the timetable which is sent using Form C informs the parties of the date, venue and time estimate for the first appointment (FA) hearing.

FPR 2010, rule 9.12 states that the court will fix a first appointment hearing not less than 12 weeks and not more than 16 weeks after the date of filing the application. In the current overworked court system, the dates are more aspirational than achievable. As a consequence, the parties may be able to use the additional time to the date of the first appointment to narrow the issues between them.

## 4.3 APPLICATIONS IN THE HIGH COURT AND FAMILY COURT, AND CROSS APPLICATIONS

### 4.3.1 Applications in the High Court and Family Court

The majority of financial remedy applications will be issued and listed in the Family Court, as access to the High Court is limited. Financial remedy applications can be listed in the Family Court to be heard in front of a High Court judge. If it is hoped that an application will be allocated to a High Court judge either in the family division of the High Court or in the Family Court, the 'Statement on the efficient conduct of financial remedy hearings allocated to a High Court judge whether sitting at the Royal Courts of Justice or elsewhere' document prepared by Mr Justice Mostyn, revised on 1 February 2016 (**www.familylawweek.co.uk/site.aspx?i=xb1743**) will be applicable.

A case will only be allocated to be heard by High Court judge if:

(a) it is exceptionally complex;
(b) there is another substantial ground for the case being heard at that level;
(c) allocation to that level is proportionate; and
(d) allocation to that level is unlikely to be proportionate unless the net assets exceed £7.5 million.

The issue of allocation to a High Court judge is complex, and the document should be read in detail if the applicant proposes that the matter should be listed at this level. Once an application is issued in the High Court it can continue along the standard procedure, although there are likely to be more complex issues that may require a close attention.

### 4.3.2 Service of the Form A

*4.3.2.1 General rules*

The court officer will give notice of the date for the first appointment and the application to the respondent within four days beginning from the date the application was filed. In practice, this is not usually done within the time limit anticipated by the rules. It is a good idea for the applicant to tell the respondent or their solicitor (where one is instructed), that an application for financial remedy has been made. This will allow them to start to complete the Form E and any avoid unnecessary delay in filing it if there is a court delay in informing the respondent that an application has been issued.

It is possible for the applicant to serve the respondent with notice of the financial remedy application instead of the court officer. This can be requested when sending the Form A to the court for issue; if requested, the court should return the sealed paperwork to the applicant to effect service.

Service is effected in accordance with FPR 2010, Part 6. The applicant's solicitor will usually send the papers by first class post or DX to the respondent or their solicitor, but only if they have agreed to accept service of the documents or have filed a notice of acting with the court. There is so much email traffic between firms these days that most solicitors believe that service by email is effective, but this is only the case where the respondent or their solicitor has agreed to accept service by email (FPR 2010, PD 6A).

A request to the court for the applicant to effect service is sometimes overlooked by the court administrators, so the applicant's solicitor should make every effort to ensure that the court is aware of the request.

The rules indicate that if the applicant is effecting service, they must serve the respondent with the application and notice of hearing, four days from the date when the application is received from the court. The applicant should file a certificate of service (Form FP6 is suitable) with the court at or before the first appointment to confirm that service was effected. This will be important evidence if the respondent does not comply with any directions and the applicant applies to the court to impose sanctions on the respondent. The court will need to know when the applicant served the respondent with the papers and how service was effected before imposing any sanctions for non-compliance.

### 4.3.2.2 Service of the Form A on third parties

The applicant is also required to serve a number of third parties with a copy of the sealed application (FPR 2010, rule 9.13). The applicant must serve the following people:

1. Where there is a trust:

    (a) the trustees of the settlement (if applicable);
    (b) the settlor of the trust if living;
    (c) such person as the court directs.

2. Where the application relates to land:

    (a) any mortgagee.

3. Where the applicant has made an application against the respondent's pension(s):

    (a) The applicant must serve a copy of the sealed application on the person responsible for the pension arrangement (PRPA) (FPR 2010, rule 9.31).
    (b) The person with pension rights (this will often be the respondent to the financial remedy application) must ask the PRPA for valuation information in accordance with Pensions on Divorce etc. (Provision of Information) Regulations 2000 SI 2000/1048, reg.2(2) (FPR 2010, rule 9.30(1), (2)).
    (c) Within seven days from the date when the person with pension rights (the respondent to the financial remedy application) receives the valuation information, they must send a copy of it to their spouse together with the name and address of the person responsible for each arrangement.

    Usually the documentation provided by the pension provider will have the name and address stated on the documentation. This is usually sent with the Form E, or perhaps will be sent afterwards depending on the pension scheme and how quickly they are able to provide such information.

It is not unusual for this information to take three months or more to be sent to the pension member. Pensions administered by central government often take the longest to send valuation information. For this reason, the information should be requested as soon as the solicitor is aware that there is a pension for which a valuation will be needed, this may even predate any application if NCDR options are considered.

(d) If the respondent, as the person with the pension rights, has already received the valuation information via NCDR processes and it is dated within the previous 12 months, there is no need for them to obtain a fresh valuation. However, if the valuation obtained is clearly different to a current valuation if one was obtained, there is nothing to stop a party from getting a current valuation to use in the divorce. A financial adviser specialising in divorce and pensions may be able to assist both the solicitor and the client with regards to these matters. Those pensions that are valued in line with stock market fluctuations (defined contribution pensions) should be carefully revalued when the need arises.

The relevant rules require pension providers to provide one free valuation for divorce purposes every 12 months; details of when charges can be made are found in the Pensions on Divorce etc (Charging) Regulations 2000 SI 2000/1049. Charges can be levied if the information has already been provided with in the previous 12 months, the pension is in payment or the member will reach normal retirement age within 12 months of the request.

It is sometimes worth paying the PRPA to produce an additional valuation if this is likely to result in a drastic revaluation of the pension. Some pension schemes will not need to levy a charge to value the pension if it is a simple task, for example with a defined contribution pension. These valuations are often easily produced and the pension provider may even have an online portal that can be used to value the pension.

Sometimes clients can be shocked at the fees levied by pension schemes for obtaining the valuation when compared to the benefits that they are likely to receive. The requirement to produce this valuation is mandatory and there is no way to circumvent the fees, even if it seems to be disproportionate to the income received from the pension.

### 4.3.3 Cross-applications

#### 4.3.3.1 The possibility of cross-applications

In the above example, it is assumed that the applicant is the person without pension rights and that the respondent is the person with pension rights. However, if the applicant has pension rights and the respondent wants to make an application against them, the respondent may need to make a cross application on Form A in order to engage the relevant rules and regulations in respect of service of information and obtaining a valuation. This is a matter that concerns practitioners – the report of the Financial Remedies Working Group (FRWG) (available from this website: **www.judiciary.uk/publications/financial-remedies-working-group-report/**) addresses the issue of 'deemed applications' (interim report, para.14; and final report, para.8). The FRWG took the view that once a party makes a financial remedy application, unless the application is limited in nature, it will be deemed to apply to all possible applications that could be made by either party. That provision hasn't been introduced formally by any amendments to forms or rules; no changes have been made to effect new service regulations regarding third parties.

For the time being, it will be necessary for parties to issue cross applications where they are needed – this involves completing the Form A, paying the necessary fee or completing the help with fees form and sending all to the court dealing with the financial remedy application for the applicant. There does not need to be a fresh timetable in respect of the cross application; as soon as the second sealed Form A is received it can be used to effect service on the relevant third parties.

Each court appears to have a different approach when the same issue is raised in respect of deemed cross applications when consent orders are submitted for approval – my advice is to find out what the court expects when submitting the consent order for approval.

#### 4.3.3.2 When is a cross-application needed?

There are many learned barristers and solicitors who take the view that there is no need for a respondent to submit an application for cross applications in a financial remedy case. I take the view that it is better to make the application than to risk relying on deemed applications to give jurisdiction to the court to deal with both parties' applications in a case where only one party has submitted an application. I have known more than one district judge threaten to take a final hearing out of the list where the respondent has failed to make an application for financial remedy and it is clear that they are the party seeking a substantial pension sharing order. If this were to happen, a costs order may follow – and in the worst case, a wasted costs order may be made against the solicitor for failing to file a cross application.

If third parties have a right to be notified of a financial remedy application, it is important that their rights are not overlooked. In reality, rarely will any third party acknowledge receipt, let alone participate with the process. Once I received a telephone call from a bewildered woman at a pension company who claimed never to have been served with a Form A in accordance with FPR 2010, rule 9.31. I doubt that I am the only solicitor in the country complying with the rules, but her bewilderment indicates a lack of familiarity by pension administrators with the divorce process.

In cases where one party makes a limited application for financial relief, the other may need to make a more general application for those orders that the applicant has not specified. For example, a very wealthy applicant might want an order to be made against them. If there is one jointly owned property, they might only tick the box on the Form A to indicate that they want a property adjustment order for only that property. The respondent, on the other hand, may wish to make an application against the applicant's pensions, other properties and for periodical payments to be paid to them.

It isn't an arduous task to complete a Form A for the respondent (soon to be the cross-applicant) and file it with the court with the relevant fee. The cost to the client will be a few units of a solicitor's time, a letter to the court and the filing fee. The application should be sent with a letter explaining that a fresh timetable isn't needed, but that a sealed Form A is required to enable service of it on the PRPA. It is a matter often overlooked in small money cases (see **3.3.4**) particularly if the spouse who owns the majority of the assets is the first applicant asking the court to make an order against them. It is unlikely to have any real impact on the ongoing procedure of the financial remedy claim, although technically the respondent's Form A does need to be served on the third parties.

In practice, once the applicant's application has been timetabled, both parties usually proceed to obtain the relevant valuation information and documentation from the relevant pension providers. The additional cross application does nothing more than satisfy a procedural need – disclosure will take place in the usual way whether there is one application or two.

## 4.4  THE FORM E

### 4.4.1  Overview

The first of the documents to be filed after the commencement of the application and any cross application, is the Form E. The rules state that this should be filed with the court and exchanged with the other party no less than 35 days before the first appointment. The Form E should be carefully completed, as it follows MCA 1973, s.25 (CPA 2004, Sched.5, Part 5) – if properly completed, each party will satisfy their obligation to give full, frank and clear disclosure.

Each party must produce a number of documents which are mandatory with the Form E. These include bank statements for each account owned jointly or solely by each party, for the previous 12 months. This would include any accounts closed within the previous 12-month period, or any account that person has an interest in. Each must provide details of any mortgage, loan or debt, and evidence of any investments.

The Form E has a checklist page at the back to ensure that the person completing the form understands that numerous documents need to be appended to the form in order to satisfy the mandatory disclosure requirements. Other documents can be attached to Form E to explain the content of any section – this is made clear on the front page of the Form E and at FPR 2010, rule 9.14(2)(b)(ii).

Occasionally solicitors fail to understand that it is their client's obligation to expose their full financial and personal circumstances throughout the litigation process. This means that sometimes disclosure at this stage is limited to providing only the mandatory documents. The Form E is the bedrock of disclosure in the litigation process and should be as full, clear and up-to-date as possible. This means that *all* relevant documents should be attached to the Form E, and such production should not be limited to those which are mandatory.

### 4.4.2 Using the Form E post NCDR disclosure

In my view it is not sufficient for the parties to agree to use a Form E that was prepared for the purpose of pre-application voluntary disclosure in accordance with FPR 2010, PD 9A. This is sometimes used as a shortcut post NCDR options to get the matter listed before the court for a FA hearing, without expending unnecessary time or cost on updating the disclosure already given. I understand the intention of the parties to want to save costs in this way. However, this approach is only likely to encourage further disclosure to be ordered by the court at the FA hearing. The Form E prepared for voluntary disclosure is likely to be woefully out-of-date, which results in more requests to update disclosure. This approach could be seen to be in keeping with the overriding objective (FPR 2010, Part 1 – see **2.3.2.1**) but I don't believe it complies with the rules regarding disclosure.

Although frequently used in practice without sanction from the court, I would worry that the filing of Form E's that have not been updated may attract the ire of a district judge. If this approach is suggested, both parties should agree to follow the approach and the agreement should be drawn to the judge's attention when filing the Form E's. At the very least, the parties should agree to update the disclosed documents – though this will not help the judge at the FA, who won't see the disclosure bundle, as only the Form E's are usually included in the hearing bundle.

If one party is ready to exchange Form E but the other party is not, the finalised Form E should be filed with the court on time. The covering letter should be clear that a copy has not been sent to the other spouse. The FPR 2010 are clear that the Form E's between the parties should be simultaneously exchanged – this is to avoid one party taking advantage of having seen the other's documents or disclosure of their position in relation to other matters. Holding back on exchange but filing with the court is the best way to comply with the rules.

### 4.4.3 Local court variations on filing Form E

Some courts do not require the Form E to be served with the documentation attached, due to lack of storage space at the court. HM Courts and Tribunals Service (HMCTS) is currently piloting various online filing projects around the country where forms can be filed digitally rather than in hard copy. Solicitors should keep up-to-date with the pilot projects in their local court. If solicitors are filing in a court they are using for the first time, they should make enquiries with local practitioners or the court to ascertain what the local practice is if it varies from the published rules.

### 4.4.4 Documents missing from Form E

Where a party has been unavoidably prevented from sending any document that is required to be filed with the Form E, that party should serve a copy of that document as soon as possible on receipt of it (FPR 2010, rule 9.14(3)). That party should also file a written explanation of their failure to file a copy with the court. This is very rarely, if ever, observed in practice, but in almost every case some documents will be missing from the Form E attachments, whether these are bank statements, pension valuations or other mandatory filing documents.

There should be no disclosure or inspection of documents between filing the application and the FA hearing other than the Form E and the pre-hearing documents. This is unlikely to be problematic, as once the forms E are exchanged, solicitors are usually busy raising questions and preparing for the FA. Further disclosure is unlikely to be requested or given in this short period.

### 4.4.5 Documents to be filed before the FA hearing

A number of documents must be filed before the FA hearing FPR 2010 rule 9.14(5) which will help the court to narrow the issues between the parties and help to timetable the matter forward to an FDR hearing;

(a) a concise statement of the issues between the parties;
(b) a chronology;
(c) the questionnaire;
(d) completed Form G to inform the court whether that party is in a position for the first appointment to proceed with an FDR; and
(e) a certificate of service (where applicable).

*4.4.5.1 Statement of issues*

The purpose of the statement of issues is to enable the court to understand the issues upon which the parties are agreed and those that are in dispute. This should assist the court at the FA hearing to narrow the issues between the parties going forward.

When drafting a statement of issues, it is important to establish whether there are any assertions made in the other party's Form E that are not accepted. If so, then this is the place to raise those objections. Solicitors who draft these documents often confuse the simple act of objecting to an assertion with a requirement to ask a question about it or to ask the other party to produce evidence to support the assertion. For example, often the parties will not agree the value of the matrimonial home. This is commonplace in both big money cases and small money cases. One party can simply assert in the statement of issues that they do not agree with the other party's valuation. There is then no need to raise a question to establish how or why the other party arrived at the value as stated in their form. A valuation of property can easily be obtained using a single joint expert (SJE); once the dispute is known, a simple application can be made for an expert to be appointed at the FA hearing (see **Chapter 7** for further detail).

### 4.4.5.2 Chronology

A chronology must be drafted and filed before the FA hearing, to assist the judge to understand the history of the parties' relationship before, during and after the marriage and divorce or dissolution proceedings. The document should include relevant information about the parties, but not to the extent that it is contentious. In small money cases the chronology is likely to be limited to the parties' and children's dates of birth; the date the parties commenced cohabitation (if applicable); the date of marriage; the date of separation; date of petition; and financial remedy application. Occasionally, solicitors will include the relevant dates of purchase for other properties, inheritances or gifts received and other financial contributions made if these are likely to be relevant.

In general, none of these issues is likely to be relevant to the issue of distribution of assets in small money cases where needs are not likely to be met using the assets and income available. This information becomes more complex and relevant in big money cases, where the finances are invariably more detailed and a summary overview of a long marriage extends to three or four pages rather than a single page. A chronology filed in a court bundle shouldn't be any longer than 10 pages, unless permission of the court has been given (FPR 2010, PD 27A, para.5.2A.1).

### 4.4.5.3 Questionnaire and request for further documents

The questionnaire should be drafted with reference to the statement of issues an important provision which links the two documents (FPR 2010, rule 9.14(5)(c)). The statement of issues explains a party's position regarding their disputed issues, and the questionnaire contains relevant questions about those issues. Sometimes it is necessary to ask for relevant documents to be produced as well as, or instead of, asking a question.

The questionnaire is not a vehicle to cross-examine the other party about their disclosure or position on certain issues. Neither is it an opportunity to go on a 'fishing expedition' for information or documents that may or may not be pertinent. Occasionally, one party will want to raise questions to embarrass the other party, or to reveal the details of a relationship that they think may have started during the marriage or civil partnership. This is not the purpose of the questionnaire in financial remedy proceedings.

The client needs to be carefully managed when the questionnaire is drafted to ensure that they don't think they have carte blanche to ask whatever questions they like. The questions need to be relevant – answers to the questions will only be directed where they are proportionate to the issues. The court at the first appointment is looking to narrow the issues in dispute between the parties. If a solicitor is persuaded to draft a lengthy questionnaire and the judge or their barrister at the FA reduces it so that only reasonable questions are answered, the client might lose trust in the solicitor, so it is better to be realistic about the questions the judge will direct to be answered at the drafting stage. Occasionally it is difficult to dissuade the client from wanting a question asked about a non-relevant issue, in which case the advocate at the FA should be aware of this and the client's reasons for including the question.

### 4.4.5.4 Other requirements

The parties should file and serve confirmation of all the persons served with the application and confirm that there are no other persons who need to be served with the application. If the applicant opted to serve the respondent with the court timetable and copy application form, the applicant must file a certificate of service at or before the first appointment.

### 4.4.5.5 Costs

The parties must file on the court and serve on the other party an estimate of costs incurred in the financial remedy proceedings no less than one day before every hearing or appointment (FPR 2010, rule 9.27).

Not less than one day before the FA, the parties must file a costs estimate of the costs likely to be incurred to the FDR if the matter doesn't settle at the FA. Form H should be used to file the costs estimates, the statement of truth should be signed by their solicitor to confirm they have discussed the costs with their client.

## 4.5 FIRST APPOINTMENT HEARING

### 4.5.1 Overview

First and foremost, the FA hearing must be conducted with the objectives of defining the issues between the parties and saving costs. The court will use its case management powers (under FPR 2010, Part 4) to decide how to proceed.

The majority of cases heard in the Family Court across the country are small money cases where the parties simply cannot afford to litigate extensively. The overriding objective (FPR 2010, Part 1, rule 1.1 – see **2.3.2.1**) is always relevant to the court when making decisions about timetabling, directions for the instruction of experts and listing the matter for a further hearing.

In the High Court, where money is usually not limited, the court will still need to timetable the application carefully to ensure proper allocation of judicial resources. Issues will need to be narrowed and case managed, although the end result may be significantly different to a small money case.

FPR 2010, rule 9.15 makes it clear that wherever the FA is heard, the court must determine:

(a) which questions submitted by each party must be answered (and when those answers should be submitted);
(b) what documents requested by each party should be disclosed (and when those documents should be provided);
(c) if there is an application by either party to adduce expert evidence whether such evidence will be permitted (see **Chapter 7**) and whether a costs limit should be imposed on the expense of obtaining the evidence;
(d) what other evidence needs to be adduced by each party (what form that evidence will take and when it will be filed and served);
(e) what further chronologies and schedules need to be filed by each party (although this is now more specifically dealt with by FPR 2010, PD 27A); and
(f) whether the next hearing will be an FDR appointment, unless part of the FA has been used as an FDR; a second FDR could be directed, or even a directions appointment.

### 4.5.2 FA order

It is very useful to use the standard order template, orders 1.1 or 1.2, after an FA to ensure that all relevant matters are dealt with. These can be found via the link to 'Standard orders volume 1 financial and enforcement orders' at: **www.judiciary.uk/publications/practice-guidance-standard-children-and-other-orders/**. The template orders are extensive, using them will ensure compliance with the *Practice Guidance: Standard Family Orders*, 29 July 2019 and amended May 2020, circulated by the President of the Family Division (**www.judiciary.uk/announcements/standard-orders-announcement-by-mr-justice-mostyn/**). The standard order templates do not have the status of forms (FPR 2010, Part 5) so their use is not mandatory but is strongly encouraged. The standard order templates will usually be the beginning and end of the drafting exercise, as they provide for all usual issues that arise – though there is scope for variation of the precedents where needed in more unusual cases.

It should be noted that all standard order templates carry the following warning notice on the front page:

> WARNING: IF YOU DO NOT COMPLY WITH THIS ORDER, YOU MAY BE HELD TO BE IN CONTEMPT OF COURT AND YOU MAY BE SENT TO PRISON, BE FINED, OR HAVE YOUR ASSETS SEIZED.

Inclusion of this notice compels compliance with the order – if this notice is included, no further penal notice will be needed in the event that the order is breached.

### 4.5.3 Costs estimates

Each party is required to file a Form H which sets out the approximate costs incurred to date by each party (FPR 2010, rule 9.27). From July 2020 the form needs to be filed and served one day before the FA.

The costs estimates need to be filed with the court and served on the other party. Each costs estimate filed includes a provision that they have been served on each party and that costs have been discussed with the party on whose behalf they are provided.

The standard order precedents were amended to accommodate the requirement in FPR 2010, rule 9.27(7) that the costs must be recorded in the recital to the order.

This is very important information for the court and the other party to know as the case progresses through litigation. Legal costs should be proportionate to the assets of the case. In the High Court case of *Goddard-Watts* v. *Goddard-Watts* [2019] EWHC 3367 (Fam), Mr Justice Holman repeatedly gave clear costs warnings to both parties as follows (para.74):

> It is recorded that in discharge of its duties under FPR rule 1, the court today very strongly indeed urged both parties to find a means of resolving their differences, including if appropriate very early forms of out of court dispute resolution, before being sucked into the vortex of yet another round of very costly and destructive litigation.

The parties had been engaged in lengthy and complex proceedings since their separation 10 years previously. The court has no power to stop the parties using the court or instructing expensive lawyers, but the judge can ensure that the parties are aware that there are other options other than litigation to resolve their disputes.

Recent changes have been made to the rules to provide clear costs estimates to each party and introduce more stringent requirements upon the parties to be transparent about costs (changes to the FPR 2010 by insertion of rule 9.27A and amendments to rule 9.27, implemented 6 July 2020).

In the event that a party doesn't comply with the costs rules, that fact must be recorded in a recital in the order, and a direction should be made to require the party who failed to file the costs estimate to file and serve it within three days of the FA.

### 4.5.4 Using the FA as an FDR

The parties can inform the court whether they will be in a position to utilise the FA hearing date as an FDR appointment (FPR 2010, rule 9.14(5)(d)). The form to notify the court is sent to the parties with the timetable and is identified as Form G.

If both parties indicate that they are in a position to use the FA date as an FDR appointment, the judge will need to agree that there is sufficient time to accommodate an FDR. An FDR appointment is usually listed for anywhere between 45 minutes to one hour, whereas an FA is listed for 15 to 20 minutes.

Given the shocking delays occurring in the Family Court, it is highly unlikely that parties who are able to proceed with an FDR appointment will be permitted to do so at the FA. It might be more cost-effective and quicker for the parties to consider early neutral evaluation (ENE) using the private FDR model (**Chapter 2**) rather than rely on the court to agree to proceed with an FDR at an early stage.

A party will only be able to proceed to FDR if they are content that disclosure is complete. This means that there are no outstanding documents sought; no outstanding questions to be answered; all valuations have been agreed; and there are no SJE reports needed or that expert evidence was acquired by agreement. This might be the case where the parties have been engaged in NCDR processes which have successfully concluded the disclosure phase but have stalled during the negotiations.

It may be that the parties only want to attend an FDR appointment for some indication of settlement options from a judge. There are some Family Court hearing centres that might entertain a financial remedy application that proceeds directly to FDR rather than FA, although this would be unusual. The financial remedy application procedure is fairly rigid and currently does not allow parties to apply to the court on Form A and move straight to FDR (although this would be useful). There may be some regional flexibilities but there are no rules the parties can rely on to move straight to the FDR stage after application. It is hoped that this issue will be revisited in the future as it is expensive for the parties to attend a timetabling hearing (FA) that is not strictly necessary in order to eventually gateway to the FDR.

If the parties are not ready to move to FDR at the FA appointment, the court has no power to compel them to do so. This matter was considered by the FRWG, but no changes have been made to the current rules. The parties must agree to move to FDR negotiations with the agreement of the judge at the FA appointment – they can't be compelled to negotiate at the FA.

In the High Court, or in cases presided over by a High Court judge in the Family Court, it is possible that the date for a final hearing may be fixed at the FA. It is also possible that the FDR will be listed with a time estimate of one day, unless the parties certify that a lesser period is sufficient and written permission of the FDR judge is obtained for a reduced time estimate. Reference should be made to the *Statement on the efficient conduct of financial remedy hearings* produced by Mr Justice Mostyn, para.7.

Every application in a High Court case must be made to the allocated judge, unless it would be impracticable to do so or it would cause undue delay. Judicial continuity in complex High Court cases is very important.

### 4.5.5 After the first appointment

Once the court has directed the parties to provide answers to (amended) questionnaires, produce copy documentation, instruct experts and obtain valuations, the court expects each party to comply with the directions as directed.

*4.5.5.1 Dealing with delay*

Sometimes the timetable is derailed, particularly with regard to the instruction of an SJE in pension matters. (These experts are now more widely known as pension on divorce experts (PODEs) following the Pension Advisory Group (PAG) July 2019 report, *A Guide to the Treatment of Pensions on Divorce*. See **5.7.2**)

Unless a delay caused by either party is likely to affect the next appointment or hearing, there is no need to contact the court or apply for sanctions against them. This is quite different to the position taken for applications commenced under the Civil Procedure Rules (CPR) 1998 SI 1998/3132, as the county court is much stricter regarding the adherence to time limits and the timetable fixed by the court than the Family Court.

However, in some circumstances the other party will not comply at all, rather than simply filing documents late. This is problematic, as disclosure will not be complete unless the directions are fulfilled. In these cases, it is important to consider those options outlined regarding the inclusion of a penal notice where the standard order template is not used or an application for committal for failure to comply with the order. See **3.6**.

*4.5.5.2 Further disclosure after FA*

FPR 2010, rule 9.16(1) states that: 'Between the first appointment and the FDR appointment, a party is not entitled to the production of any further documents'. The main exception to this rule is the production of information and documents ordered at the first appointment.

Permission can be sought by way of an application to the court for additional disclosure to be ordered by way of a supplemental questionnaire. The application can be made under FPR 2010, Part 18 (Form D11 with the filing fee) if additional disclosure is required. However, the parties often agree to provide such additional disclosure where it is reasonable and proportionate to do so, despite the rule that specifies this is not permitted. In this instance, non-compliance with the rules might achieve compliance with the overriding objective (FPR 2010, Part 1). An agreement is likely to be costs proportionate, particularly in a low asset case.

### 4.5.5.3 The schedule of deficiencies

It is fairly common for a party to draft a document called the 'schedule of deficiencies' (SOD). There is no provision in the FPR 2010 for the preparation of such a document, but it is a usual response to deficiencies in the replies to the questionnaire or production of documents. The SOD document is not usually sent to the court with an application to direct the other party to serve it, although if voluntary compliance isn't forthcoming then an order can be sought.

If the original questionnaire (as amended) isn't answered in full, then a party could be in breach of the FA order if they don't respond to a request to respond to the SOD. It is a frequent practice among family solicitors to draft the SOD document and expect a response if the original order hasn't been complied with.

The SOD can be drafted after a party provides answers to the questionnaire and appends to it documents as directed by the court at the FA. The receiving party, having analysed the further disclosure concludes that the amended questionnaire and request for further documents has not been properly answered and/or the correct documents have not been produced. The SOD is a neat way to highlight the deficiencies in answers given but to do so without raising any new requests for disclosure.

Solicitors may make the mistake of calling a document a 'schedule of deficiencies' and using it to highlight deficiencies in the replies and production of documents but *also* using the opportunity to raise fresh questions and ask for production of new documents. In my view, it would be much clearer to draft two separate documents:

(a) a SOD to deal with deficiencies in the answers to the questionnaire and production (or lack thereof) of documents;
(b) a supplemental questionnaire, asking new questions and seeking the production of additional documents; an order is required for directions to respond to the supplemental questionnaire.

If this is not achieved on a voluntary basis, then the request can be appended to an FPR 2010, Part 18 application (Form D11 with filing fee), if the questions are legitimate and proportionate.

Before a solicitor refuses a request to complete disclosure by way of the production of a SOD, they should reflect on the answers and documents produced by their client and consider whether there are any gaps in disclosure. Sometimes this may be a simple oversight, such as photocopies or scans of bank statements on one side only instead of double-sided. Occasionally the client isn't co-operative in the information they are producing, and if this is the case they should be warned that this might be interpreted in the worst way by the court and their spouse. This may increase cost and acrimony between the parties and delay any attempts at negotiation.

### 4.5.5.4 Schedule of assets

Once disclosure is complete, the solicitor should prepare or update a schedule of assets, which may be used for the purpose of negotiating a settlement, advising the client and at the next appointment.

Counsel usually prepare their own schedules where instructed. It is useful to have an ongoing asset schedule (preferably as an Excel spreadsheet rather than a Word document), to ensure that both the solicitor and client have a clear understanding of the financial picture. This is important in small rather than low asset cases where debts can increase quickly. If the housing market is declining, solicitors may find that there are no assets with any equity available over which to negotiate a settlement. Clients may find themselves in a situation where their debts outweigh their assets – this means that the client is technically insolvent, and as such there is little the court can do in a financial remedy case. If assets decline more rapidly, the solicitor may find that the client becomes bankrupt during the divorce and financial remedy proceedings. This prevents the proceedings from being resolved by a settlement between parties, as a bankrupt party doesn't have the capacity to deal with their affairs. The trustee in bankruptcy will take over that party's financial affairs during the period of bankruptcy.

In big money cases, it is equally important to maintain a schedule of assets so as to understand the ongoing tax implications of selling or transferring assets, and to ensure that stock market volatility is as accurately tracked as possible.

It may be impossible and undesirable to update the schedule on a daily basis – that level of accuracy is not needed in any event. It is important to understand the general financial position and update it as and when a court appointment is near, or when there are any notable fluctuations such as a global pandemic! It may also be sensible to update the schedule when an offer to settle is being drafted or considered for acceptance.

### 4.5.5.5 Other directions

It is worth considering that in addition to answering questions, producing documents and obtaining expert's reports, the court usually directs the parties to file and exchange the following:

(a) *housing particulars that each party thinks are suitable for their own needs following the financial division*; this includes housing for any minor children that may live with them or stay with them overnight;

(b) *housing particulars that each party thinks are suitable for the other party's needs following the financial division*; this includes housing any minor children that may live with them or stay with them overnight; and

(c) *information relating to their ability to raise and repay a capital repayment mortgage*; it is unlikely that the court would consider it acceptable to produce mortgage information for an interest-only mortgage without any evidence of how the capital sum would be repaid at the end of the mortgage term.

FINANCIAL REMEDY PROCEDURE

EVIDENCE OF SUITABLE HOUSING

The majority of cases are small money cases in which there are not sufficient capital assets and/or income to meet each party's housing needs and outgoings. These cases often focus on the ability to house the party who is the main carer for any minor children. This will either involve keeping the current (jointly) owned property if it is of a reasonable size, location and cost. The party who is likely to remain in this property will still need to produce alternative property particulars to see if there is any possibility of downsizing or relocating to cheaper, more affordable property. This may have the knock-on effect of:

(a) releasing mortgage liability to make the new property more affordable; or
(b) releasing capital to pay a lump sum to the other spouse; this may be in full or part payment of their interest in the property, depending on how much money can be released and what that party's share of equity is.

It is very important when asking a client to obtain housing particulars that they do so with a great deal of thought. This is sometimes overlooked in the general preparation for the FDR appointment or a final hearing.

The client must obtain full housing particulars (not just internet particulars from an estate agent's website), including colour photographs and a full floor plan with the square footage of all proposed properties. The properties should be in a suitable location for the children to travel to school and for the main carer of the children to access their work or support network of family and friends. There is little benefit in submitting property particulars that are of a better standard than the property that the parties lived in during the marriage, as standard of living during the marriage is an important factor (MCA 1973, s.25(2) and CPA 2004, Sched.5, Part 5, para.21(2)(c) – **Chapter 5** considers the s.25 factors in more detail).

In big money cases, housing is a significant factor and should also correlate to the parties' standard of living during the marriage. Even though there will be more money available for housing, such housing should still be of a standard that is comparable to that enjoyed by the parties, not significantly better or worse, for either party. It is highly unlikely that there will be any mortgage to repay in these types of cases, and so the size, condition and location of the property are important factors.

The cost of a property, purchase costs and stamp duty usually form the starting point of any capital distribution. In small money cases, it is likely that the challenge may be to find a fair solution for the non-occupying spouse while the property and equity is used for the benefit of the child(ren) during their minority. MCA 1973, s.25(1) and Sched.5, Part 5, para.20(b) and CPA 2004 both say that the court will give first consideration to the welfare, while a minor, of any child of the family who has not attained the age of 18. The court may well consider the welfare of adult children who are in full-time education. Inevitably, this is likely to require the non-occupying spouse to wait to be paid their full settlement capital until the children reach adulthood.

In big money cases, the costs of purchasing a property represent the starting point in reaching a fair capital, property income and pension settlement between the parties. A financial distribution is much more likely to end with a clean break (see **5.2**) than in a small money case.

Both parties should endeavour to visit as many of the properties proposed by the other spouse as possible. They should identify any work that needs to be done to the property, the size, condition and location of each. If the property is not suitable the client should be able to confidently explain why. This exercise is important both before the FDR appointment and before any final hearing, if the matter has not settled before then. The task of visiting properties by the nominator and nominee is central to every case in which the standard, style, size, cost and location of housing is an issue.

*AR* v. *ML* [2019] EWFC 56 provides a cautionary tale about the importance of submitting sensible housing particulars before a final hearing. The wife proposed that she needed £525,000 for suitable housing; however, the housing particulars she produced did not evidence that she could purchase a suitable property in her desired location for that sum. The husband proposed a smaller budget for housing and produced evidence to support his position.

In the absence of any other evidence, the judge accepted the husband's evidence, albeit that she was willing to award the wife the slightly higher sum for housing, awarding her a lump sum of £410,000. In order to better her position, the wife's counsel asked for permission to submit further evidence after the judgment was handed down but before the final order was made. Although the judge did initially allow such further evidence to be filed, the decision was successfully appealed.

The moral of the case is that solicitors should always ensure that their housing particulars support the narrative of the case that they are advancing at trial.

MORTGAGE CAPACITY EVIDENCE

When a party provides a document regarding their mortgage capacity, they should ensure that they have made every effort to get evidence which is as accurate as possible. Completing an online calculator which gives a broad indication of how much can be borrowed may not be sufficient if the party is self-employed or who doesn't have a good credit score. (An online calculator is unlikely to be the best evidence because it won't be sufficiently detailed for more complex mortgage calculations. It doesn't show the client in the best light. A client who wants an accurate mortgage indication should see a specialist mortgage adviser who will have a detailed knowledge of the mortgage market.) Any person with an unusual income or multiple income streams may need to seek advice from a specialist broker to get an accurate mortgage capacity document. A party who obtains only one document that supports their position may be criticised for failing to do their best to obtain the information needed.

It is also possible that retired parties may wish to provide evidence as to the availability of equity release mortgages available to them. There are a number of over-70 mortgage products which may be suitable to parties getting divorced later in life.

Parties should think about negotiating a settlement as soon as possible after disclosure and provision of housing particulars and mortgage information (where relevant) is complete.

## 4.6  THE FINANCIAL DISPUTE RESOLUTION APPOINTMENT

### 4.6.1  Purpose of the FDR appointment

The FDR appointment is governed by FPR 2010, rule 9.17. The Family Justice Council (FJC), whose primary role is to promote an inter-disciplinary approach to family justice and to monitor the system (**www.judiciary.uk/related-offices-and-bodies/advisory-bodies/fjc/about-fjc/**), has produced a best practice guidance document which is extremely useful when preparing for an FDR appointment: *Financial Dispute Resolution Appointments: Best Practice Guidance* (2012) (available at: **www.judiciary.uk/wp-content/uploads/2014/10/fjc_financial_dispute_resolution.pdf**).

The FDR is a meeting held for the purposes of discussion and negotiation. Much of the time will be utilised by the parties and their respective representatives in oral negotiation. Although the matter will be listed for the appointment for anywhere between 45 minutes to one hour on the day, the time spent negotiating will be anywhere from one to five hours on the day. Emphasis should be placed with the client on the high likelihood of negotiating a settlement rather than resolving the matter in the time spent before the judge. The client should be advised as early as possible that the purpose of attending is to negotiate a settlement. If the client is not prepared to reach an agreement, the appointment will be unsuccessful. The better prepared the client and advocate are for settlement, the more likely it will be that the day will end in agreement.

Eighty per cent of issues cases are likely to settle in the short period before the FDR, when negotiations usually begin; or at the FDR appointment; or in the few weeks after the FDR. Such is the emphasis on negotiation before, during and after the appointment, that the chances of settlement are very high. Parties and their representatives should commit themselves to try to settle matters at this stage. In my personal experience, the FDR appointment will not result in settlement if one of the parties has not been informed that the appointment is likely to last all day, and the onus is on the party actively to engage in negotiation. Often the client believes that the role of the solicitor is to 'sort out' the financial matters. Although solicitors can prepare disclosure, advise the client and give a view on the fairness of a proposed offer, the client has to accept an offer for a settlement to be reached. In my experience, the client has to be prepared to make decisions, and they can only do so if they are prepared in advance to settle and they are confident that the offer on the table is fair.

### 4.6.2 Filing and serving requirements before the FDR appointment

No less than seven days before the FDR appointment, the applicant must file with the court and serve on the other party details of all offers and proposals and responses. This includes offers that are marked without prejudice, or on the rare occasions where such offers are made, those marked without prejudice save as to costs. This does not mean that each letter containing proposals and responses must be copied and sent to the court, although in practice this is what is likely to happen. It is equally possible for the applicant to prepare a document setting out the offers, proposals and responses, although this would involve further work at a cost to the client. This requirement is in addition to the requirement under FPR 2010, PD 27A to prepare a bundle of documents to use at the FDR appointment. It is prudent to include details of the offers in the bundle just in case the court doesn't have the offers to hand at the FDR.

The costs rules require the parties to file and serve a costs estimate using Form H not less than one day before the FDR appointment. That estimate should be for the costs incurred in the financial remedy proceedings up to the date of that appointment. In addition, not less than one day before the FDR appointment, the parties should each file and serve a costs estimate of the costs that party expects to incur up the date of the final hearing (FPR 2010, rule 9.27(3)).

### 4.6.3 The FDR appointment itself

The FPR 2010 requires both parties attend the FDR appointment (FPR 2010, rule 9.17(10)), unless the court directs otherwise. Such a direction can be sought at the FA or by separate application using the FPR 2010, Part 18 procedure.

The Ministry of Justice paper, L. Tinder et al., 'Litigants in person in private family law cases' (2014) (**https://assets.publishing.service.gov.uk/government/ uploads/system/uploads/attachment_data/file/380479/litigants-in-person-in- private-family-law-cases.pdf**) indicates that if one of the parties is unrepresented, it is rare that the court will direct an FDR appointment. Although it isn't impossible to proceed with an FDR hearing where one party is unrepresented, it may be more difficult to negotiate with a litigant in person.

It is extremely difficult to conduct an FDR appointment if one of the parties is attending via telephone or remotely via Skype for instance – it is much more likely that a settlement will be reached if the parties are in the same building. In those cases where one party is overseas or unable physically to attend, it might be better to look at using a private ENE meeting where the person acting as the judge physically meets the parties at a location chosen and paid for by them.

Solicitors are more than capable of advocating/negotiating for the client at these appointments; there is also the option of instructing counsel or a solicitor advocate to attend if the solicitor does not feel sufficiently confident to be able negotiate a fair settlement on the day.

If counsel or a solicitor advocate is instructed, then it may be necessary to have a conference with counsel or a meeting with the solicitor advocate before the FDR appointment. This allows the client to meet their advocate, and a strategy can be agreed for settlement purposes. It is not always feasible to have a conference or meeting beforehand, but should be borne in mind as it is one of the FJC recommendations. FPR 2010, PD 9A, para.6.5 also indicates the 'the legal representatives attending those appointments will be expected to have full knowledge of the case'.

The parties are required to attend the appointment one hour in advance of the allotted time – so, for example, if the matter is listed at 10a.m. the parties and their representatives are required to attend at 9a.m. to start negotiating. The parties are required to use their 'best endeavours' to reach an agreement on those matters that are in issue between them (FPR 2010, rule 9.17(6)).

At the FDR appointment, the parties can negotiate for at least one hour before being called before a (deputy) district judge. When the parties are called in front of the judge, the judge will expect the parties to explain how far their negotiations have advanced and will, when called upon, give them an indication of where the likely settlement lies or whether the parties are on the right track towards settlement. The right steer by the judge at an FDR appointment will help the parties towards final settlement on the day. Each judge has a different way of conducting an FDR appointment, however their intention should always be to help the parties to reach a fair settlement.

While at the FDR appointment, the parties are expected to negotiate in an open manner: 'parties must approach the occasion openly and without reserve' (FPR 2010, PD 9A, para.6.2). In order to facilitate the best environment for negotiation on any offers made during the day, 'evidence of anything said or of any admission made in the course of an FDR appointment will not be admissible in evidence' (FPR 2010, PD 9A, para.6.2). This means that any oral offers discussed on the day are not made on an 'open' basis and are not admissible as evidence in future proceedings. The only exception to this rule is if there is a trial of a person as a result of an offence committed at the appointment – see *Re D (minors) (conciliation: disclosure of information)* [1993] Fam 231.

It is a fairly common error for solicitors to mention FDR negotiations in correspondence after the appointment – if this happens, then that correspondence will be treated as being 'without prejudice' and will not be admissible at a final hearing. If after the appointment a party wants to repeat an offer made at the FDR but to express in 'open' terms, it is possible to do so as long as the FDR isn't mentioned in the letter. Rule 9.27A FPR 2010 requires the parties to file open proposals within 21 days of the FDR appointment unless the court directs that another date is more appropriate.

### 4.6.4 Reaching an agreement

If the parties are able to reach a settlement during an FDR appointment, it is very important that they record the agreement and that it is approved by the judge. This can be done in two ways to achieve a binding agreement (both are explained below):

(a) the parties draft a 'heads of agreement' document which records the main terms of the agreement; or
(b) the parties draft a consent order.

If you have a heads of agreement then you must follow up with the consent order. However, you may skip the heads of agreement stage and go straight to drafting a consent order if there is sufficient time to do so at court after the settlement has been reached.

Once a settlement is reached and the heads of agreement are drawn up by the parties, it will become an imperfect order of the court as soon as the judge indicates that they approve the terms.

Whichever document is prepared, it should be signed by the parties and their legal representatives, where applicable. The judge should always approve the terms of any heads of agreement, and where an order is presented it should be signed and dated by the judge. Doing this creates what is known as a 'Rose order', named after the case of *Rose v. Rose* [2002] EWCA Civ 208.

#### 4.6.4.1 Heads of agreement

A heads of agreement document should only be drafted where it is not possible to draft a consent order at court, or where by some oversight it is not possible to submit a consent order at the conclusion of settlement negotiations. This would only happen if the decree nisi had not yet been pronounced in the divorce proceedings; in civil partnership proceedings this is the interim order stage. Generally, an FDR appointment should not proceed if the decree nisi/interim order has not been pronounced although it has been known to happen.

If proper service of the application on third parties has not been effected, then it may not be possible for the court to seal the consent order at the end of settlement negotiations. Upon service, third parties can sometimes ask to see further evidence or raise objections, so it is sensible to wait to see what their response to service is. Equally, it is a requirement of the rules that they are served with the application at the outset – if this is done there will be no need to wait at this stage of the matter.

If an agreement has been reached, the parties should not leave the court until that agreement is distilled to the main areas of agreement – this is what is known as the 'heads of agreement' document. The more detailed the heads of agreement document is, the less likely there will be any room for confusion when the parties come to draft the consent order.

Once the heads of agreement document is drafted, the parties and legal advisers should sign it and it should be placed in front of the judge who has conducted the

FDR for approval. Once the judge gives their approval to the terms of the agreement, the agreement is binding subject to submission of the consent order – 'a Rose order' is created.

Difficulties can occur if a party wants to resile from an agreement drafted in these terms; it is therefore very important that it is made very clear to the client on the day that the absence of an order on the day does not leave the door open for further negotiations. It is important for the advocates and solicitors to ensure that the heads of agreement document is as fully drafted as possible. Leaving court without the approval of the judge is fatal, as there will be no binding agreement – the judge's approval is vital.

In the case of *Rose*, the judge said (para.44):

> The whole purpose and effect of the FDR would be lost or compromised were parties free to analyse and re-evaluate the crucial decision of the previous day or the previous week and to decide on further reflection that they made the wrong choice.

### 4.6.4.2 Consent order

The parties should ideally draft a consent order using the standard order precedent order 2.1. If the parties are at an FDR appointment and are able to draft a consent order for the judge on the day, there is no need for the parties to file the D81 form to be submitted – this form should usually be filed in any other circumstances when sending a consent order to the court or filing with the digitised consent order system. This system became mandatory for solicitors to use from 24 August 2020. After this date, paper applications may no longer be sent to the regional divorce centres by a solicitor who represents the applicant in financial proceedings. Solicitors must first register for a Payment by Account with HMCTS and then register for a 'My HMCTS account' to be able to use the digitised consent order system. FPR 2010, PD 41B sets out the process of submitting a digital consent order.

## 4.6.5 No deal – further directions

### 4.6.5.1 Directions for the future progress of the case

If the parties are unable to reach a settlement at the FDR, the court must give directions for the future progress of the case. The standard order precedents for directions are useful as they detail the steps that need to be completed before trial. This will include updating financial disclosure by both parties; filing further evidence by way of a statement from each party; the possible updating of expert evidence and valuations; and, of course, fixing of the final hearing date.

In most cases, each party is directed to file a statement which can be used as their evidence in chief at the final hearing. This is always limited to 25 pages, exclusive of exhibits (FPR 2010, PD 27A, para.5.2A.1). The court can allow a statement to be longer where necessary – a direction should be sought prior to filing a statement that is longer, although permission can be applied for at the time the statement is filed. Such a statement is commonly referred to as the 'section 25 statement' as it will usually encompass the factors in MCA 1973, s.25 (CPA 2004, Sched.5, Part 5). As much of this information will already have been initially covered in the Form E, this is an opportunity to update the court and prepare for the final hearing.

The 'Statement on the efficient conduct of financial remedy hearings' document drafted by Mr Justice Mostyn and applicable to High Court cases, indicates that section 25 statements must contain only evidence – this is useful guidance to all cases in which such statements are directed to be filed. Such a statement should not 'contain argument or other rhetoric'.

A small money case is usually listed for a maximum of a one-day hearing. This is a very tight hearing schedule, which will allow for a short period of consideration for each party's oral evidence and their cross-examination. Time needs to be allowed for judicial reading of the bundle, and sufficient time for the judge to prepare the judgment and deliver it orally. It is not unusual at the end of a hearing for the judge to reserve judgment and circulate a written judgment in due course.

The advocate at FDR should give a realistic time estimate of the final hearing, but also be mindful of the likely delay in listing to a longer hearing. A hearing with a time estimate of one day will be listed much sooner than that of two days. The court needs to approve the proportionate use of court time for such a case.

For big money cases, the trial can be listed for anywhere between one to 10 days or more, depending on the complexities of the parties' finances and other issues. Quite often, complex finance cases are dealt with in the Family Court by a High Court judge; the matter may even be transferred to the family division of the High Court. All cases are started in the Family Court unless there are factors that allow them to be issued in the High Court. If the matter is being heard by a High Court judge, then a pre-trial review needs to be listed approximately four weeks before the final hearing. A final hearing template should be prepared to allow reasonable time for judicial reading and judgment writing – guidance can be found in the 'Statement on the efficient conduct of financial remedy hearings' document prepared by Mr Justice Mostyn. Paragraph 10 of the statement states what should be in the template. Sometimes individual judges or courts have their own templates that they give to advocates to complete.

The parties may, if they wish, instruct an arbitrator to hear a trial of the matter sooner than the final hearing listed date at court, which can sometimes be six to 12 months after the FDR appointment. Not all cases are suitable for arbitration – for example, those cases where there are third parties involved and those parties do not agree to be bound by the decision of the arbitrator. Both parties must agree to the instruction of an arbitrator – see **Chapter 2** for further information on the arbitration process.

Where the parties have *almost* reached an agreement at or after the FDR, they could re-engage with other NCDR processes. Mediation is most likely to be useful at this stage.

### 4.6.5.2  The requirement to file open offers

FPR 2010, rule 9.27A introduces a new requirement for the parties to file with the court and send to the other party an open proposal for settlement after the FDR appointment. The court may direct that such open offers to be exchanged at any date that can be inserted into the post FDR order; or if no date is given, those offers must be filed no later than 21 days after the date of the FDR. In the case of *OG* v. *AG* [2020] EWFC 52 Mostyn J highlighted that PD 28A, para.4.4 allows the court to make a costs order where one party 'refuses openly to negotiate reasonably and responsibly'. This applied he said whether the case was big or small. Costs orders were made to reflect the wife's unreasonableness, these were offset against a costs order against the husband.

If there is no FDR appointment, which would be unusual, the court should direct the open proposals be filed on a date ordered, or in default not less than 42 days before the date of the final hearing.

## 4.7  FINAL HEARING

### 4.7.1  General rules

The judge who conducts the FDR appointment should not preside over the final hearing (FPR 2010, rule 9.17(2)). The case of *Myerson* v. *Myerson* [2008] EWCA Civ 1376 underlines the importance of the FDR judge having no further dealings. The judge approved a consent order after an FDR; however, there were a number of subsidiary issues outstanding which could not be agreed by the parties. The judge listed those issues to be determined before her despite a provision in FPR 1991 SI 1991/1247 which specified that the judge 'hearing the FDR appointment must have no further involvement with the application, other than to conduct any further FDR appointment or to make a consent order or a further directions order'. FPR 2010, rule 9.17(2) contains an identical provision. It was concluded in the Court of Appeal that the judge should not have been involved in the dispute after the FDR appointment save as permitted by FPR 1991. The FDR judge is privy to without prejudice material at the FDR to help the parties conciliate – the litigants 'must be confident that conciliation within the court proceedings guarantees them the same confidentiality that they would enjoy had the dispute been referred by the judge to mediation by a mediation professional'.

Each party will be expected to attend the final hearing in person to give evidence, and to be subject to cross-examination (FPR 2010, rule 27.3). Where one party has been obstructive throughout the proceedings by failing to co-operate with disclosure, or failing to attend directions appointments and that party subsequently fails to attend the final hearing, the court may decide to proceed in their absence (FPR 2010, rule 27.4). The court will of course need to be satisfied that the person who has failed to attend has been given reasonable notice of the date of the hearing and that there is a good reason to proceed in their absence.

Each party will be required to provide such further disclosure as directed by the court following the FDR. In the event that no FDR took place, then those directions made at the FA should be fulfilled.

### 4.7.2 Preparation of the trial bundle

The applicant will be required to file a bundle in accordance with FPR 2010, PD 27A. If the applicant is not represented and the respondent is represented, then the respondent will be responsible for the preparation of the bundle. If neither party is represented, then the judge will use the court file in the absence of a bundle.

If the respondent is preparing the bundle, they can levy a charge to the applicant for providing the bundle to them (25p per page for photocopying costs is the most that is usually charged). It is important that an unrepresented applicant is able to follow the trial, and having a trial bundle is vital. If they do not want to pay for the bundle, there is no harm in providing them with an electronic copy of the bundle if one is available. There is no additional cost to the respondent in providing this service, and it will ultimately assist the court on the day. Electronic bundles are becoming increasingly normal for counsel who operate paperless practices, and more often for tech savvy judges, so a PDF bundle is likely to be available.

The preparation of the bundle for the final hearing is very important and should be given a great deal of thought, from the preparation for FDR appointment. Historic documents do not need to be included in the bundle unless they are likely to be referred to at the final hearing. The bundle should not exceed 350 sheets of A4 paper, or the equivalent as an electronic bundle. Practitioners regularly fall foul of the page limit, and may be subject to costs orders being made against them. The judge may remove the case from the list if there is a breach of PD 27A (FPR 2010, PD 27A, para.12.1).

### 4.7.3 The requirement to file an open statement

FPR 2010, rule 9.28 specifies that the applicant should make an 'open statement' to set out concise details of the orders the applicant proposes to ask the court to make. This is known as an 'open position' and should be replicated in counsel's summary/skeleton document. This open statement is not the same as the open offers the parties are required to file and serve after the FDR appointment. The purpose of the open statement before the final hearing is to inform the court of the parties' respective positions. The reason to file and serve open offers after the FDR is to encourage the parties to continue to negotiate a settlement following an unsuccessful FDR.

The open statement should include monetary sums and is usually cross-referenced to a schedule of assets which will be used at the final hearing. Often, but not always, this takes the form of an open offer letter to the respondent. Every effort should be made to ensure that the open statement is as comprehensive as possible and covers all matters in dispute or agreed. Often, counsel's advice is taken before filing the open statement as this will form part of the case at trial.

The respondent should set out their open statement in response no more than seven days after service of the applicant's statement. Likewise, respondent's counsel should be consulted before an open statement is filed; it should be comprehensive and include all parts of the respondent's position at the final hearing.

Each party's open statement needs to be served on the other party and filed with the court, although in practice these open statements can be added to the final hearing bundle and/or are replicated in the summary or skeleton filed by counsel. That is assuming that counsel is representing the party at the final hearing, which is not always the case.

## 4.8 COSTS RULES

Each party must file with the court and serve on the other party a statement giving full particulars of their costs, using Form H1. This should be filed no less than 14 days before the final hearing (FPR 2010, rule 9.27(4)). Each party must file and serve 'a statement giving full particulars of all costs in respect of the proceedings which the filing party has incurred or expects to incur, to enable the court to take account of the parties' liabilities for costs when deciding what order (if any) to make for a financial remedy' (FPR 2010, rule 9.27(4)).

If either party wants a costs order to be made at a final hearing lasting a day or less, or at any FA or FDR, the Form N260 should also be completed and served on the other party.

## 4.9 JUDGMENT/ORDER

Once the judge has heard evidence in chief (where needed), cross-examination and submissions in respect of each party's case, the judge will deliver a judgment and draw up an order. Where the court orders a party to draw an order (FPR 2010, rule 29.11), the parties must file an agreed statement of its terms and it must be checked by the court before it is sealed. Standard order precedent 2.1 can be used for this purpose.

A judgment or order will take effect from the date is given or made or a later date if specified by the court (FPR 2010, rule 29.15).

If there is an accidental slip or omission in a judgment or order, then it can be corrected (FPR 2010, rule 29.16). This is often known as an amendment under the 'slip rule'. This only applies to minor errors or amendments as opposed to contested matters.

## 4.10 THE FAST-TRACK PROCEDURE

### 4.10.1 Applications

Most financial remedy applications adopt the standard procedure (as above). However, there is a fast-track procedure which can be adopted in limited cases involving applications for periodical payments only. This is governed by FPR 2010, Part 9, Chapter V, rules 9.18–9.21.

The fast track procedure can apply to the following specific financial remedy applications under:

(a) Domestic Proceedings and Magistrates' Courts Act 1978;
(b) CPA 2004, Sched.6;
(c) Children Act 1989, Sched.1;
(d) Article 56 of the Maintenance Regulation (Council Regulation (EC) No 4/200925 of 18th December 2008 on jurisdiction, applicable law, recognition and enforcement of decisions and co-operation in matters relating to maintenance obligations); or
(e) Article 10 of the 2007 Hague Convention (Convention on the International Recovery of Child Support and other forms of Family Maintenance done at The Hague on 23 November 2007).

It is unusual to make standalone applications for periodical payments in any proceedings, rather than a full financial remedy application. The procedure would be more commonly used if an application is made for variation of financial remedy order for periodical payments. Where any application is made for standalone periodical payments or the variation of periodical payments orders, the Form A1 should be used. The use of this form indicates that the fast-track procedure applies.

FPR 2010, rule 9.9B indicates that the fast-track procedure will apply to a financial remedy application for periodical payments or variation of periodical payments under the above statutes. The standard procedure will apply for an order for substitution of periodical payments by way of capitalisation, property adjustment or pension sharing or pension compensation sharing order. That means a simple variation application is dealt with under the fast-track but not in cases where a more complicated order is sought.

Where an application is allocated to the fast-track procedure, the court may at any stage in the proceedings direct that the matter continue under the standard procedure (FPR 2010, rule 9.9B(4)).

Where the fast-track procedure should apply but the applicant wants the court to use the standard procedure, they should request the use of the standard procedure when filing the application. The request must set out the reasons why the applicant would like the standard procedure to apply (FPR 2010, rule 9.18A).

Where the respondent receives notification of a financial remedy application to which the fast-track procedure applies and they wish to make representations about using the standard procedure, they may file a request within seven days of service of the application. The respondent must indicate which procedure they would like the court to apply and the reasons why.

Where either the applicant or respondent has made a request to change from the fast-track procedure to the standard procedure, the court must determine the matter without notice to the parties and before the first hearing. Both parties must be notified of the court's determination and any consequential directions made as a result.

It should be noted that although the fast-track procedure applies to a small number of applications, the courts are not accustomed to directing matters to proceed under this track. This means that even those cases to which the fast-track should apply are often allocated to the standard procedure by mistake. If the applicant or respondent notices that the standard procedure has been applied when the fast-track could have been utilised, they should write to the court immediately and cite the relevant rules with regards to changing track. FPR 2010, rule 9.18A relates to the fast track procedure but allows the respondent at rule 9.18A(4)(b)(i) to make representations about applying the fast-track procedure where the standard procedure may have been allocated or an application has been made by the applicant to change track to the standard procedure.

On one occasion I have successfully persuaded the High Court to list an application for variation of periodical payments under the fast-track. Having attended court, counsel for the respondent insisted on adopting the standard procedure without notice. The court was perfectly happy to adopt the same and I was directed to draft questionnaire (not required under the fast-track procedure) while I was waiting to be heard. This is not the intended use of the fast-track procedure, which should be quicker and less onerous than the standard procedure.

An application allocated to the fast-track procedure requires a first hearing to be listed not less than six weeks and no more than 10 weeks after the date for filing the application (FPR 2010, rule 9.18(1)). This means that the hearing will be listed more quickly than a hearing under the standard procedure.

### 4.10.2 Before the first hearing

The rules indicate that the court will notify the respondent of the application within four days from the date the application is filed (FPR 2010, rule 9.18(1)). The court officer will also serve a copy of the application on the respondent and notice of the first hearing date. It is worth remembering that the court rarely adheres to these times for notification. It is better for the applicant to inform the respondent that an application has been made and send them a copy of the unsealed application to allow them to prepare for the forthcoming hearing.

The applicant may ask the court to serve a copy of the application instead of the court effecting service. If so, the court will send the papers to the applicant, who must serve the respondent within four days of receiving the application from the court and must file a certificate of service at or before the first hearing.

The date for the first hearing must not be cancelled except with the court's permission; and if it is cancelled, a new hearing date must be fixed immediately.

The fast-track procedure differs substantially from the standard procedure (FPR 2010, rule 9.19) – there is a requirement for simultaneous exchange and filing of the financial statement (which could be either Form E or E1); and it is filed no more than 21 days after the issue of the application. The same provisions regarding disclosure apply (**Chapter 3**) but there is no requirement to file any other documents before the first hearing. There is no requirement to file a questionnaire or request the documents or the statement of issues.

If a party is delayed in sending any document with the financial statement, they must send that document at the earliest opportunity to the other party and to the court, with a statement explaining why the document wasn't filed with the financial statement.

Any documents directed to be filed according to FPR 2010, PD 27A must be filed – for example, a chronology.

The same requirement to file a costs estimate in accordance with FPR 2010, rule 9.27 applies – each party must file and serve the costs estimate not less than one day before the hearing. The estimate should include an estimate of costs that party expects to incur up to the date of the hearing, and it must be discussed with the party on whose behalf it is provided.

### 4.10.3 At the first hearing

The court may be able to determine the application at the first hearing. If this is possible, then the court must do so unless there are good reasons not to (FPR 2010, rule 9.20(1)).

If the court does not determine the application, it may give directions as to:

(a) filing further evidence;
(b) production of further documents;
(c) any other matter required for the fair determination of the application.

Where possible, the court may use the first hearing as part of an FDR appointment (FPR 2010, rule 9.20(4)).

If the court directs that the first hearing will be used as an FDR, then the applicant should produce all offers and proposals and responses at the first hearing. This is a different requirement than that in the standard procedure, where details of the offers need to be produced prior to the FDR appointment rather than the offers themselves.

If no FDR takes place, the court can direct that an FDR is listed. If the court decides that an FDR appointment is not appropriate, then it may direct the parties' attendance at a further directions appointment, or fix an appointment to make an interim order where applicable. The matter may also be fixed for a final hearing without attendance at an FDR; the court must direct which level of judge should hear the case. NCDR may be appropriate – if this is the case, then the application can

FINANCIAL REMEDY PROCEDURE

be adjourned to allow NCDR to proceed. There is much greater procedural flexibility in the fast-track procedure. It is deliberately flexible because there will usually be a discrete matter for the court to decide.

The matter may conclude at an FDR, by hearing of the contested matter or by referral to NCDR processes. An order will always be made either by consent or determination of the court.

## 4.11 COSTS ORDERS IN FINANCIAL REMEDY PROCEEDINGS

The applicable costs rules are at FPR 2010, rule 28.3. The general rule in financial remedy proceedings applies, which states: 'the general rule in financial remedy proceedings is that the court will not make an order requiring one party to pay the costs of another party' (FPR 2010, rule 28.3(5)). Although costs orders may be made, it would be rare to do so – the court would consider the provisions at FPR 2010, rule 28.3(7) to decide if an order should be made as the proceedings progress or at a final determination of the matter. PD 28A para.4.5 states that if a party intends to seek a costs order they should make this plain in open correspondence or skeleton arguments before the hearing and there is an obligation to file Form N260. Those factors are as follows:

(a) any failure by a party to comply with these rules at FPR 2010, rule 28.3(7), any order of the court or any practice direction which the court considers relevant;
(b) any open offer to settle made by a party;
(c) whether it was reasonable for a party to raise, pursue or contest a particular allegation or issue;
(d) the manner in which a party has pursued or responded to the application or a particular allegation or issue;
(e) any other aspect of a party's conduct in relation to proceedings which the court considers relevant; and
(f) the financial effect on the parties of any costs order.

If one of the parties fails to attend a hearing, or comply with directions made, then they are more likely to have a costs order made against them. Although costs orders are not common, it is possible to secure orders at the FA or FDR stage if the parties do not comply with their obligations.

It is possible to succeed in an application for a costs order if an open offer is made during the proceedings which was rejected by the other party and which is close to the order made by the court. This provision should encourage parties to negotiate on open terms as early as possible. This provision doesn't prevent negotiations taking place on a 'without prejudice' basis; however, those negotiations will not result in a costs order being made as no offer to settle which isn't an open offer is admissible other than at the FDR appointment (FPR 2010, rule 28.3(8)). PD 28A clarifies that the court is entitled to make a costs order where one party refuses to openly negotiate reasonably and responsibly as this amounts to conduct.

It is much more difficult to succeed in securing a costs order under the provisions at (c)–(e), as these require detailed consideration of allegations relating to costs which are likely to require more of the court's time after an order is made to determine the issues. It may only be cost-effective to pursue a costs order under those provisions if it is clear that the party seeking costs will be successful or it is costs proportionate to make an application for costs. In small money cases it unlikely that a costs order will be made as (f) makes it clear that an order will only be made after considering the financial effect on the parties of an order. Sadly, the lack of resources in small money cases means that there is likely to be no real benefit in making a costs order, either because the paying party won't be able to pay, or because it would derail the purpose of the final order, which is usually made to secure housing for minor children.

CHAPTER 5

# Available orders

## 5.1 INTRODUCTION

It is important for the client to understand that the court has a limited range of powers under Matrimonial Causes Act (MCA) 1973 or Civil Partnership Act (CPA) 2004. It is useful to explain those powers to the client at the point that questions arise about the distribution of the parties' assets including property, income and pensions and managing the payment of any debt.

Often a client wants to achieve a fast outcome, and they imagine that this will be easily achieved by implementing a formula for distribution of assets and income. Save for the calculation of child maintenance paid via the Child Maintenance Service (CMS) (**Chapter 6**), no such formula exists. The distribution of assets is undertaken by reference to the statutory factors at MCA 1973, s.25, considered below. The factors allow for a great deal of flexibility. This ensures that in every financial remedy case, each relevant factor is considered to produce a fair outcome. As can be seen historically with the child maintenance formula, problems can occur because of the rigidity of a formula-based approach – hence, it is unlikely that this will ever be implemented in financial remedy proceedings.

This can make it difficult for the client to understand what will happen financially following divorce or civil partnership dissolution. It can also be difficult for the solicitor to give advice, because so much is dependent upon having full disclosure from both parties and sufficient experience in applying the MCA 1973, s.25 factors to be able properly to advise on what will be a fair outcome, whether the parties reach an agreement between themselves or in the event of a contested dispute.

This is difficult to predict, as there are regional variations and personal interpretations by individual judges of what a 'fair' outcome looks like. Lord Nicholls of Birkenhead delivering the main judgment in *White* v. *White* [2000] UKHL 54 began the judgment with an assessment of fairness, which is necessarily broad:

> Everyone would accept that the outcome on these matters, whether by agreement or court order, should be fair. More realistically, the outcome ought to be as fair as is possible in all the circumstances. But everyone's life is different. Features which are important when assessing fairness differ in each case. And, sometimes, different minds can reach different conclusions on what fairness requires. Then fairness, like beauty, lies in the eye of the beholder.

Naturally, if the parties wish to reach a resolution via non-court dispute resolution (NCDR), while they may achieve a faster fair outcome, this might not be the same fair outcome that would have been achieved in litigation. As long as the agreement is within the bounds of reasonableness and sufficiently fair to both parties, the court will approve an order. It is helpful to note that in each case, there may be a number of different outcomes, all of which could be considered to be fair to the parties and which would be approved by the court. A mistake that solicitors sometimes make is to search for a 'single right answer', overlooking that there may be a range of solutions that might be acceptable to both parties and the court.

Sometimes, one party will feel that the breakdown of the relationship is not of their choosing and therefore the distribution of assets should favour them. As we will see below, issues of conduct are one factor in the distribution of assets (MCA 1973, s.25(2)(g)), but this very rarely (if ever) results in one party receiving all or the majority of the assets to the detriment of the other. The issue of conduct is more often than not a red herring in the balancing act of the statutory factors considered by the court. Only rarely will bad conduct ever be at a level that the court will be persuaded to alter the distribution of assets to reflect the conduct.

A second common grievance is that one party asserts that they financially contributed more than the other, perhaps through higher income or capital contributions. They feel that this should entitle them to an award that is more favourable to them than the other party. The other party may have contributed via unpaid work, or by looking after children by adopting a traditional 'homemaker' role. This falls under the statutory heading of 'contribution' (MCA 1973, s.25(2)(f); and the equivalent CPA 2004 provision) below – since the landmark House of Lords decision in the case of *White* v. *White* above, different financial and non-financial contributions are treated as being equal: 'There should be no bias in favour of the money-earner and against the home-maker and the child-carer.' This can be difficult for the money-earner to accept, particularly if they have been a very high earner, as they struggle to equate their spouse's non-financial contributions with their financial contributions.

The financial claims that can be made by either party are easily divided into four distinct areas:

(a)  income;
(b)  capital;
(c)  property; and
(d)  pensions claims.

We will look at each claim in turn so that the solicitor understands the scope of the court's powers which will help them to advise the client and importantly to draft a robust order, which aims to ensure that the future division of assets is clear so the parties can effect the terms without needing to revert back to the court. The implementation of orders is key. Drafting an order once an agreement is reached is vital and often executed poorly. The judge who receives the order to approve will not necessarily be checking that the order is properly drafted, and so it is unfortunately commonplace for poorly drafted orders to be sealed. This will inevitably cause problems if the order isn't complied with by a party and the other party brings enforcement proceedings.

**Appendix B1** sets out the statutory references for each available order the court can make and the corresponding precedent clauses that might be considered when drafting an order. The operation of each order is important, as it can help the solicitor to give practical information to the client and structure a settlement. The provision of information to the client is important, but shouldn't be confused with giving advice. Standard leaflets or letters shouldn't be overly relied upon, as it is much more useful for the client to receive bespoke advice.

This chapter will cover an overview of the following:

- clean break;
- the remarriage/civil partnership trap;
- income orders;
- duration of orders;
- lump sum orders;
- property orders;
- pension orders; and
- MCA 1973, s.25/CPA 2004, Sched.5, Part 5, para.21(2)(f).

The chapter discusses negotiations at all relevant stages.

## 5.2 CLEAN BREAK

The court is under the duty to consider whether a 'clean break' is appropriate in each case on or after the decree absolute is pronounced (MCA 1973, s.25A; CPA 2004, Sched.5, para.23). This does not mean that the court must ensure that there is a clean break in every case, as this isn't always possible.

A 'clean break' means that all of the parties' claims are terminated in the order. That is, once the terms of the order are implemented, neither party will be able to make a financial claim against the other in life or in death. It may be that as soon as the order is sealed by the court and the decree absolute or final order is pronounced, the clean break takes effect. Occasionally the clean break won't take effect until the transfer or sale of property, or the payment of a lump sum – this is known as a 'deferred clean break'. This is also the case where an order is made for periodical payments which have a definite termination date or event upon which they come to an end. Further, it is possible to have an immediate clean break on capital and pension claims, and a deferred clean break on income.

In high net worth 'big money' cases, a clean break can take place where the parties have sufficient capital, property, pensions and income to ensure that each is able to meet their needs comfortably. There is no reason for them to be tied to each other financially, and so a clean break is desirable. (Capitalisation of maintenance and the Duxbury calculation are dealt with in detail below.)

At the other end of the wealth spectrum, it is also possible to effect an immediate clean break. This can be where parties have little or no capital, property and pensions; or have equivalent incomes; or there is no real prospect that one will ever be able to afford to pay spousal maintenance to the other. In these cases, the parties can resolve whatever financial matters are in hand quite easily with a clean break.

In the 'average case', in between the two wealth extremes, it might only be possible to effect a clean break after many years. The parties may need to continue to hold the former family home in joint names, with a joint mortgage as the party who occupies the property isn't able to release the other from the mortgage obligations and the home needs to be preserved for the benefit of the children of the family until they reach adulthood; thus, the parties are bound to each other. In these cases, there might also be a maintenance order to ensure that the parent who provides the majority of care for the children has sufficient income to remain living in the property. This order may be for a specific period (a 'term maintenance order') rather than indefinitely (a 'joint lives maintenance order'). While the intention to clean break the parties' claims will be written into the terms of the order, the effect will be delayed for many years in the future.

It is not unusual for parties to enter into an order for 'dismissal purposes only' – in such a case, the order would have no substantive orders for property, capital, pensions or income; the order would merely record that each party's financial claims against the other are dismissed. This is very important if the client wants certainty that no future claim can be made against them – for example, if the business they hope to start becomes successful, or they are likely to inherit substantive assets, or they win the lottery!

A clean break order is important as it marks the end of the parties' financial ties to each other. They both have certainty that the other won't ever be able to make an application for money, property or pensions once the clean break takes effect. Each can walk away with no ties – this means that each can inherit assets, build a successful business or receive gifts from third parties knowing that their former spouse or civil partner will never be able to claim any of the post-divorce windfall. This is only possible if the parties enter into the terms of an order which dismisses future claims against the other in life and death.

However, in more than 50 per cent of all divorce matters, the parties to a divorce or civil partnership never enter into an order. This means that their financial claims continue to exist until either party remarries or they decide to enter into the terms of an order which will ultimately dismiss their claims.

In the case of *Wyatt v. Vince* [2015] UKSC 14, the parties were divorced on 26 October 1992, after a short marriage with one child together. At the time of their divorce, neither party had any capital, property, pensions or income of any note, and they had mainly lived on state benefits during their relationship. The husband then became a new-age traveller for a number of years, after which he became very wealthy having developed a commercial supply of wind energy. At the time of the judgment, his company was valued at £57 million. His ex-wife lived in a small mortgaged home that she purchased under the right-to-buy scheme. Although she worked, she was from time to time dependent on state benefits. She lived at her home with three adult children from other relationships who contributed little to the household. The property they lived in was in a poor condition and in need of repairs that she couldn't afford.

The parties never entered into the terms of an order to dismiss their claims against each other. In 2011, the wife made a financial remedy application. She had never remarried, and so she was perfectly entitled to make these claims, despite the fact that the parties had been separated for more than 30 years.

They eventually settled her financial claims, after undoubtedly expensive litigation that reached the Supreme Court to ensure that her claims were made properly after such a long period of divorce. The terms of the settlement are recorded as *Wyatt v. Vince* [2016] EWHC 1368 (Fam). The husband agreed to pay a significant sum to the wife; such sum was much lower than the legal costs incurred by the parties.

## 5.3 THE REMARRIAGE/CIVIL PARTNERSHIP TRAP

### 5.3.1 Overview

A party to a marriage or civil partnership who hopes to have financial orders made in their favour, must make an application for those orders to be made before their remarriage or subsequent civil partnership. If they do not make such an application, they will fall foul of MCA 1973, s.28(3)/CPA 2004, Sched.5, Part 10, para.48, which state that if no application is made prior to remarriage or subsequent civil partnership, then that party is not entitled to apply for a financial provision order or a property adjustment order.

This is known as 'the remarriage trap', which operates as a complete bar on making financial applications save for an application for a pension sharing order.

There is no time limit to bring financial claims – MCA 1973, ss.23(1) and 24(1) provide that orders for financial provision and property adjustment may be made on granting a decree of divorce or at any time thereafter. It is not unusual for parties to wait for some time after the divorce proceedings have finalised to turn their attention to the division of finances – an extreme example of which can be seen in *Wyatt v. Vince* above.

See **Appendix B2** where there is a flowchart to follow in the event that you have client who might be caught by the remarriage trap and for those clients who may still be able to apply for financial remedy applications.

### 5.3.2 How to make an application

A petitioner who ticks the relevant boxes in the current petition to indicate that they intend to pursue financial orders will be able to pursue any available claims they preserved after remarriage.

Any petition which predates 6 April 2011 (when the new petition forms were introduced) didn't have an 'opt in' section for financial claims: it contained an automatic claim for financial relief. It was possible in the previous petition to delete the claims for 'ancillary relief' (more commonly called 'financial remedy' after the introduction of the FPR 2010) but it would have been rare for a solicitor representing a petitioner to delete those claims. This ensured that their client wasn't caught out by the remarriage trap.

In order to avoid a situation where a client doesn't have a copy of an old petition to see if claims were preserved and now wishes to pursue a claim for financial relief, the court should keep a copy of the file with the petition for 125 years. However, it should be noted that in the case of *Wyatt* v. *Vince*, the entire divorce file was missing and the petition was never located.

As maintenance automatically ceases upon remarriage or subsequent civil partnership, this will not be available on an application after the potential applicant's remarriage. While solicitors usually ensure that the petitioner's claims are preserved by ticking the relevant boxes in the current petition, those who opt to do their own divorce do not usually understand the importance of stating their intention to make a financial claim in the petition. See **Appendix B2** for further information regarding the remarriage trap problems that arise.

The respondent to a petition has no form to complete in which they can notify the court and the other party of their intention to pursue financial orders as a result of the divorce. The acknowledgment of service is the only form the respondent needs to complete in the divorce/dissolution process and a petitioner can sometimes proceed in the absence of this form being returned. If the respondent decided to issue a cross petition, then they would be able to tick a box about their financial claims. Most respondents do not cross petition or defend a petition and so are unlikely to be nudged to protect themselves from the remarriage trap unless they take legal advice when receiving the petition. When the new 'no fault' process is introduced in Autumn 2021 the respondent will not be able to cross petition or defend a petition. It has been suggested that the acknowledgment of service be changed to allow the respondent to indicate a desire to pursue financial claims, but this change may not come about for some time if at all.

A respondent could issue a Form A to preserve their financial claims, although this usually instigates a full court timetable being produced, including a date for the first appointment. A covering letter could indicate that the respondent doesn't wish to proceed with the timetable or a hearing. This may successfully protect the respondent from the remarriage trap, but would incur a court fee and possible further fees to suspend the timetable and vacate the hearing. This is not something that is commonly undertaken and may cause confusion in the court office resulting in a court listing regardless. While it is not ideal, if the respondent is hoping to preserve their financial claims after divorce or dissolution, this may be a way to do it.

### 5.3.3 Pension sharing applications post remarriage

Oddly, a party can apply for a pension sharing order after remarriage or subsequent civil partnership even if no formal application is made prior to remarriage. The Pension Advisory Group (PAG) 2019 report, *A Guide to the Treatment of Pensions on Divorce* (**www.nuffieldfoundation.org/wp-content/uploads/2019/11/Guide _To_The_Treatment_of_Pensions_on_Divorce-Digital_2.pdf**) addresses these issues. (I was a member of the PAG and fully endorse the content of the report.) Appendix V, para.V.13 states that a pension attachment order falls within the definition of financial provision. However it also states:

> There is no logical reason for pension sharing to be excluded from the remarriage trap. It is believed that the omission of pension sharing by way of amendment from the subsection may result from an oversight on the part of the draftsman.

## 5.4 INCOME CLAIMS

### 5.4.1 Types of income claims

Income claims are claims for regular payments of money to be paid from the income of the payer to the recipient. The regularity of payment is either weekly or monthly, and principally these claims are between spouses or civil partners. The statutes allow periodical payments to be made to children, but these payments are rarer and considered separately (**Chapter 6**).

Income claims between parties are often referred to as 'spousal maintenance', although they apply in the same way to civil partnership claims.

There are three types of income claims:

(a) *maintenance pending suit* – which is known as maintenance pending the outcome of proceedings in civil partnership proceedings (MCA 1973, s.22/ CPA 2004, Sched.5, Part 8, para.38);

(b) *interim maintenance* – which would be applicable if the decree absolute or final order has been pronounced in the divorce or dissolution proceedings, but the final financial remedy proceedings have not been agreed or decided upon; and

(c) *periodical payments* or *secured periodical payments* – which commence upon the pronouncement of the decree absolute/final order and the making of the final financial remedy order (MCA 1973, s.23/CPA 2004, Sched.5, Part 1, para.2).

```
┌─────────────────┐     ┌─────────────────┐     ┌─────────────────┐
│ Petition issued │ ──▶ │ Decree absolute │ ──▶ │ Financial remedy│
│                 │     │ pronounced      │     │ order           │
└─────────────────┘     └─────────────────┘     └─────────────────┘
```

- Earliest date a maintenance application can be made or backdated.

- Maintenance pending suit comes to an end and converts to interim maintenance.

- Interim maintenance ends and periodical payments begin (quantum and term to be decided).

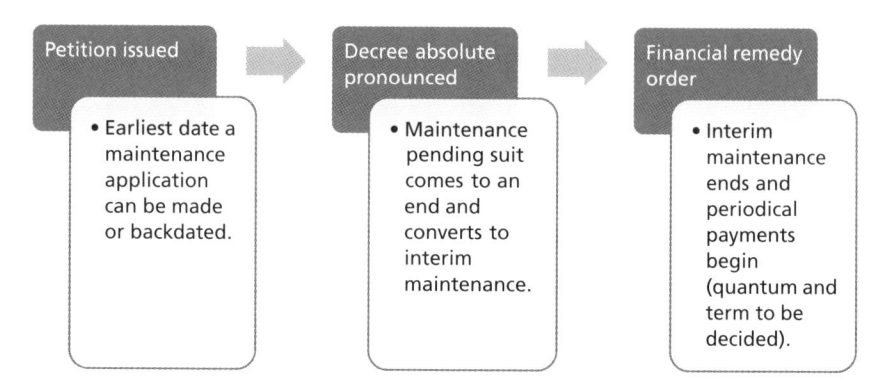

**Figure 5.1** Diagram to show a timeline for the changing types of maintenance order available in marriage or civil partnerships

### 5.4.2 Duration of income orders

#### 5.4.2.1 *General rules*

An application for maintenance pending suit can be made as soon as the petition is issued – this will only be the case where need has arisen and non-court dispute resolution (NCDR) has been rejected or has not been broached. Maintenance pending suit will automatically cease upon the pronouncement of the decree absolute, or final order in civil partnership proceedings. It is important to note that maintenance pending suit applications cannot include a provision for the payment of legal services. A separate application would need to be made under MCA 1973, s.22ZA/CPA 2004, Sched.5, Part 8, paras.38A–38B, although the two applications are often made together on the Form D11 and listed together by the court.

Interim maintenance takes over from maintenance pending suit, although it can be applied for even if maintenance pending suit was not needed. It will commence after the pronouncement of the decree absolute. Interim maintenance terminates upon a final financial remedy order being made which will either dismiss maintenance or in all likelihood contain a provision for periodical payments for the recipient.

The earliest a periodical payments order (or a secured periodical payments order) can be made is at the same time as the issue of the petition. A periodical payment order automatically terminates upon the death of either party (MCA 1973, s.28(1)(a), (b)).

A secured periodical payments order terminates automatically upon the remarriage of the recipient or the recipient's death, but not upon the death of the payer. This makes the order more advantageous to the recipient of maintenance, but it is rare, as a clean break with capitalised maintenance would be preferred to a secured periodical payments order.

Other terminating events can be negotiated between the parties. These can include the following:

- cohabitation (usually continuous) of the receiving party for a specified period;
- the youngest child ceasing full-time secondary or tertiary education;
- a specified date by which the receiving spouse will be expected to have secured suitable full-time employment;
- another specified date (for example, the sale of jointly owned property);
- a further order.

Sometimes the parties agree that if the recipient of the maintenance cohabits with another person for a certain continuous period, maintenance will cease. This is by no means accepted to be a 'usual' trigger event. Cohabitation does not bring with it any security for the person losing maintenance as the new relationship might not last and so this terminating event should be carefully considered before agreeing to include it in the terms of settlement.

If no additional terminating events are agreed between the parties, only the statutory events will terminate the maintenance order. This is usually known as a 'joint lives' maintenance order. It is very unusual these days to agree such an order, as the focus is on promoting financial independence and achieving a clean break. MCA 1973, s.28(1) makes it clear that a maintenance order should be made for a term 'as the court thinks fit'. No other guidance is given, save that the MCA 1973, s.25 factors should be considered.

Generally, maintenance orders are made in cases where one party is the main carer for the minor children of the family. A briefing paper – E. Hitchings and J. Miles, 'Financial remedies on divorce: the need for evidence based reform' (2018) (available at: **www.nuffieldfoundation.org/project/final-settlements-in-financial-disputes-following-divorce**) – gives a clear view on when periodical payments orders are usually made. The prevalent practice seems to be towards achieving a clean break on income, however this may under-protect 'economically vulnerable wives'. Such wives may have had their earning capacity impacted by their role as the main carer, and they may need additional financial support, where this is possible. There may also be another reason why such a wife would be vulnerable – for example, she may be unable to work due to disability, or a controlling partner may have prevented her from entering the workforce, even in the absence of having children or after children have flown the nest. It is important to realise that such women may need ongoing income orders and that a clean break is not appropriate.

The briefing paper indicates that in the majority of cases where periodical payment orders were made, the husband was the payer and in a high-level occupation. However, in the study it appeared that there are only periodical payments orders made in 16 per cent of cases. There was an immediate clean break in the majority of cases; a deferred clean break in 7 per cent of cases; and joint lives orders in 5.5 per cent of cases. Practitioners often concern themselves with the issue of periodical payments, but the statistics show that (rightly or wrongly) in reality this is not a common order.

It may be that there is insufficient surplus income when the order is made to justify a substantive maintenance order. In these cases, a nominal order (£1 per annum or less) will be made which could be varied upwards if the payer's income position improves. Variation applications (MCA 1973, s.31; and CPA 2004, Sched.5, Part 11) are complex and expensive and so an application should only be made where there is a real possibility of an order being changed. Sadly, such applications are made too frequently and there are serious costs implications if an application is wrongly made or defended where a compromise should have been reached. Arbitration is the perfect forum for these disputes, and may be cheaper than pursuing a court application for variation.

Furthermore, if there is a pension sharing order in place, then it would be double recovery to agree the terms of a maintenance order after income could reasonably be expected to be drawn from the pension, as in those circumstances the paying party may have lost part of their pension income from the pension sharing order and would then be forced to pay maintenance after retirement from the remaining pension.

In the appeal of the first instance decision in *D* v. *D (financial provision: periodical payments)* [2004] EWHC 445 (Fam) the court limited the wife's periodical payments to a term of 10 years in substitution of a joint lives order. In the terms of the original order, she was to receive £10,000 per annum for the parties' joint lives and a pension sharing order. The husband's appeal related only to the term of the maintenance order and not its quantum. The husband sought a 10-year term to be imposed with an MCA 1973, s.28(1A) bar (see below).

The term of 10 years was imposed to coincide with the husband's retirement. The term was left open to the possibility of extension, i.e. no MCA 1973, s.28(1A) bar was imposed as it would be wrong after a long marriage and the wife's dependency during it, to prevent the court from considering the matter again if in the intervening time the wife suffered financial embarrassment.

Global maintenance orders can be made by the court – these are sometimes called a 'Segal order'. This order combines the liability for a spousal and child periodical payments order into one sum. The order usually reduces pound for pound in the event that a CMS assessment is made. The court may not have the jurisdiction to make a child periodical payment order, but does have the ability to make a global maintenance order. Such an order must always contain a substantive spousal maintenance order to be made by the court – the court shouldn't make the order if the spousal element is minor compared to the child periodical payments sum. There is no need to specify in the order how much of the sum is for each element of the order.

### 5.4.2.2  MCA 1973, s.28(1A) bar – the non-extendable term

Where the parties have agreed, or the court has made, a periodical payment order with a term as opposed to a joint lives order, the court should consider whether to impose an MCA 1973, s.28(1A) bar. This provision operates to ensure that there is a definite end to the term of maintenance ordered by the court. By inserting this provision into the terms of the order, the court specifically directs that a party in receipt of maintenance shall not be entitled to apply under MCA 1973, s.31 for an extension of the term. This recipient may, however, still apply for an upwards or downwards variation of the quantum of the maintenance (see below) during the existence of the order.

Where a s.28(1A) bar is imposed, there is no circumstance in which the term of the order can ever be varied to make the term longer. It is possible for the paying party to apply to terminate the maintenance earlier, but there would need to be good reason to make the application to succeed in doing so.

### 5.4.2.3  The extendable term

If a termed periodical payments order is made and no specific reference is made to the MCA 1973, s.28(1A) bar provision, the maintenance order is known as an 'extendable term order'. Both the term of maintenance and the quantum can be varied.

Practitioners should note that the term can only be varied if an application to do so is made before the periodical payments order terminates. For example, if the first terminating event is 1 January 2021, an application to extend the term must be made under MCA 1973, s.31 before that date. If an application is made at any point after 1 January 2021, the term will have expired and it is not possible to make any application to extend the term. Obviously, an application to vary quantum can only be made during the subsistence of the maintenance order.

#### 5.4.3  Quantum

### 5.4.3.1  General rules

Along with the questions of whether there should be maintenance, and if so for what duration, is the equally important question of how much money should be paid.

A nominal order, as referred to above, can be for a sum of £1 per annum or less; some orders refer to 5p per annum as the appropriate sum. It is not expected that the payer of maintenance will actually make a payment of this sum. It is both nominal and notional, although I have known clients in the past to take great delight in sending 1p coins to their ex-spouse, usually fixed to a Christmas card! The purpose of a nominal sum is to ensure that where the paying party has no surplus income to support the receiving party, the maintenance claim is kept open. The nominal sum will either be an extendable or non-extendable termed order or a joint lives order.

MATRIMONIAL FINANCE HANDBOOK

**Is maintenance needed?**

- Is it reasonable for there to be maintenance in this case? (If yes then)
- If no, then there should be a clean break on income orders

**Can the payer afford to pay a maintenance order?**

- Is there surplus income to pay substantive maintenance? (If yes then)
- If no, then review if there should be a clean break on income or a nominal maintenance order

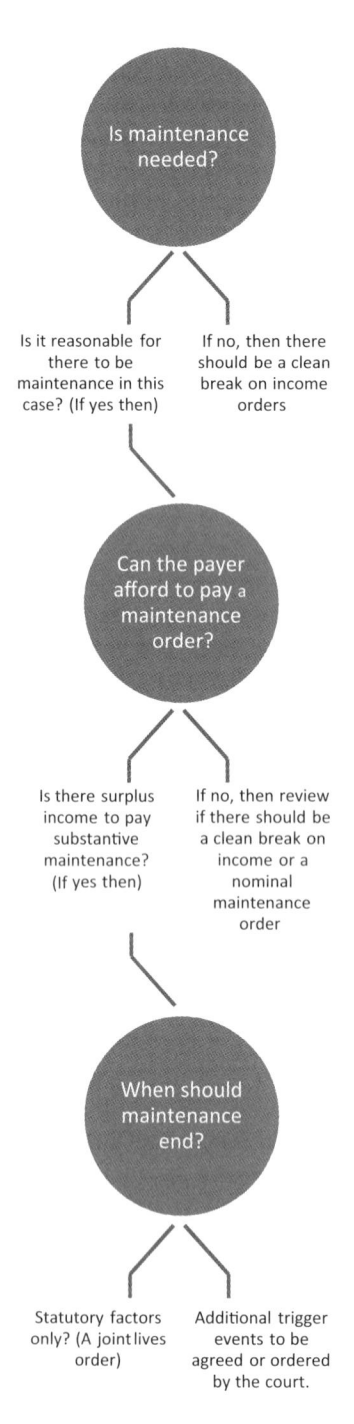

**When should maintenance end?**

- Statutory factors only? (A joint lives order)
- Additional trigger events to be agreed or ordered by the court.

**Figure 5.2** The process of consideration when assessing a potential maintenance claim

During the term of the maintenance order, the receiving spouse could apply for the quantum to be varied upwards in the event that the paying party suddenly has a change of income. In practice, it is rare to see a nominal order increased to a substantive sum, unless circumstances have changed dramatically, for example the recipient has become incapacitated, although in the case of *North* v. *North* [2007] EWCA Civ 760 the court considered just such an application to vary and capitalise an historical nominal maintenance order for the ex-wife.

A substantive maintenance order is one where a specific sum of money is paid on a regular basis. The order usually specifies how the monies are paid by identifying a bank account into which the payment will be made and specifying a date when payments will start.

Where it is fair for a substantive maintenance order to be made, the difficulty can be in assessing the appropriate sum. There is little guidance in MCA 1973 outside s.25 which is applied by the court exercising its discretion. On a practical level, maintenance is decided by balancing the income/earning capacity of the parties against the needs as set out in their evidence.

It should be noted that a person's income is not shared according to entitlement – the sharing principle does not apply to future income (*Waggott* v. *Waggott* [2018] EWCA Civ 727).

### 5.4.3.2 Practice points

For the practitioner representing the paying party, it is important to ensure that their client's net income is accurately presented and, more importantly, that the schedule of outgoings (the money they need to meet their reasonable needs) is properly drafted. This ensures that any surplus income can be identified as being available for the payment of maintenance. A common mistake can be for the paying party to show a huge surplus of net income, but then argue that they should not be paying maintenance. In some cases, this may arise by not paying sufficient attention to the schedule of outgoings and understating the payer's future budget. If a surplus is available and the other spouse cannot make ends meet from their own income, then a maintenance order is likely to be made, unless capitalisation is a possibility.

Even if a surplus is not shown, the schedule of outgoings will need to be reasonable – for example, if the paying party has large sums of regular savings/investments/pension contributions, the court may deem it to be more appropriate for that money, or part of it, to be paid as maintenance to the other spouse.

For the practitioner representing the receiving party, it is important that they represent income from all sources available to that party. Often the availability of child benefit and/or tax credits is overlooked, and this can be problematic if equivalent sums of maintenance are being requested from the paying party. Each party has an obligation to maximise their income in earning capacity from all sources.

In my experience, the receiving party can sometimes underestimate the income required to meet their needs, perhaps because during the marriage their spouse had controlled the finances and paid the bills. The solicitor should ensure that the client completes the schedule of outgoings carefully.

The receiving party can sometimes wholly overestimate the annual outgoings needed, in which case the court and other party will immediately start to reduce or delete particular items in the schedule as being unreasonable. This is much more likely to happen in high net worth cases than in small asset/income cases, where inflated 'aspirational' budgets are commonplace, in my experience.

In the case of *McCartney* v. *Mills McCartney* [2008] EWHC 401 (Fam), the wife estimated her annual income needs at in excess of £1.2 million, but the court was persuaded that the budget exceeded the parties' standard of living during the marriage. She was awarded £600,000 per annum for her reasonable expenditure. The court indicated that it was unreasonable that after a short marriage to a very wealthy man she should expect to continue to live at the same rate as she did during the parties' marriage. Her maintenance award, which was ultimately capitalised, was awarded to allow her to adapt to 'a standard of living that she could expect as a self-sufficient woman' (para.240).

The advice to practitioners is to ensure that clients are being reasonable when preparing their budgets – they should not attempt to exceed the standard of living they enjoyed during the marriage and should be advised not even to expect the same standard of living after divorce.

In the vast majority of cases, judges will advise the parties to 'cut their cloth' – meaning that each party needs to learn how to live with the money available to them. Most people getting divorced need to maximise their income from all sources, including (if needs be) returning to work if one party has been out of the workplace. Emotionally, this can be a struggle where one party does not have skills and did not expect to have to return to work. The earlier a client can be advised of the need to maximise their income, for their own benefit, the quicker a settlement will be negotiated. In small money cases, it can be very difficult for the main carer of the children to consider returning to work when this hadn't been part of their plan during the marriage. Unfortunately, the only way to make ends meet may be for that person to obtain a part-time position. Their income together with universal credit, child benefit and any child maintenance being paid will probably constitute their entire income. Spousal maintenance is rarely paid due to affordability factors, and that spouse cannot simply hope to rely on their partner to support them even if this was the arrangement during the marriage.

### 5.4.3.3 Other quantum considerations

If the person ordered to pay periodical payments dies whilst still making payments, the recipient is likely to be able to make a claim against their estate under the provisions of the Inheritance (Provision for Family and Dependants) Act 1975, as a dependent ex-spouse. The consent order should deal with the parameters of such an inheritance claim and there are precedents that can limit the claim that can be brought against the estate.

In the alternative, thought should be given during the disclosure and negotiations, to the possibility of the payer taking out maintenance protection insurance to ensure that the recipient is not left without much-needed income in the event of the payer's death. These matters need to be negotiated prior to the making of an order if the recipient wants the certainty of payment. The payer should usually take financial advice alongside legal advice when negotiating the terms of the financial remedy settlement. It is likely that such a financial adviser would encourage taking out appropriate insurance.

Some thought should also be given to the security of the parties while the divorce and negotiations are ongoing. Until the final order is made, the parties are able to make claims under the Inheritance (Provision for Family and Dependants) Act 1975 in the event of the death of one of the parties. It is sensible for the parties to take financial advice as early as possible in the divorce or dissolution process so that they can ensure no rash decisions are made until the final solution is reached. The parties can be inclined to cancel insurance policies upon separation, but this may not be a sensible decision. Careful financial planning needs to be considered, both during and after the relationship breakdown.

It should also be noted that the payment of spousal maintenance may reduce the receipt of universal credit. When negotiating, this cannot be overlooked, particularly where income is critical to ensure that the recipient can pay their bills and feed the family.

### 5.4.4  Capitalisation of an income stream

#### *5.4.4.1  Overview*

Occasionally, the parties will agree that rather than one party paying maintenance to the other, it would be sensible or desirable, instead of paying maintenance, to provide a capital sum (see **5.4.4.3**) which would allow a clean break to take effect immediately.

First, the parties would need to ascertain whether a maintenance order is needed, and then decide the term and quantum. If there is indeed an income need, it can be exchanged for a capital sum. For the various methods of calculating capitalisation, see below.

It is much more likely that capitalisation will take place in high net worth cases, where there is sufficient capital to exchange for a substantive maintenance order. In small money cases, there is much less likely to be a true maintenance provision, and therefore a clean break will be reached in the absence of capitalisation because no maintenance order would have been made. This can sometimes be a mistake made by practitioners in small money cases, to assume there is an income order needed without a proper consideration of the facts of the case.

### 5.4.4.2 Variation applications

MCA 1973, s.31(7A)–(7F) and CPA 2004, Sched.5, Part 11, paras.50–52 permit capitalisation of an income stream if an application to vary a maintenance order is made by either party. This can either be by way of a capital lump sum being paid, or a property adjustment order being made.

More recently, these provisions have been amended to allow one or more pension sharing orders to be made in place of a maintenance order. It should be noted that where a pension is shared during the financial remedy proceedings, it cannot be used to capitalise maintenance at a later date. Therefore, if pension A was shared in the financial remedy proceedings but pension B was untouched, only pension B would be available in variation proceedings for capitalisation.

If the financial remedy order pre-dates the availability of pension sharing (1 December 2000), then this cannot be used as a remedy in a variation application which post-dates pension sharing. For example, an application for variation is made on 1 January 2021. The petition was issued as dated 1 December 1998 (this precedes the availability of pension sharing orders). While capitalisation could take place with reference to a lump sum or property adjustment order, pension sharing will not be available.

### 5.4.4.3 How to capitalise a maintenance order

In high net worth cases, it is possible that where a substantive maintenance order is made, a capital sum could be ordered to replace the income stream. An example of this can be seen in the case of *McCartney* v. *Mills McCartney* above. This is not a solution in lower asset cases, as there simply will not be sufficient capital to substitute an income stream, even if the income stream is a small one.

The method of capitalisation is not fixed; however, the courts tend to default to using the 'Duxbury calculation'. This calculation derives from the case *Duxbury* v. *Duxbury* [1987] 1 FLR 7. The calculation assumes, among other factors, that there will be uniform income yield of 3 per cent pa, uniform capital growth of 3.75 per cent pa, uniform inflation at 3 per cent and a consistent tax regime increasing in line with inflation. It anticipates a consistent level of drawdown, and that the recipient will survive to the average age of their contemporaries. The Duxbury tables can be found in the At a Glance publication which is published by the Family Law Bar Association (FLBA). There are many family law professionals who do not believe that these tables are fit for purpose, particularly as the methodology rarely changes. The tables assume a joint lives maintenance order, and so does not accommodate capitalisation of a termed maintenance order very easily. The main objection to this calculation is that it does not allow for the costs of wealth management but assumes that an income stream will be derived from the capital sum in fairly risky investments, which most recipients wouldn't be comfortable investing in.

It is very easy these days to engage the services of a financial planner or independent financial adviser (IFA) who can fairly easily project a capital sum to replace an income stream using current financial assumptions, rather than the fixed predictions that Duxbury offers. This is likely to be much more accurate and will easily allow for capitalisation in termed maintenance cases. Some family law professionals doubt whether the judiciary would be amenable to using more modern methods of capitalisation.

Lord Justice Moylan sitting in the Court of Appeal in the case of *Tattersall* v. *Tattersall* [2018] EWCA Civ 1978 indicated that the judge is not restricted to using the Duxbury tables to effect calculation of a capital sum to replace an income stream. He said (para.42): 'Although I would expect judges typically to use Duxbury, a judge can decide to use a method of calculation other than Duxbury. To do so is not, in my view, an error of law.'

In this particular case, the judge used the Ogden tables (used in personal injury cases) to capitalise maintenance – these tables are not typically used in family law matters. Lord Justice Moylan doubted whether there would have been much difference in using those tables to the Duxbury tables. In fact, Ogden tables usually expect a lower level of risk when investing the capital sum to produce the income stream. Ogden tables also allow for the costs of investment, which is an obvious error in the Duxbury tables.

## 5.5 LUMP SUM ORDERS

### 5.5.1 Overview

MCA 1973, s.23(1) and CPA 2004, Sched.5, Part 2 empower the court to make an order that one party shall pay to the other lump sums as specified in the order. We will be looking at the payment of lump sums to children in **Chapter 6**.

Clearly, in order to pay a sum of money, the party must have that money to pay, or have the ability to raise the money by the payment date. If the client commits themselves to making a lump sum payment on a certain date, the failure to do so will attract penalties in the form of interest payments.

Often in the context of the overall division of assets, one party may agree to 'buy out' the other party's interest in a jointly owned property. Before an order is made to that effect, every effort should be made to ensure that the mortgage can be secured to borrow the necessary sum or investments liquidated for that purpose. In this scenario, a default provision for sale will sometimes be drafted into the terms of the order (MCA 1973, s.24A/CPA 2004, Sched.5, Part 3, para.10). This will ensure that the recipient receives either the lump sum or proceeds of sale equivalent to the lump sum plus whatever interest is allowable.

In high net worth cases, a lump sum might represent a housing fund for the recipient plus a capitalised maintenance fund which will produce an income. In a small money case, the lump sum (if made) may be a small percentage of what one party may expect as their share of capital assets. The majority of assets may be utilised for housing minor children and a lump sum will likely represent a small percentage of their fair share.

```
                    ┌─────────────────────────┐
                    │   One lump sum order    │
                    │    (which can be        │
                    │ adjourned in rare cases)│
                    └─────────────────────────┘
                                 │
        ┌────────────────────────┼────────────────────────┐
        │                        │                        │
┌───────────────┐    ┌────────────────────┐    ┌──────────────────────┐
│  One lump sum │    │ A series of        │    │ One lump sum payable │
│ e.g. £100,000 │    │ individual lump    │    │ by instalments, e.g. │
│  paid on a    │    │ sums, e.g. five    │    │ £100,000 paid as     │
│ specified date│    │ lump sums of       │    │ instalments of       │
│               │    │ £20,000 paid on    │    │ £20,000 over five    │
│               │    │ different dates    │    │ months               │
└───────────────┘    └────────────────────┘    └──────────────────────┘
        │                        │                        │
┌───────────────┐    ┌────────────────────┐    ┌──────────────────────┐
│ The lump sum  │    │ The lump sums are  │    │ MCA 1973, s.31(2)(d)/│
│ is not subject│    │ not subject to     │    │ CPA 2004 equivalent. │
│ to variation  │    │ variation          │    │ The instalments are  │
│               │    │                    │    │ capable of variation │
└───────────────┘    └────────────────────┘    └──────────────────────┘
```

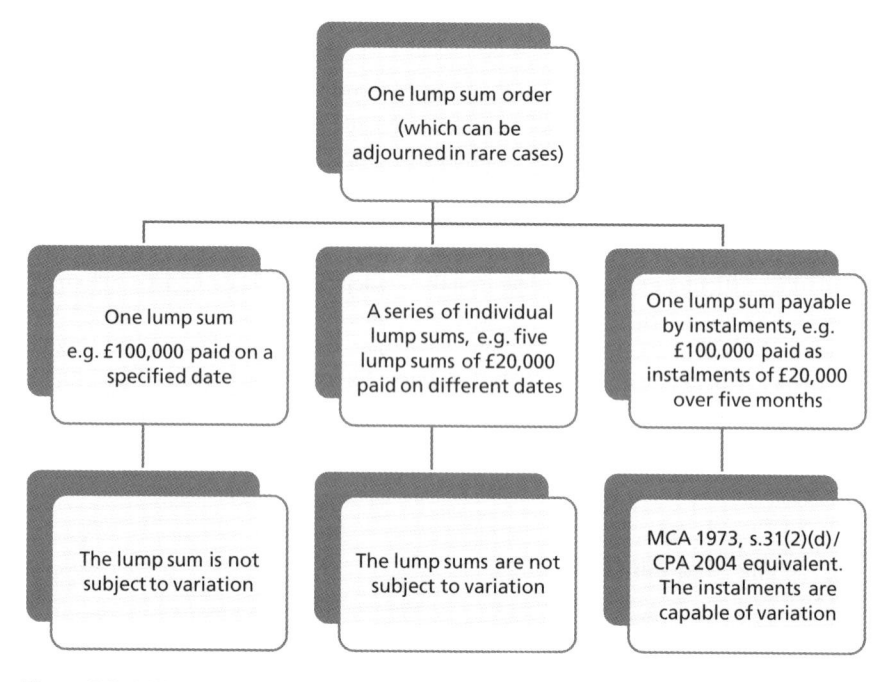

**Figure 5.3** Different options for lump sum payments and possibility of variation

*Hamilton v. Hamilton* [2013] EWCA Civ 13 is an important case, as it stresses the importance for parties to understand the difference between (a) a series of lump sum payments and (b) lump sum payment by instalments.

A lump sum can be expressed as either a single sum paid on a specific date, for example £250,000 paid on 1 January 2021; or it can be expressed as a *series of payments*. If there is a series of payments, the overall sum to be paid will be £250,000, but payment will be made on the first of each month starting from January 2021. The final payment will therefore be made on 1 May 2021. Each lump sum of £50,000 is an independent payment where there is a series of lump sums. There is no power of the court to vary, discharge or suspend a lump sum order.

If payments were expressed to be *instalments*, there would be one lump sum payment of £250,000 to be paid in instalments on the first day of each month starting from January 2021. On the face of it, this appears to be no different than the previous example. However, where there is one lump sum payment which is paid in instalments, each instalment is subject to the court's power to vary, discharge or suspend any instalment payment (MCA 1973, s.31(2)(d)/CPA 2004, Sched.5, Part 11, para.51).

It is important when drafting a consent order to make it clear whether it is intended that there will be a series of individual payments or whether subsequent payments are by instalment. The standard order precedents provide clear templates for each scenario. (These can be downloaded via the link to 'Standard orders volume 1 financial and enforcement orders' at: **www.judiciary.uk/publications/practice-guidance-standard-children-and-other-orders/**.) For example, standard order 2.1, para.28 says:

> The parties agree and declare that the lump sum order set out in paragraph [para number] below should be considered to be [a series of lump sum orders]/[a lump sum order payable by instalments].

It is therefore very important that the parties consider whether they want the flexibility to be able to return to court to vary the lump sum orders, or whether certainty is more important. If this is likely to be an important factor, it should be highlighted at the negotiation stage, rather than at the drafting stage.

### 5.5.2 Interest payable on a lump sum order

Judgments Act (JA) 1838, s.17 applies to all High Court judgments and Family Court judgments of more than £5,000. Thus, any lump sum order for more than £5,000 automatically carries interest at the judgment rate (8 per cent) from the date of non-payment to be paid until the date of payment. It is common for an order to contain a provision regarding the payment of interest if the lump sum if it is not paid on time; the issue of the payment of interest and the percentage that is levied in the event of non-payment can be subject to negotiations.

In cases where the lump sum is less than £5,000 the standard order precedents do not allow the court to levy interest charges in the event that payment is not made on time. However, there is a provision in the precedents for the paying party to pay further lump sums calculated as a daily rate from the date of default until the date of payment. This is a way of ensuring that a penalty is paid for late payment where the court has no jurisdiction to order interest payments to be made.

Although unusual, the court has the jurisdiction to order the payment of interest on lump sum orders from the date of the order until the date of payment (MCA 1973, s.23(6)). This is rather more uncommon than the payment of interest upon default of payment. See the case of *Moher* v. *Moher* below.

However, if no thought is given at the time of drafting to the payment of interest, then the statutory default provisions will apply in the event that the lump sum is not paid on time.

When drafting, it is important to know with certainty when the lump sum payment will be due. The parties can agree to make payment on a specified date, although if the order has not been approved by that date there can be some reticence to make payment of the lump sum in the absence of a financial order and the decree absolute which puts into effect the financial order.

A way to circumvent the confusion would be to express the payment of a lump sum to take place 28 days after the date of the order or the date of the decree absolute, whichever is later. This ensures that the lump sum does not accidentally become notionally payable on a date before an order has been approved by the court and the decree absolute pronounced. See the case of *Moher* v. *Moher* below with reference to the payment of interest in these cases.

One practical difficulty with this can be in rare cases where the financial order/decree absolute are approved, but the court forgets to send them out. I hope that this should be a thing of the past with the online divorce portal and online filing of consent orders – it has, however, caused me moments of great stress to discover that an order was approved but sitting in the file at court rather than being sent to the parties to implement the terms.

### 5.5.2.1  *Moher v. Moher [2019] EWCA Civ 1482*

It is well known that a lump sum order cannot take effect until the decree absolute has been pronounced. However, if an order contains the provision for a lump sum, it should be clear when interest should start to run. Interest can start to run from the date of the financial provision order which can predate the decree absolute. The situation could arise where interest has started to accrue even though the decree absolute has not been pronounced and therefore the order has not taken effect.

For example, the financial order states that the lump sum of £250,000 with interest to run at 8 per cent to be paid on 1 April 2021. The order is dated 25 March 2021; the decree absolute isn't pronounced until 1 May 2021. The lump sum is paid on 2 May 2021 as the order took effect the day before. Some may say that the paying party owes interest at £54.79 per day (8 per cent of £250,000 is £20,000 per annum.) This would be a total interest payment of £1,643.70 for 30 days' non-payment. On the other hand, the paying party may say that the order didn't take effect until 1 May 2021, no interest is due. The paying party must pay interest if it is clearly stated that interest will run from a particular date, even if that date pre-dates the order taking effect when the decree absolute is pronounced.

To be clear, in *Moher* v. *Moher*, Moylan LJ indicated that the order should state the payment should be made on the relevant date 'or the date of decree absolute, whichever is the later' (para.42).

### 5.5.3  Adjourned application for lump sum order

It is possible that an application for a lump sum order can be made with other financial remedy applications but that the lump sum application will be adjourned to another date. This might happen if there is a possibility of a capital payment in the future, from which a lump sum might be generated.

*D* v. *D (lump sum: adjournment of application)* [2001] 1 FLR 633 is a case in which the wife successfully persuaded the district judge to adjourn her application for a lump sum. The sum of the husband's bonus was not yet known, and so the wife invited the judge to adjourn her application, which he did on a general basis. On the husband's appeal against the adjournment, the court dismissed it save for the fact that the adjournment was made for a specific period, until the amount of the bonus was known, rather than a general adjournment.

### 5.5.4 Interim lump sum orders

In many cases, it would be useful for the financially vulnerable party to be able to make an application to the court for an interim lump sum order. This money might be used to fund legal expenses or to pay for specific items, school fees, and holidays or even for a new car. Where one party holds all the investments and earns all the money, it can be very difficult for the other party to continue living to the same standard without some financial assistance from their spouse. Although a maintenance pending suit/maintenance pending the outcome of proceedings (MPS/MPOP) order may be available, sometimes there is no regular income but quite a lot of capital available for distribution. Additionally, some items of expenditure don't fall within the strict interpretation of regular expenses, and so the making of an interim capital order would be useful.

Unfortunately, the jurisdiction of the court to make an interim lump sum order is limited and so this power is very rarely ever used. MCA 1973, s.23(3) permits an application to be made by a party to get an interim lump sum order. This interim lump sum is limited to meeting liabilities or expenses which are reasonably incurred in maintaining the party or any child of the family before the application is made. Undoubtedly, the cost of making such an application would be disproportionate to the likely recovery.

## 5.6 PROPERTY ADJUSTMENT ORDERS

### 5.6.1 Types of property adjustment orders

There are a number of different orders that can be made for property adjustment. We do not include in this section the provision of a fund of money to enable one party to purchase a property, as this would be a lump sum order with the intention of purchasing a property rather than a property adjustment order.

The following types of property order are available:

(a) the transfer of a property or properties;
(b) the settlement of a property;
(c) the sale of a property or properties;
(d) the variation of an ante-nuptial or post nuptial settlement made on the parties to a marriage; and
(e) continuing to hold the property jointly while redistributing the parties' beneficial entitlement.

The most common order when dealing with property is either a transfer or a sale. Although the court has the power to settle property, this rarely happens in practice. The variation of ante-nuptial or post-nuptial settlements is also rare, and by its nature usually only likely to happen in high net worth cases. Where these orders are likely, counsel's advice should be sought at an early stage.

### 5.6.2 Property transfers

The most common type of property order to be made in divorce or civil partnership dissolution cases is likely to be the transfer or sale of property.

MCA 1973, s.24(1) and CPA 2004, Sched.5, Part 2, para.7(1) give the court the power to make an order to transfer the property from one party to the other. Naturally the party who is ordered to make the transfer should have an interest in the property either in possession or reversion. The court has the power to order the transfer of property for the benefit of a child of the family; this happens rarely and is considered further in **Chapter 6**.

A property adjustment order will not take effect until the divorce or civil partnership reach their conclusion with the pronouncement of the decree absolute or final order.

There is no definition of 'property' in either the MCA 1973 or CPA 2004. This provision applies to the transfer of houses, land, shares, policies and other types of property – this list is not exhaustive.

Real property, such as land or buildings, can be owned in one party's sole name, in joint names with their spouse or civil partner or in joint names with a third party. In each case of joint ownership there are two options, to own the property as beneficial joint tenants or as tenants in common.

The ownership of real property between a party to the divorce and a third party can cause significant difficulties from a procedural point of view. Essentially, the beneficial share of the party to the divorce must be agreed or established before the dispute between spouses can be agreed or adjudicated. Once established, the beneficial share of the third party is of no consequence in the financial remedy proceedings.

In practice, the third party is often a family member, new partner or friend and rarely are the beneficial interests clearly defined in a deed of declaration of trust. Sometimes where there is a deed of declaration of trust, the beneficial interest of the spouse involved in court proceedings isn't reflective of their financial contribution to the purchase of the property. In these cases, the deed of declaration might need to be challenged to establish the true beneficial interest of the spouse.

The existence of a third-party interest might complicate the financial remedy procedure – the Family Court is often faced with this type of issue and should be able to navigate the complexities quite easily. Where a property is owned with a third party, that party may need to be joined to the proceedings if there is a dispute about their beneficial interest in the property. This is considered further in **Chapter 3**.

### 5.6.3 Sole ownership

Where a person owns a property in their sole name, the fact of sole ownership does not exclude the property from consideration in either a divorce or a civil partnership dispute. The court has the jurisdiction to include the property and divide it between the parties in any way that is seen to be fair.

Occasionally, a property will be legally held by one party in their sole name but there may be a deed of declaration of trust which indicates that the beneficial ownership is different. The court will take those factors into consideration as a relevant circumstance, when dealing with the division of assets (MCA 1973, s.25(1)). A deed of declaration of trust entered into by spouses before the marriage does not oust the power of the court to distribute assets between them, but may be an influential factor.

Likewise, the court will take into account the existence of a properly contracted pre- or post-nuptial agreement, which might help the parties and the court to divide the property in accordance with their intentions. The leading case of *Radmacher* v. *Granatino* [2010] UKSC 42 sets out the approach of the court where a pre-nuptial agreement is entered into by the parties. The court will need to decide what weight to attach to the agreement – in doing so, the court will consider whether each party intended to enter into a binding agreement with the other. There should be no duress, fraud or misrepresentation which would impair the validity of the agreement. Other 'unconscionable conduct' may operate to minimise or eliminate any weight attached to the agreement reached. Furthermore, if the terms are unfair from the start, the weight attached to the agreement will be reduced.

When considering issues concerning pre- or post-nuptial agreement, the excellent book by Stephen Parker, *Family Law Agreements and Consent Orders* (Law Society Publishing, 2019), is invaluable.

### 5.6.4 Home rights

When advising the non-owning spouse or civil partner, it is important to consider whether registration of a 'home rights' notice is appropriate (Family Law Act (FLA) 1996, s.30). Where one spouse is entitled to occupy a property and the other is not, the spouse who is not entitled to occupy has certain 'home rights' – these include the right not to be evicted or excluded unless by order of the court. If that spouse is not in occupation, they are entitled to enter and occupy with permission of the court.

These 'home rights' will only apply if the property was a matrimonial/civil partnership home or was intended to be their matrimonial/civil partnership home. Only one residential property can be registered for the protection of 'home rights' in any one marriage or civil partnership.

Where the property is registered, the Form HR1 (**www.gov.uk/government/publications/notice-of-home-rights-registration-hr1**) should be completed and sent to the relevant land registry office for the property. There is no fee payable to register the notice.

The notice will only be applicable in protecting 'home rights' for the duration of the parties' marriage or civil partnership. As soon as a decree absolute or final order is pronounced, the 'home rights' notice can be cancelled from the register by production of the document ending the marriage or civil partnership (decree absolute/final order), together with the Form HR4. This is an important consideration when applying for decree absolute or if requesting an undertaking from the petitioner not to proceed with the decree absolute/final order before financial matters can be finally resolved.

Before making an application for a notice to be registered, the client should always be notified that their spouse will be made aware of the application as soon as it is registered. This can sometimes be a matter of concern, particularly if the parties continue to live together and it is possible that the owning spouse will react badly to receiving the notice.

Any person searching the register, for example a prospective purchaser or mortgagee, will become aware that the named person has a right to occupy the property. This does not necessarily prevent any dealings with the property, but anyone who enters into a transaction involving the property will be subject to the right of occupation of the named party. This has the practical effect of stopping genuine third-party sales as the prospective purchaser will not buy unless the occupier confirms that they will vacate the property and withdraws the notice. If the occupier confirms that they will voluntarily vacate the property, they can complete the HR4 form and cancel their home rights notice.

Home rights can be brought to an end by the court, if it is appropriate to do so. In the case of *BR* v. *VT* [2015] EWHC 2727 (Fam) the wife's home rights were terminated in order to allow a sale of the property to proceed. It is rare for an application of this nature to be made and granted – the issue of interim sales of property is a thorny one.

The case of *WS* v. *HS* [2018] EWFC 11 also considers the interim sale of a property on appeal. The order was set aside as the application hadn't been properly made before the district judge. Mr Justice Cobb reviewed past decisions where interim sale orders had been made and concluded that 'the court's jurisdiction to make an interim order for sale doesn't arise from FPR rule 20.2(1)(c)(v) as decided by Mr Justice Mostyn in *BR* v. *VT*'. Mr Justice Cobb indicated (para.27) that the court may have the jurisdiction to order a sale of a property under MCA 1973, s.24 to give effect to an order made under MCA 1973, s.22ZA (legal services order – see **Chapter 1**).

### 5.6.5 Property sale

*5.6.5.1 Points to note*

It is important for practitioners to note that an order for sale cannot be made without first an order for periodical payments or secured periodical payments, lump sum or property adjustment order being made (MCA 1973, s.24A(1)/CPA 2004, Sched.5, Part 3, para.11). In practice this means that the court has no jurisdiction to make a standalone order for sale. This shouldn't be overlooked when negotiating or drafting an order for sale.

It should also be noted that the court will frequently approve an order with a standalone order for sale – if problems arise with the sale there could be problems with enforcement of the order as the court had no jurisdiction to make the order in the first place.

### 5.6.5.2 Trigger events

Once the parties agree the terms of an order for sale, the actual sale of the property does not need to be immediate. Sometimes the sale might not be scheduled to take place until a specified event has occurred – these are known as 'trigger events' because the occurrence of an event will trigger the sale of a property. Common trigger events can be:

- where one party wishes to buy out the other party's interest – in the first instance there should be a transfer of a property by a certain date; if the transfer fails by the nominated date, the property should be sold;
- a lapse of time – e.g. 28 days, 42 days etc.;
- a child of the family finishing full-time secondary/tertiary education;
- the spouse who remains in the property remarries or cohabits with another person for a fixed period;
- the spouse who remains in the property dies;
- the spouse who remains in the property (and children if any) voluntarily vacates the property;
- further order of the court.

The trigger event creates an obligation for the property to be sold at some point in the future, and creates an opportunity for the spouse (with children) to remain living in the property.

### 5.6.5.3 Mesher order

You will often hear lawyers talking about a 'Mesher order' – so-called after the case of *Mesher* v. *Mesher and Hall* [1980] 1 All ER 126 (1973).

When a Mesher order is made, the property will be held jointly on trust by the parties as beneficial tenants in common. Their beneficial interests will be specified in the terms of the order. The order will also specify who will be responsible for the payment of outgoings, mortgage, insurance and property maintenance and repairs. One party will be permitted to occupy the property rent-free to the exclusion of the other party.

This type of order is made when it is impossible to transfer the property to the occupying spouse. The parties are then forced to co-own the property for the benefit of the occupying spouse and their children. I have never known a Mesher order to be made where there are no children who require housing.

The Mesher order will specify when the property will be sold, which will usually be:

(a) when the minor children of the family no longer require the home as their primary residence;
(b) when the spouse occupying the property remarries or cohabits with another person for a fixed period (a sale can only take place with permission of the court if there are minor children still in occupation);
(c) on the death of the occupying spouse or the children;
(d) on the voluntary vacation of the property by the occupying spouse for a fixed period or as their primary residence; or
(e) further order of the court.

Standard order 2.1 para.58 (Trust of Land) is the correct precedent to use when drafting an order based on a Mesher agreement.

Mesher orders are unwieldy to draft and more unwieldy to manage, as the parties are required to have contact with each other for many property-related reasons. Sometimes a Mesher arrangement is the only way securely to house the children, and the non-occupying spouse must wait for their share of the proceeds of sale. When they eventually receive the proceeds of sale, they will have to pay capital gains tax on the funds, if there has been a gain on their share. This should be accounted for when negotiating the share that they will receive in the future.

It is not unusual for the non-occupying spouse to be forced to make an application to the court to force a sale of the house when a trigger event occurs. This can cause problems many years after the divorce itself and may cause a rift between adult children and the parent wanting to get at their equity. This is another reason why Mesher orders can be unattractive for the non-occupying spouse, but may be more attractive to the occupying spouse if they know it can be difficult for the other spouse to force a sale of the property.

The non-occupying spouse is likely to have a capital gains tax liability to pay when they realise their interest upon a sale of the property, as they may not have been in occupation of the property for many years but remain a joint owner. This potential tax liability should be taken into account when negotiating their interest in the property. Even if they secure a 50 per cent interest in the property, their share will be subject to tax, whereas the occupying spouse may be entitled to claim principal residence relief in respect of their share of the property.

### 5.6.5.4 Martin order

A Martin order is named after the case of *Martin* v. *Martin* [1977] 3 All ER 762. This type of order would be appropriate where the occupying spouse has no means to house themselves other than to live in the home, and the non-occupying spouse has no immediate need for housing and can wait until the trigger events take place before a sale and distribution of the proceeds of sale.

The property will be sold at some point in the future, however the trigger events for sale are usually limited to:

(a) death of the occupying spouse;
(b) remarriage of the occupying spouse;
(c) permanent vacation of the property by the occupying spouse;
(d) further order of the court.

The sale of the property isn't linked to the age or occupation of the property by minor children. This is a recognition that the occupation of the property is primarily for the spouse, and not the children.

As with the Mesher order, the parties set out the terms of occupation, who will pay the outgoings and mortgage (if any) and who will maintain the property until sale.

The parties' respective beneficial shares will be set out in the terms of the order so that when a sale takes place, there is no doubt about each party's interest. There is likely to be a capital gains tax liability to be paid by the non-occupying spouse, and this may need to be considered when negotiating their beneficial interest in the property.

It may be that in the worst-case scenario, the non-occupying spouse predeceases the occupying spouse. In this case, their beneficial interest in the property will be received by their own estate for distribution.

Obviously, a Martin order is used only sparingly, as the non-occupying spouse may never see any equity in their lifetime.

## 5.7 PENSION ORDERS

### 5.7.1 Types of pension orders

There are now four different types of pension orders that are applicable in both marriage and civil partnership breakdown, plus one other way of dealing with pensions. They are as follows, in order of the dates they were introduced:

(a) pension attachment order (PAO) introduced for petitions filed after 1 July 1996;
(b) pension sharing order (PSO) introduced for petitions filed after 1 December 2000;
(c) pension compensation attachment order (PCAO) introduced for petitions filed after 6 April 2011;
(d) pension compensation sharing order (PCSO) introduced for petitions filed after 6 April 2011; and
(e) offsetting – which is not an order, but is the most common way that pensions are dealt with in divorce and civil partnership breakdown.

By far the most common type of order is a PSO, which physically carves up the pension between the parties. This is a clean break option; once the PSO has been implemented, it cannot be varied. After implementation, both parties will have their own pension funds and these will not be affected by the death or remarriage of the other.

By contrast, a PAO is variable and isn't a clean break option. The non-member spouse will need to wait to receive their pension benefits, which can't be accessed until the pension member chooses to draw the benefits. This means that the non-member spouse is at the mercy of their ex-spouse to draw an income in retirement. This option is further complicated by the fact that the order is subject to variation and is adversely affected by the remarriage of the non-member spouse. In 21 years of practice, I have never been involved in a case in which a PAO was made.

There are some unique cases in which these orders would be beneficial, such as pension gap cases where the pension member already receives their pension income and they have a much younger spouse who needs to share that income immediately. However, these examples are few and far between – a financial planner should be consulted if a PAO is being contemplated.

The two compensation orders ((c) and (d) above) operate in the same way as the usual sharing or attachment orders, however the compensation orders are made only in cases that involve the Pension Protection Fund (PPF) (a statutory public corporation accountable to parliament which protects people with a defined benefit pension when an employer becomes insolvent). Appendix K of the PAG report deals with the PPF involvement in pensions on divorce.

Finally, offsetting is often the option that many clients prefer, despite the inherent problems that arise when trying to reach a fair solution. The PAG report (Part 7) defines offsetting as the 'process by which the right to receive a present or future pension benefit is traded for capital or money now'. The difficulties that arise revolve around how to determine fairly a way to swap different types of asset.

### 5.7.2 'A guide to the treatment of pensions on divorce'

Any lawyer dealing with a pension in the context of divorce or civil partnership dissolution should read the PAG report, *A Guide to the Treatment of Pensions on Divorce*, which was published in July 2019.

The President of the Family Division, Sir Andrew McFarlane, endorses the report: 'For too long the division of pension assets, which may often be of significant value, has been confused by jargon, complicated structure and changing provisions'. The report serves as the basis for a single source of knowledge and information on the issue of pensions on divorce and civil partnership, in order to avoid regional and court or judge specific variations to the division of pensions in both divorce and civil partnership.

I do not propose to repeat here what is said there, particularly as the report is free to access online (**www.nuffieldfoundation.org/wp-content/uploads/2019/11/ Guide_To_The_Treatment_of_Pensions_on_Divorce-Digital_2.pdf**). There will be a lay guide published to share with clients in November 2020 and this should be available on the Nuffield Foundation website.

### 5.7.3 What type of pension is it?

One of the main difficulties that practitioners face when dealing with pensions is a lack of knowledge and understanding about financial products. The most basic of those issues is the difference between a defined contribution (DC) pension and a defined benefit (DB) pension. In addition, there are public sector pensions and the state pension.

From the very beginning of a financial remedy case, the practitioner should be alert to the possible complexities that pensions can bring with them. The first question to address is what type of pension you are dealing with. Once the complexities are understood, the practitioner can decide what experts are needed to help the client and lawyer to navigate the potential pitfalls. Lawyers are not financial advisers and are not authorised to give financial advice – it is therefore important to be able to work with financial advisers and other financial experts. The client might be loath to incur any additional expense in addition to that of their solicitor, but in order to provide a good service and avoid negligence claims, some input is likely to be needed from authorised financial professionals.

A DC scheme is a pension scheme where the pension rights are related to the amount of money contributed to the scheme and any investment return. The schemes are sometimes referred to as 'money purchase' schemes. There will therefore be a sum of money regularly deposited into the pension which will be utilised to buy investments. The value of this scheme is subject to the daily fluctuations of the stock market. It should be easy to obtain a reliable valuation of this type of investment.

A DB scheme is a pension scheme where the pension rights are related to a formula at retirement, usually related to the final salary or a career average salary of the pension holder. Although the pension member might make regular contributions to the pension scheme, the benefits they will receive on retirement are linked to either their salary at retirement ('final salary scheme') or a calculation of their average salary according to the trustees' rules. It is more complex to obtain a reliable valuation of this type of scheme, as the pension actuary is attempting to value the liability to the company of paying the member's pension income.

The public sector schemes offered by the government are DB schemes. They are valuable to the member, and because they are unfunded schemes, they create their own unique problems. These schemes are a promise of an income in retirement by the government – there is no pot of gold set aside for the payment of these pension incomes. This is unique to public sector pensions, and as a result there can be no external pension share of the pension. Appendix I of the PAG report is dedicated to the complexities of certain public sector schemes and should be read with care.

Fundamentally, these three types of pension scheme are so different to each other that although they are classified as pensions, they are like night and day.

The state pension will be a significant source of income during retirement and cannot be overlooked for either party. A state pension forecast can easily be obtained. The entitlement to a state pension is based on national insurance contributions. Part 11 of the PAG report goes into detail about the state pension.

### 5.7.4 Pension valuation

When disclosing the value of the pension, parties are expected to obtain the cash equivalent (CE), some pension trustees and practitioners still refer to this value as the cash equivalent transfer value (CETV). Whichever terminology is used, the meaning is the capitalised value of pension benefits. When the CE is calculated for a DC scheme, it represents the value of investments on the date that the valuation is given. However, for a DB scheme it is the value placed on the member's benefits by the scheme actuary. That actuary will use assumptions to value the cost to the scheme to pay the benefits in the future. Different schemes might value the same benefits differently.

### 5.7.5 Pension on divorce experts

Often a single joint expert (SJE) and shadow expert will be needed if there are complex pensions that need to be considered before offers of settlement are proposed or the parties attend the FDR for the purpose of settling the case. The matter of experts is dealt with in more detail at **Chapter 7**. Pension on divorce experts (PODE) are few and far between – at the time of writing I would estimate that there are no more than 30 experts in the whole country. For that reason, and the fact that it can take 16–20 weeks for the experts to get the relevant information they need from the pension company, it can take 26 weeks or more to secure an expert's report on pensions. The PAG report will guide the practitioner as to whether a report is really needed or if the parties can reach a settlement without one.

I would always recommend that the parties consult a financial planner/IFA to take advice before negotiations commence to check that the pensions are what the parties think they are. Ideally, the parties will engage the services of a financial neutral as early as possible in the process to get information about pensions. This new concept, a Pension Information Assessment Meeting with a financial neutral, can save costs in the long term and ensure the parties fully understand the nature of the pension investments. Some pensions look like simple DC pensions but can have attached guarantees that make them extremely valuable.

## 5.8 MCA 1973, S.25 AND CPA 2004, SCHED.5, PART 5

The court, when deciding financial remedy applications, must take into account the statutory factors at MCA 1973, s.25 and CPA 2004, Sched.5, Part 5. The checklist of factors doesn't help the practitioner to understand how any particular case will be resolved unless they have sufficient experience to understand how the court will balance those factors. Each judge has the discretion to take those factors into account in any way to arrive at what they consider to be a fair distribution of assets and income in every case. None of the factors has any greater weight than another.

Evidence of each factor will be submitted to the court during disclosure. The Form E is designed to extract the MCA 1973, s.25 information from the party completing it. **Chapter 4** mentions that the court will generally direct each party to file a witness statement before a final hearing – this is referred to as the 'section 25' statement, which gives each party the final opportunity of addressing the factors below.

When the parties engage in negotiations, it is important to consider the factors and assess which may be more important in each case and how that will impact on the settlement.

MCA 1973, s.25(1) states:

> **It shall be the duty of the court in deciding whether to exercise its powers . . . to have regard to all the circumstances of the case, first consideration being given to the welfare while minor of any child of the family who has not attained the age of eighteen.**

The important factors in this provision to consider are:

- *'All the circumstances of the case':* Whatever instructions your client gives you regarding the finances will be considered by the court. The existence of pre- and post-nuptial agreements and any deed of separation will be considered as a factor in determining the case. It may be that if there are properly contracted agreements the court may not need to depart from them. However, the function of the court is to arrive at a fair result for both parties with first consideration to minor children. If that means that the agreement needs to be departed from, the court will do so as it isn't obliged to put the terms of the agreement into effect blindly. It is important for a solicitor to ensure that all relevant matters are properly set out in the Form E and any s.25 statement.
- *'First consideration being given to the welfare while minor of any child of the family':* Children over the age of 18 won't be the first consideration of the court; they may still be a consideration, but not the first consideration. Children of the family include stepchildren who have lived with the couple as children of the family. The court will not make an order which favours one of the adult parties to the detriment of the children. This acutely manifests itself in the need to house children and the party who is their main carer to the detriment of the other party, particularly in small money cases. This is very difficult to explain to the party who is likely to suffer a detriment, but the priority for the children is clear.

MCA 1973, s.25(2) states:

> ... the court shall have regard to the following matters –
>
> (a) the income, earning capacity, property and other financial resources which each of the parties to the marriage has or is likely to have in the foreseeable future, including in the case of earning capacity any increase in that capacity which it would in the opinion of the court be reasonable to expect a party to the marriage to take steps to acquire;

The important factors in this provision to consider are:

- The court will consider income from all sources, including benefits, universal credit, earned income and any cash in hand income if declared or evidenced by the other party.
- Other financial resources may include the mortgage capacity of the parties, access to trust funds assets or income and any other resources available.
- Where this factor refers to 'has or likely to have in the foreseeable future' it can be argued to support a case that a person may inherit money from a family member. However, generally future inheritances are not relevant as a person in England and Wales may change their will at any time until the point of death. However, in other jurisdictions this may not be the case and a person may be guaranteed by the operation of law to inherit money from another person, however it may not be clear when that person will die and whether their estate would have any value at the time of their death. Where a person has died and their estate distribution is known, then it would be reasonable to account for that inheritance as being part of one party's assets. If a person entitled to a bonus which will be received in the foreseeable future, this is likely to be taken into account.
- With regard to earning capacity, where one party has failed to maximise their ability to earn money, the court can take into account what it believes is reasonable income rather than what is actually being earned. Obviously, this is all subject to the evidence provided to the court on the subject.

> (b) the financial needs, obligations and responsibilities which each of the parties to the marriage has or is likely to have in the foreseeable future;

The important factors in this provision to consider are:

- A party's financial needs are set out in the Form E, divided into income needs and capital needs. This will represent the capital sum required to remain in or purchase a home/holiday home, together with the costs of purchase. It may include the capital required to buy furniture etc., and perhaps capital expenditure to purchase a car. In each case, whether a small money or high net worth case, housing costs are likely to be a central feature with regard to distribution of capital and income.
- Obligations and responsibilities refer to money that one party may need to pay off debts; any responsibilities that each party has that are relevant to the case. It may be that one or both parties have children who are not considered to be children of the family and that they have responsibilities toward those children.

- Small money cases are often referred to as 'needs cases'. This refers to this factor which may be the most important factor in small money cases – where it may be difficult to meet the most basic housing needs of the party with care of the minor children or a party who clearly has priority needs due to disability or other reasons.

    (c) **the standard of living enjoyed by the family before the breakdown of the marriage;**

This factor is likely to be more important in high net worth cases, where the parties have a discernible standard of living which each party wishes to maintain following the divorce or dissolution proceedings. The provision of capital for housing and corresponding income orders will in all likelihood reflect the parties' standard of living rather than their basic needs. There is no guarantee that a party will be able to replicate that standard of living after the divorce, no matter how wealthy the parties were during the marriage.

It will be of relevance to a lesser extent in small money cases where needs are likely to be basic.

   (d) **the age of each party to the marriage and the duration of the marriage;**

This provision recognises that age of the parties is particularly relevant when looking at their ability to enter into the terms of a mortgage, in the event they are seeking to transfer or purchase a property which is subject to a mortgage. It is also relevant to the distribution of pension assets – the nearer to retirement the parties are, the more likely it is that they will have substantial pension assets and little time to accrue further pensions.

The duration of the marriage is not simply limited from the date of the marriage to the date of separation – any period of cohabitation which predates the marriage and runs seamlessly to the marriage will be relevant when considering the length of the parties' relationship. For example, a couple who have been married for two years and are in their early 40s will probably receive a different asset distribution to a couple who had been married for 30 years and are in their 60s.

   (e) **any physical or mental disability of either of the parties to the marriage;**

This provision requires the court to take into account any physical disability of either party. In the Form E, the parties are required to set out the details of their health which may be used to evidence any physical or mental disability. It may be that as a result of such disability one party expects a more favourable capital, property, pension or income distribution. They will need to make this out in order to persuade the court that this is appropriate. More often than not, one or both parties will indicate that they are suffering from depression as a result of the divorce or dissolution proceedings. Unless the depression is so serious that it prevents the party from working or caring for themselves, it is unlikely to affect the distribution of assets or income.

(f) **the contributions which each of the parties has made or is likely in the foreseeable future to make to the welfare of the family, including any contribution by looking after the home or caring for the family;**

This provision is interesting, as it indicates that the court is willing to look at the different contributions of the parties; this is subject to the decision in the case of *White* v. *White* in which the court found that financial contributions and non-financial contribution should be considered to be equivalent. Therefore, one party earning millions of pounds per annum will be matched in their contribution by the other party caring for their children.

The court, in rare circumstances, will consider 'special contributions' which are made by one party and justify a departure away from the yardstick of equality – for example, in the case of *Sorrell* v. *Sorrell* [2005] EWHC 1717 (Fam). In this case, the court found that the husband was more than just a successful businessman. He was 'exceptionally talented' and had built his company to the success it was at the time of the hearing. The judge found that his genius was the generator of the wealth. As such, to reflect that contribution and to achieve a fair result, there was a departure from the yardstick of equality in his favour, and he received 60 per cent of the assets. Such cases are few and far between, and are likely only to involve multimillionaires.

The court will consider contributions that each party is likely to make in the foreseeable future to the welfare of family, and this may justify a departure from equality. The court is interested in unmatched contributions between the parties, bearing in mind that financial and non-financial contributions can be considered to be different but equal. When the contribution is made during the relationship and the source of the funds, an inheritance for example, will all be relevant when asking the court to consider this factor.

(g) **the conduct of each of the parties, if that conduct is such that it would in the opinion of the court be inequitable to disregard it;**

This provision regarding conduct rarely justifies a departure away from the yardstick of equality when dividing assets. The client may be keen to raise numerous allegations of what they consider to be misconduct when completing the Form E. However, the Law Society's *Family Law Protocol* (2015) states that allegations should only be raised when the conduct is sufficiently exceptional to be relevant. A solicitor is expected to give robust advice on any allegations of conduct that do not meet this very high bar. For example, whereas allegations of domestic abuse may be sufficient to include in a divorce petition based on behaviour, this would not be enough to include in financial remedy proceedings. If one party had attempted to murder the other and was found guilty of such a criminal act, it would meet the necessary test. Case law suggests that the conduct should be of the type that is 'inequitable to disregard'.

Practitioners should be mindful of this guidance and dissuade a client of pursuing allegations of conduct where they are unlikely to succeed. Allegations of litigation misconduct will be considered, and may result in a costs order being made rather than a departure from the yardstick of equality. It is also possible that the court will consider allegations of financial misconduct, where it is alleged that one party has spent family money for their personal use. These are sometimes difficult lines to take in small money cases where the costs of litigating the point will be disproportionate to the sums.

(h) **in the case of proceedings for divorce or nullity of marriage, the value to each of the parties to the marriage of any benefit ... which, by reason of the dissolution or annulment of the marriage, that party will lose the chance of acquiring.**

Before the introduction of pension orders, this provision was used to take into consideration a party's pension that could not be subject to any other order. Since the introduction of PAOs and PSOs, this provision may be used for the loss of benefits that cannot be shared between the parties. For example, I have known this provision to be relied upon where one party has accrued substantial air miles which were used for the benefit of the family but that could not be divided between them and would be lost to the other spouse in the event of divorce.

These factors are used by the court whenever financial remedy applications are considered, unless applications are made in respect of children in which case additional factors are taken into account (MCA 1973, s.25(3)). These are considered further in **Chapter 6**.

Experienced solicitors and barristers will be able to predict how these factors interact with each other in any case to allow them to negotiate a settlement or represent a client at a financial dispute resolution (FDR) appointment where negotiations are expected. Inexperienced practitioners will struggle to understand how the factors interact with each other because they are different in each case. It is difficult to predict how different judges and different courts will interpret the importance of these factors in any case, which can lead to difficulties in accurately advising the client before the FDR. At the FDR appointment, a judge should give an indication of how they think the factors determine a distribution of the parties' assets, and this should help the parties to reach an agreed settlement at or sometime after the FDR appointment.

# CHAPTER 6

# Financial remedy for children

## 6.1 INTRODUCTION

Maintenance for children can be sought from parents, and in restricted circumstances from stepparents, through different statutes. The first port of call is the Child Maintenance Service (CMS), if they have the jurisdiction to assess child maintenance.

If the parents were married or in a civil partnership, then it might be possible to seek financial orders for children/stepchildren during the divorce or dissolution process. Stepchildren may only benefit from financial orders when they are provided for as part of a married/civil partnership relationship. This is considered in more detail at **6.3**.

If the parents were unmarried, then it might be possible to seek financial orders for children using Children Act (CA) 1989, Sched.1. These provisions are considered at **6.4**. The children and stepchildren of married parents may take advantage of the provisions for financial orders available under this statute, but it would be much more advantageous to pursue applications as part of the divorce or dissolution process. A child can make an application against their parents for financial support during education or training, although such applications are extremely rare in practice.

When giving advice to a client about maintenance and other financial orders for children, the solicitor needs to understand the subtle differences between each statute and the child maintenance scheme and the procedure that would be used to secure maintenance or other financial orders. **Appendix C1** sets out a flowchart that looks at the various options available for the payment of maintenance for a child.

This chapter can only provide an overview of the various options for financial provision for children. This chapter will cover the following:

- the CMS;
- financial orders for children following a divorce or dissolution; and
- financial orders for children using CA 1989, s.15 and Sched.1.

## 6.2 THE CHILD MAINTENANCE SERVICE

### 6.2.1 Overview

The Child Support Act (CSA) 1991 sets out the statutory framework for the payment of maintenance for the majority of children. A solicitor should understand the basic structure of the scheme; how and when maintenance will be paid; and where to signpost a client if maintenance should be paid under the terms of the scheme. The possibility of a maintenance variation should be considered by the solicitor – beyond that, the solicitor is unlikely to get involved in a child maintenance assessment. The complexities of applications to the tribunals are not considered in this chapter – if the solicitor is interested in more advanced reading, the Child Action Poverty Group publishes an excellent *Child Support Handbook* (27th edn, 2019) which considers child support in great detail.

Under the terms of the current scheme, parents are expected to attempt to enter into a private maintenance agreement. This can be done using the Child Maintenance Options service (**https://www2.dwp.gov.uk/contact-cmoptions/en/new-contact.asp**). The service is free, and must be used before an application can be made for a child maintenance calculation to be carried out by the CMS. It can be accessed online or via a telephone helpline: 0800 408 0308.

It can be difficult for the parents to reach an agreement about child support when a relationship breaks down, but the CMS provides guidance and an online calculator (**www.gov.uk/calculate-child-maintenance**) which can assist the parties to work out what maintenance is payable. It is useful for the parents to consider the information online at GOV.UK: 'Making a child maintenance arrangement' (**www.gov.uk/making-child-maintenance-arrangement/using-child-maintenance-service**) as it sets out the basic information needed by each parent.

The duration which child maintenance may be agreed is for children under the age of 16 or up to the age of 20 if they are in approved education or training. This doesn't include university education, and generally ends once A-levels are complete or NVQ up to level 3 achieved.

Any agreement reached by the parents which isn't recorded in an order or calculated by CMS isn't enforceable against the non-resident parent in the event of non-payment. It isn't always necessary for the parent with care to have an enforceable arrangement with the non-resident parent if they are on good terms. However, if the parents have a difficult relationship, it may be better in the short-term to use the CMS to calculate child maintenance, which will be enforceable if the non-resident party fails to make a payment.

Alternatively, the parents could use a private agreement for the payment of maintenance. If the payer stops making payments, the person with care should apply immediately for a CMS calculation. As the CMS can't backdate enforceable arrears to a date before their calculation, the person with care should make sure that they apply immediately for the calculation to avoid a gap in the receipt of maintenance.

### 6.2.2 Definitions

It is important to understand the relevant definitions in CSA 1991 with reference to the CMS regime – they can be found in CSA 1991, s.3:

(1) A child is a 'qualifying child' if–

   (a) one of his parents is, in relation to him, an absent parent; or
   (b) both of his parents are, in relation to him, absent parents.

(2) The parent of any child is an 'absent parent', in relation to him, if–

   (a) that parent is not living in the same household with the child; and
   (b) the child has his home with a person who is, in relation to him, a person with care.

(3) A person is a 'person with care', in relation to any child, if he is a person–

   (a) with whom the child has his home;
   (b) who usually provides day to day care for the child (whether exclusively or in conjunction with any other person); and
   (c) who does not fall within a prescribed category of person.

The absent parent is also referred to as the 'non-resident parent' or the 'paying party'. The person with care is also sometimes referred to as the 'receiving party'.

It is also important to know that 'other relevant children' are taken into account in the maintenance calculation – this is a child(ren) for whom the non-resident parent or their partner receive child benefit or would receive child benefit.

### 6.2.3 When does the CMS have jurisdiction to make a calculation?

A child must be 'a qualifying child' and all parties must be habitually resident in the UK for the CMS to have jurisdiction to make a calculation. The relevant parties are the child, the person with care and the non-resident parent (CSA 1991, s.44). 'Habitual residence' is defined as a person being ordinarily resident in the UK for an appreciable period of time. In most cases it is obvious whether the parties are habitually resident in the UK for the purpose of accessing the CMS. Those cases where habitual residence might be trickier to assess are more unusual cases where, for example, the child has parents in the Forces or a parent is stationed abroad but the employer is in the UK.

In the event that the CMS does not have jurisdiction to make a calculation, the court may be able to make an order for child maintenance as part of divorce or dissolution proceedings. If the parties weren't married or in a civil partnership, an application may be made under the provisions of CA 1989, Sched.1. These provisions are considered in this chapter at **6.4**.

It is not possible to prevent a person from making an application to the CMS, and any clause in an order that purports to exclude the proper jurisdiction of the CMS is void. However, where there is a child maintenance order made by agreement on or after 3 March 2003, it will prevent an application being made to the CMS by either party until 12 months have elapsed from the date of the order. Often the parties to divorce or dissolution proceedings will agree an order regarding the payment of child maintenance rather than make an application to the CMS, or continue with a CMS calculation if one has already been made. The child maintenance order will be enforceable by the court until an application is made to the CMS, as long as that application is made more than 12 months after the order.

It is important to understand when negotiating a settlement and drafting an order, that a child periodical payments order (CPPO) will be time limited even if the order doesn't specifically set that out. The CPPO doesn't lapse at the end of the 12-month period – it will continue to be effective between the parties until one of them applies to the CMS for a calculation of maintenance. For example, the CPPO in a consent order might state that the agreed maintenance payment for a child is payable until that child reaches the age of 18 years old or completes full-time secondary education. However, either party can make an application to the CMS after 12 months, at which time the court order ceases to be enforceable and the CMS calculation become enforceable.

The parties can enter into the terms of a global maintenance order (sometimes called a Segal order) following divorce or dissolution proceedings, which combines the payer's obligation to pay both child and spousal maintenance as one global sum. It is worth noting that although either party can make an application to the CMS after 12 months, there will be no net gain to the recipient of maintenance as a global order pays a fixed sum as a combination of spousal and child maintenance. This is considered further at **Chapter 5**.

### 6.2.4 Who can apply?

For ease, in this chapter we shall consider in a straightforward scenario where the parents have separated and one parent seeks child maintenance from the other. It is possible for other people to apply if they have care of the child, but we won't be considering those more complex applications in this chapter.

The person with care can apply – for example, the mother. However, the father (as the absent parent in this example) can apply for a calculation to be made against him if the parents have not been able to reach an agreement. It is not unusual for an absent father to want to have a maintenance calculation made against him so that there is no possibility that he isn't paying the right sum. Or, to prevent a mother from insisting more maintenance should be paid and withholding contact time with the children as a negotiating stance.

It costs the applicant £20 for the CMS to calculate the child maintenance due. The fee can be waived if the applicant is under the age of 18 or the CMS accepts that the applicant has experienced domestic violence or abuse. A person who has experienced domestic abuse from the other parent is not expected to try to agree maintenance with them before approaching the CMS for a calculation.

### 6.2.5 Who is the paying party?

The absent parent is the paying party – in our example this is the father. Where there is a dispute about the parentage of a child, CSA 1991 permits the father to dispute parentage and DNA tests can be carried out to establish whether or not the alleged father is the biological parent. The consent of all parties is needed to carry out the DNA tests. If the alleged father is not the biological parent, then the cost of the test is refunded to him. If he is found to be the father, then he is responsible to pay for the tests of all parties. The tests are undertaken by the CSA and cost £239.40 at the time of writing, though this could be higher if more than one child takes the DNA test.

In certain circumstances the CMS can assume that the alleged father is the parent – if, for example, a declaration of parentage is in force against him, or he was married to the mother at any time between the child's conception and birth (the list is extensive). Although the father can still dispute parentage in these cases, the assessment will remain in place until evidence to rebut the assumption is provided to the CMS.

Disputes about parentage can arise at the time of an initial calculation being carried out or at any time afterwards. If a child maintenance calculation is already in place, this must be paid by the father, even if parentage is in dispute. If it subsequently transpires that he is not the biological parent, then the assessment will be cancelled and it is possible that any payments may be refunded from the date parentage was disputed. However, that money would first need to be recouped from the mother of the child.

### 6.2.6 How is child maintenance calculated?

Child maintenance is calculated by taking into account:

(a) the child maintenance rates (including relevant other children);
(b) shared care arrangements; and
(c) the maximum CMS assessment.

#### 6.2.6.1 Child maintenance rates

There are four rates of child maintenance:

(a) the nil rate;
(b) the flat rate;
(c) the reduced rate; and
(d) the basic rate/basic rate plus.

In applying these rates, 'gross weekly income' is defined as the income declared to HMRC – this will include any benefits received if applicable. Pension payments made by the absent parent will affect the sum of gross income. There are some limited options for a paying parent to ask for further reduction of the gross income –

FINANCIAL REMEDY FOR CHILDREN

e.g. to take of travel costs if they have to travel a long distance. The regulations in this respect are complex.

**Table 6.1** Gross income receipt and rate of maintenance paid by the non-resident parent

| Which rate? | Gross income per week | Payment per week |
|---|---|---|
| Default | Not known or not provided | Between £38 and £61 |
| The nil rate | Less than £7 | Nil |
| The flat rate | Less than £100 | £7 |
| The reduced rate | Between £100 and £200 | £7 up to income of £100 and then between 17% and 31% of income between £100 and £200 |
| The basic rate | Between £200 and £800 | Between 12% and 19% |
| The basic rate plus | £800–£3,000 | Basic rate up to £800 and then between 9% and 15% for income over £800, up the maximum sum |

THE NIL RATE

The following people don't pay maintenance:

- prisoners;
- a child under 16 (but this could be under 20 if the child is in full-time non-advanced education);
- a 16- to-19-year-old who has left school but is registered for certain types of government-approved training courses;
- a person aged 16 or 17 and they or their current partner are receiving certain benefits: income support; income-based jobseeker's allowance (JSA); income-based employment and support allowance (ESA); or universal credit (UC) which is calculated on the basis that they have no income;
- a person living in a care home or independent hospital, or a person being provided with a care home service, and who is either getting help with the fees, or who is getting the same benefits as those people who qualify for the flat rate;
- a person whose gross income is less than £7 a week.

THE FLAT RATE

The flat rate will apply to an absent parent who does not qualify for the nil rate and has a gross weekly income of less than £100 per week. If an absent parent or their current partner is entitled to certain benefits, then they will pay the flat rate. Those benefits are as follows:

- pension credit;
- income support;
- income-based JSA;
- income-related ESA;
- UC calculated on the basis that the recipient has no income.

If the absent parent receives the following benefits, they will also pay the flat rate of £7 per week:

- state retirement pension;
- carer's allowance;
- incapacity benefit;
- contribution-based JSA;
- contributory ESA.

### THE REDUCED RATE

If the absent parent doesn't qualify for either the nil rate or flat rate, they will pay the reduced rate. Their gross weekly income will be between £100 and £200. They will pay £7 (the flat rate) for all income up to £100 per week gross. Thereafter they will pay a percentage of their remaining income between £100 and £200. The percentage will be between 17 per cent and 31 per cent, depending on how many qualifying children they have and if there are any other relevant children they are responsible for. The CMS calculator should be used to calculate the specific sum due in any given case, as this gives the client a more accurate idea of how much they can expect to receive.

### THE BASIC RATE/BASIC RATE PLUS

The basic rate applies if the other rates do not. If the absent parent has a gross income over £200 per week and below £800 per week, the basic rate will be used to calculate their liability for child maintenance. Any gross income over £800 per week will be calculated using the 'basic plus' calculation up to the maximum gross weekly income of £3,000 per week.

There are two stages to be applied when calculating the basic rate – the first stage is to reduce the non-resident's gross weekly income if they have 'relevant other children' they are responsible for:

**Table 6.2** The basic rate deduction for relevant other children

| 1 relevant other child | 2 relevant other children | 3 or more relevant other children |
|---|---|---|
| Reduce gross weekly income by 11% | Reduce gross weekly income by 14% | Reduce gross weekly income by 16% |

Stage two of the calculation is to work out the child maintenance to pay using the basic and basic plus calculations:

| Number of qualifying children | Percentage of gross income up to £800 per week | Percentage of gross income over £800 per week |
|---|---|---|
| One | 12% | 9% |
| Two | 16% | 12% |
| Three or more | 19% | 15% |

Of course, the easiest way to calculate child maintenance is to use the online calculator as there are reductions allowable for absent parents who share care with the person with care.

### 6.2.6.2 The effect of shared care arrangements

If the parents share care for their child equally, there will be no liability for child maintenance (Child Support Maintenance Calculation Regulations 2012 SI 2012/2677). The presumption is that the parent getting the child benefit is the 'receiving' party. Note that parents should not use the online calculator if they share care equally – there is a caveat before you use it that says that there will be nothing to pay if you are sharing care equally with the other parent.

If, however, the non-resident parent does not share the care of the qualifying child (such arrangements are rare) then there will be a child maintenance liability. The liability will be calculated using one of the four rates detailed above. The liability may be decreased by a percentage calculated by reference to the number of nights the qualifying child spends with the non-resident parent.

The minimum number of nights that will affect the calculation is 52 nights over a 12-month period – any fewer nights with the non-resident parent will have no effect on the calculation. If the non-resident parent cares for the child during the day only, this will not affect the calculation. It should be noted that the calculations are more complex where there is more than one qualifying child.

**Table 6.3** How overnight stays with the non-resident parent reduce the amount of child maintenance payable

| Number of nights per year | Fraction to subtract from child maintenance calculation |
| --- | --- |
| 52–103 | One-seventh |
| 104–155 | Two-sevenths |
| 156–174 | Three-sevenths |
| 175 or more | One-half |

*6.2.6.3 The maximum CMS assessment*

It is important to note that the CMS can only assess maintenance up to a maximum gross income of £3,000 per week. Once a maximum calculation is made, the court will have jurisdiction to assess additional 'top-up' maintenance for the qualifying child. The case of *Dickson* v. *Rennie* [2014] EWHC 4306 (Fam) is authority that the CMS must have made a maximum assessment before the court has jurisdiction to make a 'top-up' order. It is not sufficient that the parties accept that the court has jurisdiction to make a top-up order (CSA 1991, s.8(6)).

The court will have jurisdiction to assess child maintenance in tandem with the CMS if the child is disabled or being educated or receiving training and incurs expenses which need to be paid. These are considered further below.

### 6.2.7 How is maintenance paid?

Maintenance can be paid in one of two ways:

(a) direct pay (arranged between the parents); or
(b) collect and pay (CMS collects and pays the parent with care).

*6.2.7.1 Direct pay*

The parents can use the CMS to calculate maintenance after which the parents can agree to make the payments between them. This can be done via standing order to a named account, PayPal, cheque, cash or other agreed payment method. It is important that each parent keeps proper records of the payments that are made, so that if there are any enforcement proceedings, each party knows what was paid and if there are any arrears. For this reason, using cash to pay maintenance might not be the best way for a paying parent to keep records of their payments.

If the paying party stops paying maintenance after agreeing to use direct pay, the receiving party can switch to collect and pay services.

### 6.2.7.2 Collect and pay

If one of the parties elects to pay maintenance using the collect and pay service, the CMS will do so if the non-resident parent agrees, if they believe that without collect and pay the non-resident parent will not pay, or if the paying parent defaults on a direct pay arrangement. The CMS will levy additional fees to collect payments from the payer and pay them to the payee. Collect and pay might be necessary where the payee has suffered domestic abuse or harm and doesn't wish to have any direct contact with the payer.

The CMS will charge the payer an additional 20 per cent to collect payments, and deduct 4 per cent from the recipient's maintenance. The additional fees act as a deterrent for most couples who should be able to use direct pay. If the non-resident parent wishes to move to direct pay, they can make a request to do so at any time, without the agreement of the parent with care.

One advantage of using collect and pay is that the CMS keep records of what is paid, and those records can be used if enforcement proceedings are needed.

### 6.2.8 Variation of a CMS calculation

In certain circumstances a CMS calculation can be varied on application by either party. The grounds upon which a variation is possible are restricted, and will only be made if 'just and equitable' to do so. If either party believes that variation will be needed they can flag this when the application is made or after calculation has been produced.

This is an area in which solicitors can help the client to make a difference to the amount of income they receive or pay respect of their child. It is a technical area, and should therefore be considered very carefully before advising a client. In an ideal world, a client who may need a variation will seek advice before a referral is made to the CMS so that the factors that may lead to a variation can be considered by the CMS before an assessment is produced. If the CMS make an assessment, it will take effect until a variation is dealt with – this may cause problems if the receiving party is hoping to engage the jurisdiction of the court following a maximum assessment.

The non-resident parent may apply for a variation on the grounds that they have special expenses that need to be taken into account but which would otherwise not affect the child maintenance calculation. There are strict time limits for applying, so the practitioner should read the letters from the CMS carefully to avoid missing a deadline. The expenses are as follows (CSA 1991, Sched.4B(2)):

- costs incurred travelling to work;
- costs of maintaining contact with a qualifying child or children;
- costs of long-term illness or disability of a 'relevant child';
- debts incurred before the couple separated;
- boarding school fees paid for a qualifying child or children;
- costs of repaying a mortgage on a home in which the person with care and a qualifying child(ren) reside.

It is possible that the person with care will want a calculation to be varied on the grounds that the non-resident parent has additional income that has not been taken into account in the assessment process. No variation will take place if the gross weekly income of the non-resident parent exceeds £3,000, which is the maximum sum that the CMS will assess against.

The variation may be made on the basis that the non-resident parent has one or more of the following:

- unearned income of more than £2,500 per year;
- is on the nil or flat rate, but has a gross weekly income of more than £100;
- has diverted income – for example, they control their income and have unreasonably reduced the amount of income that they should receive, diverting it to someone else or for another purpose;
- notional income from assets worth over £31,250 – this might be appropriate where the non-resident parent has high value assets and appears to have an affluent lifestyle;
- pension contributions that are allowed to be deducted set at an artificially high level.

An application for variation can be made by either party, either by telephone or in writing. The application has to state the grounds upon which it is made, otherwise it will not be accepted. The application commences a process of review and reconsideration by the CMS which may result in a variation.

Either parent can ask for an assessment to be made on the payer's current income if that person has had a change in income (up or down) of 25 per cent or more. Otherwise, there is an historical base if the last tax return or P60 is used and then there is an annual review each year on the anniversary of the effective date. It is said by many commentators that there is some scope for abuse when using historic income figures to pay maintenance. If a variation or review results in a cancellation of the maximum assessment, the court will no longer have jurisdiction to make CPPOs and any order already made will be adversely affected.

### 6.2.9 Enforcement of CMS payments

If arrears arise, whether using direct pay or collect and pay, enforcement proceedings can be taken at the discretion of the CMS. If the direct pay service is used, the person with care must notify the CMS that arrears have accrued, and the CMS may decide to take enforcement action. If the collect and pay service is used, the CMS will know as soon as arrears accrue and should take action.

Some types of enforcement action can be taken as soon as arrears arise, for example:

- a deduction from earnings order;
- deductions from bank and or building society accounts.

FINANCIAL REMEDY FOR CHILDREN

If the paying party wishes to appeal a deduction from earnings order, this can be done in limited circumstances at a magistrates' court. If an appeal is sought against a deductions order from bank or building society accounts, this is done by application to the Family Court.

Other types of enforcement action require the CMS to obtain a liability order first, for example:

- an order to take control and sell goods belonging to the payer;
- to disqualify the payer from driving, or holding or applying for a passport or travel authorisation;
- to imprison the payer.

If these orders are made, they can be subject to either appeal or judicial review depending on the order made.

## 6.3 APPLICATIONS FOR FINANCIAL ORDERS FOR CHILDREN FOLLOWING DIVORCE AND DISSOLUTION PROCEEDINGS

### 6.3.1 Overview

Children of a marriage or civil partnership can benefit from a number of orders that can be made for them. **Appendix C2** sets out all the financial remedy orders available. In summary, these are:

(a) child periodical payments orders (CPPOs) or child secured periodical payments orders (CSPPOs); these orders could be subject to a variation application;
(b) lump sum for a child;
(c) property adjustment orders, which include transfers of property, settlement of property or variation of ante-/post-nuptial settlement. Property can be transferred to another person to hold on behalf of the child. Multiple property transfer orders could be made under this provision.

These orders are all explained in detail in **Chapter 5** but are equally available for children and stepchildren of the marriage or civil partnership. An application for financial remedy orders for children or stepchildren is usually made as part of the parties' Form A financial remedy application.

It is very unusual for any specific financial orders to be made for the benefit of a child or stepchild; if a lump sum order was made then it is likely that trustees would need to be appointed to administer the money which would incur additional expense. It is possible that a small sum could be placed into a bank account in the name of the child, although this would be rare. There are no reported cases of a lump sum order being made on more than one occasion for a child or stepchild, although Matrimonial Causes Act (MCA) 1973, s.23(4)/Civil Partnership Act (CPA) 2004, Sched.5, Part 1, para.2(1)(f) do seem to allow for this.

It is equally rare for a property adjustment order to made for the benefit of a child/stepchild, although this is possible under MCA 1973, s.24(1) and CPA 2004, Sched.5, Part 2, para.7(1). Only in high net worth cases is this likely to be a real consideration.

Other financial remedy orders may be made in high net worth cases which benefit children directly, but in the majority of cases maintenance is likely to be the only order made as part of the divorce or dissolution proceedings.

As maintenance is usually calculated by the CMS, there are limited opportunities for the court to make maintenance orders – for example when the CMS doesn't have jurisdiction to carry out an assessment because one or more of the parties is not habitually resident in the UK, or a maximum assessment has already been made by the CMS. Once a maximum assessment is made, this gives the court the jurisdiction to make a 'top-up' order in respect of maintenance. In the recent case of *CB* v. *KB* [2019] EWFC 78, Mr Justice Mostyn set out guidance on the calculation of top-up orders by the court. The starting point, he said, should be the CMS formula:

> I suggest that in every case where the gross annual income of the non-resident parent does not exceed £650,000, the starting point should be the result of the formula ignoring the cap on annual gross income at £156,000. For gross incomes in excess of £650,000, I suggest that the result given by an income of £650,000 should be the starting point with full discretionary freedom to depart from it having regard to the scale of the excess.

As this is an initial decision from a High Court judge, we might find the Court of Appeal has a different view in due course.

There are other times when the court can calculate CPPOs, provided for by CSA 1991, s.8:

- for the benefit of stepchildren who were maintained by the paying party during the marriage or civil partnership;
- if the child is receiving instruction at an educational establishment, or undergoing training for a trade, profession or vocation (whether or not while in gainful employment). The order must be made solely for the purpose of meeting some or all of the expenses of instruction or training. This is often referred to as a 'school fees order' because it is most often made to meet the cost of private school fees and extras;
- where the child is disabled. The CPPO is made for the sole purpose of meeting some or all of the expenses attributable to the child's disability. CSA 1991, s.8(9) states that 'a child is disabled if he is blind, deaf or dumb or is substantially and permanently handicapped by illness, injury, mental disorder or congenital deformity or such other disability as may be prescribed';
- a top-up order where the maximum assessment for child support has been made by the CMS.

The court can't otherwise make CPPOs without the parties' agreement, as it will have no jurisdiction to do so. By way of reminder, the court can make a CPPO where the parties have agreed maintenance between them; this order will prevent the parties from making an application to the CMS for 12 months. Where there is already a CMS assessment in place, it would need to be withdrawn for the CPPO to be effective.

The court can also approve a global maintenance order which encompasses maintenance for both the former spouse or civil partner and child maintenance (see **5.4.2.1**). After 12 months have elapsed, either party can apply to the CMS for a maintenance calculation but this will not impact the global sum paid to the recipient. This is considered further in **Chapter 5**.

### 6.3.2 Factors the court must take into consideration

The court must take the following factors into consideration when deciding whether to make an order for the benefit of children (MCA 1973, s.25(3)/CPA 2004, Sched.5, Part 5, para.22):

(3) As regards the exercise of the powers of the court under section 23(1)(d), (e) or (f), (2) or (4), 24 or 24A above in relation to a child of the family, the court shall in particular have regard to the following matters–

    (a) the financial needs of the child;
    (b) the income, earning capacity (if any), property and other financial resources of the child;
    (c) any physical or mental disability of the child;
    (d) the manner in which he was being and in which the parties to the marriage expected him to be educated or trained;

In addition to those new factors the court will consider the factors at s.25(2)(a), (b), (c) and (e), which are considered in every financial remedy case in any event. The court does not consider the factors at s.25(2)(f) (contributions), s.25(2)(g) (conduct) and s.25(2)(h) (loss of a benefit) when considering CPPOs.

The court must also consider MCA 1973, s.29/CPA 2004, Sched.5, Part 10, para.49: the duration of financial provision orders in favour of children, and age limit on making certain orders in their favour. No order for financial provision or property transfer can be made for a child who has already attained the age of 18 years old. Orders should not extend beyond the child's 18th birthday unless the child is at an educational establishment or training or there are special circumstances that justify a longer order.

CPPOs cease to have effect if the payer dies. It is therefore sensible for the parties to consider whether an insurance policy should be maintained or taken out to protect those payments so that the person with care benefits from an insurance payment if the payer dies during the term of the order. These financial considerations can sometimes be overlooked, but can be very important during negotiations or case preparation. If the wife wants to take a policy with the husband as the insured party, with her paying the policy premiums, it is essential to get it recorded in the order so that husband will co-operate with the practical requirements of going for a medical and filling out the forms, and to get a quote for the policy before settling the terms of the order. If no agreement can be reached about the provision of a policy payment, the receiving party could make an application under the Inheritance (Provision for Family and Dependants) Act 1975, if the paying party dies without leaving reasonable financial provision for the child.

### 6.3.3 Procedure

The Form A should be completed by one of the parties to the divorce or dissolution to indicate that the applicant wants to the court to make orders in respect of a child or stepchild. The application will be listed alongside other financial remedy applications between the spouses or civil partners, and the standard procedure will be used (see **4.2**). It is possible, although unlikely, that an application for periodical payments only could be made using Form A1, which would be listed using the fast-track procedure.

Practitioners should note that the Form E doesn't specifically provide for the financial needs of the child. There is a section in the form for capital and income needs of a child to be completed, but their income or assets are not specifically taken into account. When preparing an application for financial relief for a child, these factors should be added to the disclosure to ensure that the court has all relevant information to consider the application in respect of children. It may be necessary for the court to direct the filing of a further statement in respect of those matters not specifically dealt with in the standard Form E disclosure. Form E1 does have a specific section for the resources of the children to be taken into account, this should usually be completed in fast-track cases.

Any agreement reached between the parties regarding these claims should be reflected in the terms of any consent order sent to the court for approval.

### 6.3.4 Costs

The usual rule in financial remedy proceedings is that there shall be no order for costs (FPR 2010, rule 28.3) (**Chapter 4**). Although the court has a discretion to make a costs order in the event that one party has conducted themselves in a way that would justify an order being made, costs orders are uncommon in financial remedy proceedings.

## 6.4 APPLICATIONS FOR FINANCIAL ORDERS FOR CHILDREN UNDER THE CHILDREN ACT 1989, S.15 AND SCHED.1

### 6.4.1 Overview

Applications under CA 1989, s.15 and Sched.1 are more limited in nature than those claims made following divorce and dissolution. Where a claim could be made under either MCA 1973/CPA 2004 or CA 1989, Sched.1, it would probably be more favourable to choose to make the application using MCA 1973/CPA 2004. No application can be made in respect of stepchildren of cohabiting parties under CA 1989, Sched.1, though stepchildren who are the result of a married or civil partnership can benefit from orders under this statute.

The orders available under CA 1989, Sched.1, para.1(2) are as follows:

(a) CPPOs;
(b) CSPPOs;
(c) a lump sum for the child;
(d) a settlement of property for the benefit of the child (only one such order can be made against the same respondent and the same child); and
(e) the transfer of property for a child (only one such order can be made against the same respondent and the same child).

Where property orders are made, a property is usually only settled for the benefit of the child for a specific period of time, unlike property orders made following divorce or dissolution. Often, property is settled for the child until they finish their secondary or tertiary education.

This can have a profound effect on any other children living in the property and the parent with care when the property reverts to the settlor. Only one property order can be made for the benefit of a child, so the applicant must take into account all the possible needs for housing for that child when the application is made. When representing the settlor of a property, even in the event of an out of court settlement, the making of an order would prevent future applications being made.

If no property is transferred or settled for the benefit of the child, then a capital sum may be made available to enable a property to be purchased for the benefit of the child; this will revert to the respondent when the child no longer requires housing as a minor or in education or training. A lump sum application or order can't be used to circumvent the lack of jurisdiction to make an income order.

### 6.4.2 Who can apply?

The applicant can be either of the parents, a stepparent (where the parties were married or in a civil partnership with each other) or a person who is a guardian, special guardian or a person named in a child arrangements order as a person with whom the child lives.

Although rare, a child over the age of 18 years old, can make an application for an order if they are receiving an education or undergoing training for a trade, vocation or profession. The application is made against one or both parents for periodical payments and/or a lump sum order. This is rare, as the child is not likely to be able to fund such an application.

There are additional concerns about a child making an application against a parent for financial support. Solicitors should note that a child who had an order made in their favour immediately before they turned 16 years old may not make an application under s.2(2). This may be applicable where the parties were married or in a civil partnership and entered into an order concerning the child as part of the financial remedy order. The financial remedy order might have covered the child's educational needs to the end of their secondary education, but may not have taken them to tertiary education. In such a case, the child won't be able to make an application under CA 1989, s.15 and Sched.1 and won't be accommodated for tertiary education under the terms of the financial remedy order.

### 6.4.3 Who is the respondent?

One or both of the parents could be subject to orders in favour of the applicant as these are usually made for the benefit of the child. Orders can be made directly in favour of the child, particularly if the child is the applicant. More often, the applicant is a parent or guardian who obtains an order for the benefit of the child.

If the parents are subject to an application from their child, no order can be made if the parents live in the same household as each other (CA 1989, Sched.1, para.2(5)).

A stepparent could be subject to an order. Remember that only married couples or civil partners are considered to be stepparents.

Applications under this statute are infrequent, as the respondent will need to have sufficient income, capital or property to be able to satisfy the order. Reported decisions generally concern high net worth individuals who can easily afford to make the payments.

### 6.4.4 Duration of the orders

Periodical payment orders can only be made for a child who is under the age of 18 and should usually terminate on their 17th birthday or their 18th birthday at the latest (CA 1989, Sched.1, para.3(1)). The orders can extend beyond the child's 18th birthday if the child is receiving instruction at an educational establishment or undergoing training for a trade, profession or vocation; or if there are special circumstances that justify extending the term of the order. Orders which extend to the end of the child's tertiary education are common.

A CPPO will terminate in the event that the paying parent dies. Therefore it would be sensible for an insurance policy to be taken out to ensure payment of a lump sum to the parent receiving a CPPO in the event the paying party dies. If the parties don't agree this as part of a settlement, the receiving party could make an application under the Inheritance (Provision for Family and Dependants) Act 1975, if the paying party dies without leaving reasonable financial provision for the child.

An order will also terminate if the parents resume cohabitation with each other for a period of six months or more.

### 6.4.5 Factors the court must take into consideration

The court must take into account the following factors when deciding what order to make, if any, on an application under CA 1989, Sched.1. The factors are as follows (CA 1989, Sched.1, para.4(1)):

> ... the court shall have regard to all the circumstances including–
>
> (a) the income, earning capacity, property and other financial resources which each person mentioned in sub-paragraph (4) has or is likely to have in the foreseeable future;
> (b) the financial needs, obligations and responsibilities which each person mentioned in sub-paragraph (4) has or is likely to have in the foreseeable future;
> (c) the financial needs of the child;
> (d) the income, earning capacity (if any), property and other financial resources of the child;
> (e) any physical or mental disability of the child;
> (f) the manner in which the child was being, or was expected to be, educated or trained.

The child's welfare is a very important consideration in deciding these applications, and although it is an application under the provisions of the CA 1989, the child's welfare is not paramount. Nor is the child's welfare the court's first consideration, as it would be if the application was made under the MCA 1973/CPA 2004. Any applications that can be made under other legislation will have different statutory factors considered by the court which could result in a more favourable outcome for the applicant.

Where the application is made against a stepparent (married or in a civil partnership with a parent), the following additional considerations are taken into account (CA 1989, Sched.1, para.4(2)):

- whether that person has assumed responsibility for the maintenance of the child and, if so, the extent to which and the basis on which they assumed that responsibility and the length of the period during which they met that responsibility;
- whether the stepparent did so knowing that the child was not their child; and
- the liability of any other person to maintain the child.

### 6.4.6 Procedure

Application to the Family Court may be made using the Form A which was recently redesigned so that it could be used in these proceedings. It should be completed carefully to ensure that the court is aware what application is being made and which statute is relied on. The standard procure would apply if financial remedy applications are made using Form A (see **Chapter 4**). However, if periodical payments only are sought, then application Form A1 may be used which will be allocated to the fast-track procedure (**Chapter 4**). This allows the application to be dealt with in a straightforward cost-effective way, without unnecessary costs incurring.

Where the fast-track procedure is applicable, the Form E1 may be used to provide disclosure as this is a much shorter form which does not require the parties to disclose pension information and includes sections for the financial resources of the child to be disclosed. Often the court timetable does not specify which form should be completed, whether the Form E or the E1. In my view it is sufficient to use the Form E1 for disclosure where the fast-track procedure is utilised.

For applications involving lump sum and/or property orders, the standard procedure will apply. The Form E is probably the most useful form to use for disclosure in these cases as disclosure is more comprehensive, but the Form E does not provide for the financial resources of the child to be taken into account. This should be accommodated for when completing the form so that the statutory factors can be taken into account by the court. Form E1 may be used by the parties – the court usually leaves it to the parties to decide which disclosure form should be used in the circumstances. The Form E1 excludes pensions, orders against which cannot be made in any event and provides for capital and property disclosure to be given in full.

In my experience, most practitioners have little experience in dealing with the Form E1 and object to its use even though it is appropriate in these cases. Often in my experience, practitioners open Form E1 by accident and only notice the difference between the two forms as pensions are notably excluded. The 'Final report of the Financial Remedies Working Group' (15 December 2014) (**www.judiciary.uk/publications/financial-remedies-working-group-report/**) suggests (para.6(iv)) that there should be only one financial disclosure form instead of the three current versions: Form E, Form E1 and Form E2 (which is used in variation applications). The problem is not the existence of different forms, but the fact that practitioners often do not know that the other forms exist and the court fails to specify which form to use for disclosure.

If an agreement is reached between the parties, it should be recorded by way of a consent order using the standard order precedents and sent to the court or using the online portal (this is mandatory where the applicant is represented by a solicitor) for approval with the statement of information in support of the consent order (Form D81).

### 6.4.7 Costs orders

The costs rule in these proceedings is not the usual rule in financial remedy proceedings – it is found at FPR 2010, rule 28.1: 'The court may at any time make such order as to costs as it thinks just.' This rule affords either party a greater prospect of recovering costs than in divorce or dissolution proceedings. There is no guarantee that a costs order will be made as an order for costs will be made at the discretion of the judge.

The applicant should be made aware of the potential costs implications before proceedings are commenced to ensure that they understand that there is a risk that a costs order may be made against them if their application does not succeed or if they do not negotiate sensibly. Likewise, a respondent should be advised not to defend an application blindly and to take sensible steps in the negotiations to reach a compromise. Without prejudice correspondence may be marked 'save as to costs' as the court may be asked to make a costs order if the matter is contested and one party believes that their offer justifies a costs order being made.

If an application can made under either MCA 1973/CPA 2004 legislation or CA 1989, s.15 and Sched.1, the adverse costs rules might tip the balance against an application being made under CA 1989.

## 6.5 CONCLUSION

Financial remedy provision for children is complicated and very technical. Any practitioner considering lump sum or property applications in respect of a child should carefully research the area before embarking upon an application.

The operation of the CMS should be straightforward, and in many cases does not require intervention or detailed consideration by a solicitor. However, in the event that a client requires assistance, the solicitor should look further into the nuances of the calculation and perhaps consider further action where needed.

Finally, the practitioner should note that an application under CA 1989, s.15 and Sched.1 often crosses over with Trusts of Land and Appointment of Trustees Act (TLATA) 1996, s.14. For example, where the parties have cohabited, owned a property together and have children outside a marriage or civil partnership.

These cases are complicated and require careful consideration before any applications are made, not least because TLATA 1996 applications are made to the county court and governed by the Civil Procedure Rules (CPR) 1998 SI 1998/3132, whereas CA 1989, Sched.1 applications are made to the Family Court and governed by FPR 2010.

We do not consider the complexities of TLATA 1996 applications here, but flag this as an area the practitioner should understand as intersecting with family law work. Ideally, both applications would be dealt with in the Family Court by a judge who can deal with both family and civil work.

CHAPTER 7

# Experts in financial remedy proceedings

## 7.1 INTRODUCTION

It is often necessary to involve experts in financial remedy applications to settle valuation or other disputes between the parties. These disputes arise by the parties attributing different values to assets during the disclosure process – the value of the former matrimonial home, for example. An expert may also be needed if the court and lawyers need to gain a better understanding of a complicated asset – this would be common for business or pensions valuations.

It is not cost-effective for a party to pay an expert to get involved at an early stage when completing the Form E or providing voluntary disclosure during the non-court dispute resolution (NCDR) processes. First, the parties should give an approximate value of the asset – it may be that they can agree a figure or can agree a range which is acceptable, and depending on the asset this is the first port of call. In most financial remedy cases, there is a home that needs to be valued, and an approximate valuation can in the first instance be easily obtained by looking at similar properties nearby. The parties may be able to agree the value of the home or narrow range which is acceptable to both of them. An expert will only be needed if each party has given a very different valuation for the same asset, or in the case of complicated assets an expert is needed to explain complicated features and give direction to help resolve the dispute.

Experts are not only instructed during court proceedings – it is entirely possible to instruct an expert in arbitration proceedings, or even during mediation or collaborative law practice (CLP). It is important when instructing a single joint expert (SJE) to agree that if court proceedings are commenced in the future, the expert's report should be used as evidence. It is for the court to decide whether an SJE is needed, but it seems cost-effective to reach an agreement that it is the intention of both parties to do so if NCDR is unsuccessful in resolving matters.

It is unusual in financial remedy matters to instruct a sole expert, meaning that one party instructs an expert to produce a report for court without the participation of the other. It is much more usual that an SJE be instructed by the parties. FPR 2010, PD 25D, para.2.1 states that wherever possible, expert evidence should be obtained from an SJE. For this reason, we will only be considering the instruction of an SJE in this chapter.

Sometimes practitioners may need to take advice from a second person who could be considered an expert in their field after the production of a report from an SJE. Such person is referred to as a 'shadow expert' – this person gives advice to one party; their expertise is not for the benefit of the court, and is usually given to supplement the understanding and decision-making of one party alone. It is very unusual for the other party or the court to be aware of the shadow expert's existence – as the name suggests, the expert sits in the shadows. It can be very useful to have a shadow expert if there is, for example, a complex pension report or forensic accountant's report that requires more detailed consideration with the client. The SJE is neutral and produces their report with the overriding objective of helping the court – it may be that a shadow expert can give further insight into settlement options proposed by the SJE.

It is also invaluable for the shadow expert's input on the issue of further questions that may need to be put to the SJE following the production of the report. These matters can be technical, and therefore further advice is likely to be needed.

If the matter involves a pension on divorce expert (PODE), a financial planner with experience in this field can offer further insights, questions for the expert and potential solutions that perhaps the SJE has alluded to but not clearly set out as being favourable for one party. If a forensic accountant is instructed for the purpose of a business valuation, an accountant may be able to assist in the capacity of a shadow expert to clarify any matters that are complex, and suggest questions to ask the expert following production of the report.

In **Chapter 2**, we considered the role of the 'financial neutral' – often a financial planner with experience of working with parties going through a divorce or dissolution. That person gives advice to the parties on a neutral basis, often in the collaborative field. They do not provide a report for court purposes, but provide information and advice to the parties to help them to reach a settlement. This professional is different to the shadow expert, as they operate to assist both parties outside the court process. Recently it has been mooted that a financial neutral could provide the most help to divorcing parties at the start of their divorce in a PIAM (pension information and assessment meeting). This is a novel idea but has many advantages for the parties and those advising them.

This chapter will cover an overview of the following matters under FPR 2010, Part 25 and PDs to Part 25:

- choosing and instructing an expert;
- the court's decision to appoint an expert;
- the letter of instruction;
- duties of the expert;
- experts' costs; and
- after the final hearing.

## 7.2 CHOOSING AND INSTRUCTING THE EXPERT

It is important for practitioners to understand that in financial remedy proceedings no expert evidence may be put to the court in any form unless permission of the court has been obtained (FPR 2010, rule 25.4). This provision contrasts with the prohibition in children proceedings which prevents an expert from being instructed without the court's permission.

Most expert evidence takes the form of a report (FPR 2010, rule 25.9) but this may extend to emails, letters and oral evidence if directed by the court.

An application for permission should be made in accordance with FPR 2010, rule 25.6(d), which states that an application must be made no later than the first directions hearing (first appointment (FA)). As is usual, an interim application is made using the Part 18 procedure, and the Form D11 application notice should be utilised with the correct fee or the help with fees form should be completed. The form must specifically state:

(a) the field in which the expert evidence is required (e.g. property valuation, forensic accountant, pensions etc.);
(b) where practicable, the name of the proposed expert;
(c) the issues to which the expert evidence is to relate;
(d) whether the expert evidence could be obtained from an SJE;
(e) the other matters set out in PD 25C (which relates to children proceedings) or PD 25D (which relates to financial remedy proceedings), as the case may be.

PD 25D para.3.11(a)–(h) sets out additional matters with regard to the instruction of the expert must be put in evidence before the court:

(a) the discipline, qualifications and expertise of the expert (by way of C.V. where possible);
(b) the expert's availability to undertake the work;
(c) the timetable for the report;
(d) the responsibility for instruction;
(e) whether the expert evidence can properly be obtained by only one party;
(f) why the expert evidence proposed cannot properly be given by an expert already instructed in the proceedings;
(g) the likely cost of the report on an hourly or other charging basis;
(h) the proposed apportionment (at least in the first instance) of any jointly instructed expert's fee; when it is to be paid; and, if applicable, whether public funding has been approved.

A draft order must be attached to the application notice – in financial remedy proceedings this will generally be the order pursuant to the first appointment (order 1.1 or 1.2 financial directions order) using the standard order precedents (FPR 2010, rule 25.7(2)(b)). The orders can be found via the link to 'Standard orders volume 1 financial and enforcement orders' at: **www.judiciary.uk/publications/practice-guidance-standard-children-and-other-orders/**.

The practitioner should note that any experts instructed with regards to applications for the maintenance of a minor, follow the rules for experts instructed in children proceedings. The rules for the instruction of an expert in children proceedings are different to those in financial remedy proceedings – permission must be sought to instruct an expert in children proceedings, whereas permission only needs to be sought to place an expert's report before the court in financial remedy proceedings. The standard order precedents make the distinction clear.

The party wishing to instruct the expert should give the other party a list of the names of one or more experts with the relevant speciality whom they consider to be suitable. It is usual for a list of three experts to be nominated, together with their curriculum vitae and, if possible, an estimate of costs. The other party should then choose one of the experts from the list provided. PD 25D, para.3.3 sets out a list of matters the expert may need to know before they are instructed.

To ensure full transparency, each party should disclose to the other whether they have already consulted any of the experts on the issues in question. Generally speaking, it is sensible for each party not to have independent conversations with the expert regarding their instruction. Of course, some enquiries need to be made to obtain an estimate of costs and to confirm that the expert is able to accept instructions. These enquiries may be made by email, copying the other solicitors or making such correspondence available to them.

Although the rules anticipate that these enquiries will be made before the FA, often the information concerning the expert to be instructed is not obtained until after the FA. The standard order precedents therefore provide precedents where the expert has been identified before the FA and precedents where the expert has not been identified at the FA. It is, in my view, uncommon for the parties to agree the identity of an expert before the FA, but it is in fact time- and cost-saving to do so. If there are any disputes about the proposed experts or the wording of the letter to the expert, these can be resolved at the FA rather than by way of correspondence after it.

If a party wishes to make an application at a hearing for permission to instruct an expert but there is not sufficient time to make the application, the court and other party should be notified of the intention to make an oral application and the reasons for it. The parties should provide the court and the other party with as much information as required by FPR 2010, rule 25.7 and the application may be made orally at the hearing. All applications of this nature should only be made in genuine cases where the need for an expert becomes apparent shortly before the hearing (PD 25D, para.3.8).

If the parties do not know whether expert evidence will be needed until after the FA, for example if answers to questionnaire are needed first, an application should be made at the FA to extend the time by which permission is requested (PD 25D, para.3.9).

## 7.3 THE COURT'S CONSIDERATION

When the court considers whether or not to appoint an expert, it shall have regard to FPR 2010, rule 25.4(3): 'The court may give permission . . . only if the court is of the opinion that the expert evidence is necessary to assist the court to resolve the proceedings.'

This gives the court a wide discretion when deciding an application for an expert to be appointed whether it is necessary in any particular case. The overriding objective of the court is to deal with cases justly (FPR 2010, Part 1 – see **2.3.2.1**), and this applies when an application is made for the inclusion of expert evidence.

FPR 2010, rule 25.5 gives further detail regarding the court's power to restrict expert evidence. First, the court will have regard to any failure to comply with the application to obtain the court's permission for a direction about expert evidence. The court is also to have regard to the following factors (FPR 2010, rule 25.5(2)):

(a) the issues to which the expert evidence would relate;
(b) the questions which the court would require the expert to answer;
(c) the impact which giving permission would be likely to have on the timetable, duration and conduct of the proceedings;
(d) any failure to comply with rule 25.6 or any direction of the court about expert evidence; and
(e) the cost of the expert evidence.

Practitioners sometimes complain about the variable decisions of the court regarding the appointment of an expert, in particular with regards to complex pension issues. The Pension Advisory Group (PAG) 2019 report, *A Guide to the Treatment of Pensions on Divorce*, gives very detailed guidance on this matter, which should help practitioners and the judiciary to make predictable decisions regarding the appointment of expert evidence.

If the court directs the instruction of an SJE, the order will specify the name of the expert unless the parties are directed to choose the expert following the appointment. This is more usual in financial remedy cases – one party will be directed to propose three experts and the other party will choose one of the three nominated. The court will specify a date by which the expert is to provide a written report; prior to the FA it is prudent to check that the expert will accept instructions and what time limit they believe is achievable. In order for them to estimate the time limit, they will need some information about the case, and it is a good idea to copy the other solicitors in on the correspondence so that they know what information you are giving to the expert. If the matter is particularly contentious, you may need to agree the wording of some initial communications with the experts so that there is no suggestion that you have tried to influence the expert or the ultimate report.

## 7.4 THE LETTER OF INSTRUCTION

FPR 2010, PD 25D, para.4.1 sets out the information required for the letter of instruction: 'The party responsible for instructing the expert shall, *within 5 business days after the permission hearing*, prepare (in agreement with the other parties where appropriate) file and serve a letter of instruction to the expert' (emphasis in original).

In reality, the timetable is likely to be much longer than PD 25D anticipates. The standard order precedents allow the parties to choose which party will instruct the expert (usually the party who applied for permission), the date when the letter shall be prepared and when it should be sent to the expert. It also identifies the date when the expert shall prepare the report and submit it to the court and the parties. PD 25D, para.4.1 states that the letter of instruction shall:

(a) set out the context in which the expert's opinion is sought (including any ethnic, cultural, religious or linguistic contexts);
(b) set out the questions which the expert is required to answer and ensuring that they:
    (i) are within the ambit of the expert's area of expertise;
    (ii) do not contain unnecessary or irrelevant detail;
    (iii) are kept to a manageable number and are clear, focused and direct; and
    (iv) reflect what the expert has been requested to do by the court;
(c) list the documentation provided, or provide for the expert an indexed and paginated bundle which shall include:
    (i) an agreed list of essential reading; and
    (ii) a copy of FPR 2010, PD 25D and PDs 25B and 25E; and where appropriate PD 15B (PDs will usually be sent by email link rather than papers, as good experts who are frequently instructed prefer not to receive multiple copies of PDs).

In the event that the parties are unable to agree the content of the letter of instruction to an SJE, FPR 2010, rule 25.12(2) allows the court to determine those instructions on the request of either party; the request must be copied to the other relevant parties. PD 25D, para.6.1 states that the court should settle the letter of instruction without delay and usually without a hearing. Unfortunately this indication of swift action is not likely to be seen in practice.

In the recent case of *CM* v. *CM* [2019] EWFC 16, Mr Justice Moor indicated that family law arbitration could be used to settle issues relating to a letter of instruction to an expert more cost-effectively than an application to the court (para.10)

> If, however, in a future case, there is a genuine issue as to drafting, I consider it would be exactly the sort of matter that should be referred to an arbitrator who is accredited by the Institute of Family Law Arbitrators.

Template letters of instruction for other experts are available in the companion toolkit to this book, the *Matrimonial Finance Toolkit* (M. Ruparel, Law Society Publishing, 2017).

The Pension Advisory Group's guide (see above) contains a template letter of instruction to a PODE at appendix E, which should be used by all practitioners when instructing an expert in pension on divorce matters.

## 7.5 DUTIES OF THE EXPERT

FPR 2010, PD 25B sets out the expert's duties, the content of their report and the requirement to attend court. An important matter is at para.3.1: 'An expert in family proceedings has an overriding duty to the court that takes precedence over any obligation to the person from whom the expert has received instructions or by whom the expert is paid.' Clients are sometimes sceptical about one person providing expert opinion to the court, but the rules make it clear that the expert's duty is to the court and not to the parties. This should allay any fears the client has about the expert's objectivity.

The specific duties of the expert are listed at para.4.1 – the expert should only act within their expertise and should notify the court if another expert is needed to answer any questions that are asked which fall outside their expertise.

Paragraph 9.1 details the information that should be provided in the expert's report which should be verified by the following statement of truth (para.9.1(j)):

> I confirm that I have made clear which facts and matters referred to in this report are within my own knowledge and which are not. Those that are within my own knowledge I confirm to be true. The opinions I have expressed represent my true and complete professional opinions on the matters to which they refer.

The report should confirm that the expert has no conflict in acting as an expert, or that any potential conflict was disclosed before accepting instructions. This is another common concern expressed by a client – that the expert secretly knows the other party and that they are colluding to misrepresent the information in the report.

The court will not direct an expert to attend a hearing to give evidence unless it is necessary to do so in the interests of justice (FPR 2010, rule 25.9(2)). It is unusual for an SJE to be asked to attend a hearing to give evidence in financial remedy proceedings, save for in high net worth cases where it may be cost proportionate for the expert to attend.

In the majority of cases, the parties accept the report of the expert, even if queries are first raised by way of questions (FPR 2010, rule 25.10). Those questions may only be put to the expert on one occasion without permission of the court and must be proportionate. There can be a tendency for parties to ask the expert questions that constitute cross-examination questions and not questions to clarify the report. The default position is that the parties will raise questions within 10 days from service of the report. This may not be long enough to consider the report with the client, possibly take a shadow expert's opinion and draft questions to the expert. A longer period is allowable if it is directed by the court when permission is given to instruct the expert.

The order should specify how long the expert has to answer the questions.

## 7.6 EXPERTS' COSTS

The parties should agree how the costs of the expert may be shared between them. One party may agree to pay the costs of the report in the first instance – this allows the report to proceed, but also leaves the door open for the recovery of some of those costs at a later date.

The parties usually agree to pay the costs of the report in equal shares. If this is the case, then the solicitors should inform the expert of the agreement to share the costs when sending the letter of instruction.

When agreeing to pay the expert's costs, the parties should consider how any answers to questions will be paid if they are raised. If one party alone raises questions on the report, then it seems fair that they should pay for those questions to be answered by the expert. These matters should be set out clearly in the order which appoints the expert so that there is no confusion at a later date.

## 7.7 AFTER THE FINAL HEARING

The party who was responsible for instructing the SJE should send the expert a written explanation of the court's determination and what use the court made of the expert's evidence. Most experts say that this requirement is never fulfilled by solicitors, but that it would be useful for them to receive this information. The rules state that unless otherwise directed, this should be done within 10 days of the final hearing.

The expert is also entitled to receive a copy of the court transcript or final order within 10 business days of receiving it. Once again, solicitors tend not to send the order to the expert, and so often the expert doesn't know how helpful their report was.

# CHAPTER 8

# Negotiations and consent orders

## 8.1 INTRODUCTION

It can be difficult to understand how to commence negotiations in financial remedy cases, whether orally or in writing. The mistake that solicitors often make is to put forward an offer without reference to the orders available (**Chapter 5**) and the evidence produced of assets, income, pensions and property. The successful resolution of many financial remedy cases depends on an achievable, realistic resolution of the parties' financial needs and a fair distribution of the assets. Fairness is a broad concept, so what may seem fair to one party may not seem fair to the other.

Both parties will need to be told to compromise during negotiations – the practitioner needs to explain to the client that the first offer is unlikely to be the last offer, and that the parties would be expected to move towards each other's positions. A frequent mistake made in some negotiations is for the offer to be unachievable if it is founded in what the client wants rather than what is attainable from the available assets. It may be easier to negotiate a settlement in high net worth cases, as the parties will easily be able to afford the necessary experts, valuers and experienced counsel to craft negotiations. However, it is also likely that the parties will be more inclined to spend money on legal costs to 'get what they want'. This contrasts starkly with the position of the parties in small asset cases – the assets are limited, as are the third parties who will be engaged by the parties to help negotiations. An early resolution of small money cases will be cost-effective for the client.

An example of an unachievable offer would be: if the equity in the property is £500,000, it makes no financial sense to propose that a mortgage-free property is purchased for the value of £600,000. Unless there are other investments that could be sold to top-up the capital required, the offer is impractical and therefore unrealistic and unachievable. This may sound obvious, but I often see offers that are simply impossible to accept as they are based on hope rather than reality.

In all cases, disclosure should be complete before negotiations start – the parties may struggle to negotiate if there are still contentious issues between them about third party interests or valuation disputes.

Sometimes a client will instruct a solicitor to make an offer without any disclosure. This may be on the basis that the parties have reached an agreement between them. If this is the case, the solicitor may act, but should be cautious, and any offer made should be 'without prejudice'. The parties may think they have an agreement, only to discover (for example) that they have overlooked the importance of pensions and the need for maintenance orders. The client may be willing to sign a disclaimer which protects the solicitor from a negligence claim in the event that the settlement transpires to be unfavourable to them.

It seems to me to be a waste of money for a client to instruct a solicitor to act as draftsman rather than adviser. There are services available that can draft consent orders for couples via an online portal – they charge the parties a few hundred pounds to draft the consent order. If there is a high level of risk in drafting a consent order (which may not be approved by the court) and which may obviously prejudice one party, the solicitor should consider whether they want or need to take on such risk unless they are able to mitigate against that risk.

The client should always be advised that the court will not simply agree any settlement reached between the parties – the function of the judge is to approve those orders that are fair in all the circumstances of the case. While only a small proportion of orders may be rejected by the court for being unfair, there is a risk that it may happen.

This chapter will cover an overview of the following:

- negotiations;
- consent order considerations;
- implementation;
- enforcement proceedings.

## 8.2 NEGOTIATIONS – OPEN/WITHOUT PREJUDICE/WITHOUT PREJUDICE SAVE AS TO COSTS

### 8.2.1 Background

The current costs regime encourages the parties to make 'open offers', as these can support a costs application if one party rejects a sensible open offer. There is some resistance among practitioners to make open offers, even though this regime was originally introduced in 2006 under the previous Family Proceedings Rules 1991 SI 1991/1247 and then carried over into the current Family Procedure Rules (FPR) 2010, Part 28. The making of costs orders is uncommon (**Chapter 4**) and so there is little to encourage practitioners to make or accept open offers. When they are used, they can be a powerful statement to the other party that the party making the offer is confident that their offer is good enough to be made on open terms. FPR 2010, PD 28A, para.4.4 makes it clear that a refusal to negotiate on open terms can lead to a costs order being made.

Practitioners continue to make offers marked 'without prejudice', and as can be seen from **Chapter 4**, these offers are only admissible at the financial dispute resolution (FDR) appointment and won't help the party who makes it to secure a costs order. 'Without prejudice' offers are often made on more favourable settlement terms than an open offer – the underlying message is that the client should accept the more favourable without prejudice offer rather than face the court with the less favourable open offer on the table. 'Without prejudice' offers hide in the shadows – a quiet (often toothless) threat that if the offer isn't accepted, the alternative could be worse.

Letters marked 'without prejudice save as to costs' will only affect the making of a costs order in cases such as applications under Children Act (CA) 1989, s.15, Sched.1 or interim applications (maintenance pending suit or maintenance pending the outcome of proceedings (MPS/MPOP), for example) which follow costs rule FPR 2010, rule 28.1 rather than the general rule in financial remedy proceedings at FPR 2010, rule 28.3(5).

Solicitors shouldn't respond to a 'without prejudice' or 'without prejudice save as to costs' letter with an open letter. An open letter shouldn't refer to any 'without prejudice' offers, whether oral or written. It is possible for a party to respond to an open offer with a 'without prejudice' letter – however, if the court ever assesses liability for costs, it will only see the open offers in financial remedy proceedings. If a practitioner responds with a 'without prejudice' response, it will look as though the open offer was not acknowledged or responded to. This may be damaging in the assessment of a costs order, always remembering that an order is unlikely to be made in any event.

The process of negotiation is often a lengthy process of the parties going back and forth with different offers to see if they can agree a mutually acceptable compromise. During the process, the solicitor should be alert to the differences in the parties' offers, the 'net effect' of how much each party will exit with and the possible costs consequences of proceeding with litigation. This is a careful balancing act which must be carefully monitored throughout the process.

In the case of *ABX* v. *SBX* [2018] EWFC 81, Mr Justice Francis criticised the costs incurred by the parties in a case he described as 'not ... particularly complicated' (para.2). The parties had incurred costs of £1.1 million by the final hearing, whereas the total net assets in that case were between £1.5 million and £5.4 million, and significant parts of those assets were illiquid and may never be realised. He said 'it will be obvious to anybody reading this Judgment that the costs incurred in this case are wholly disproportionate to the size of the assets' (para.2). Whether in high net worth cases or small money cases, solicitors are expected to act in a proportionate manner and advise their clients accordingly. There is of course no guarantee that the client will act upon that advice.

### 8.2.2 Structure of an offer to settle

**Appendix D1** sets out a checklist of factors that the solicitor should consider when putting together an offer to settle. The checklist follows the main clauses in the standard order precedents 1.2. I find that if solicitors don't cross-check their offers with the precedents that will be used to draft an order, important matters may be missed. It therefore makes sense to look at the headline clauses so that they inform the settlement proceedings. I would also recommend having the schedule of assets and income to hand to ensure that no asset, debt, credit card or life policy is overlooked during negotiations. (The standard order precedents can be found via the link to 'Standard orders volume 1 financial and enforcement orders' at: **www.judiciary.uk/publications/practice-guidance-standard-children-and-other-orders/**.)

Many of the clauses and the terms of settlement rely on the parties having taking financial advice – for example, the provisions about insurance and pensions. I have stressed the importance of the client taking financial advice throughout this book, so that when a settlement is reached there are no nasty surprises waiting for the solicitor or their client. Even simple financial products can be more complicated than a solicitor anticipates.

Matters to consider are:

- housing;
- lump sum;
- pensions;
- income orders;
- costs orders.

### 8.2.2.1 *Housing*

First, an affordable property needs to be provided for the person with care of the child or children. If there are no children, then the court would hope to be able to house the parties equally – or if this isn't possible, then the assets would be distributed fairly, taking into account the Matrimonial Causes Act 1973, s.25/Civil Partnership Act 2004, Sched.5, Part 5, para.21(2) factors (see **5.8**).

Housing need is informed by the evidence in the parties' Form E's and affordability. In high net worth cases, the property should be of a similar standard to that of the property the parties lived in during the marriage, it should not be a better home than the former marital home, and should meet the party's needs.

In small asset cases, the property may be subject to a mortgage, and enquiries about the mortgage must be made before the offer is sent. Can the proposed occupier afford to pay the mortgage, and be able to transfer it into the name of the occupier, or is it only likely that a Mesher or Martin order will be possible (see **5.6.5.3** and **5.6.5.4**)? Often I see offers that are made with no regard to whether the mortgage company will release the non-occupying spouse from the mortgage covenants despite the fact that the offer assumes that consent to a transfer and a release from the mortgage will be given.

Issues concerning capital gains tax, stamp duty and legal fees should not be overlooked, as these can amount to thousands of pounds.

### 8.2.2.2 Lump sum

Once a sensible position is found for housing, the person making the offer should consider whether the occupying spouse can pay the other spouse a lump sum representing the other party's share or part share in the property. If not, the other spouse will expect that their share of the equity will be paid at some point in the future, for example when the property is sold (see the options available in **Chapter 5**).

### 8.2.2.3 Pensions

In the alternative, the non-occupying spouse's interest in the property may be offset against their pension entitlement, if they have any. Offsetting property against pensions is a difficult calculation – the Pension Advisory Group (PAG) 2019 report, *A Guide to the Treatment of Pensions on Divorce*, Part 7 deals with the various red flags with offsetting in detail. Practitioners should be careful when undertaking this negotiation in the absence of an expert's input. Numerous pension negligence claims have been made against solicitors who agree pension offsetting without a full understanding of the true value of defined benefit or public sector pensions, which offer extremely valuable benefits. The article by Grant Lazarus, 'You need the house, love – let him keep his pension' [2019] Fam Law 373 (April) offers a very useful insight into negligence claims against solicitors for offsetting pensions against equity in the home.

Pension orders may still need to be made if an offset isn't possible or only a partial offset of equity in the property can be achieved. Practitioners should take great care to understand what orders can be made and make offers having taken financial advice or having instructed an expert.

### 8.2.2.4 Income orders

The party making the offer should consider whether the occupying spouse can live in the property without an income order. If they can, then a clean break on income will be possible.

If not, then serious consideration needs to be given to the quantum and duration of any income order for the spouse and children. Any income order may reasonably be subject to a MCA 1973, s.28(1A) bar as explained in **Chapter 5**.

In a high net worth case, once income orders are considered, it may be possible to capitalise the order, thereby achieving a clean break (MCA 1973, s.25A). In small money cases, there will either be no other capital against which a capitalisation could take place, or the income will be vital for the receiving party to rely on. In any case where an income order is made, the negotiations may benefit from a thought to providing insurance to protect the receiving spouse if the payer dies.

## 8.2.2.5 Costs orders

It is unlikely that the parties will need to agree any costs orders, save that each party pays their own costs. If there were costs orders made in the divorce or dissolution proceedings, it is good practice to mention them during financial negotiations.

### 8.2.3 Practical matters

The parties should always consider practical considerations, such as:

- When the orders will take effect?
- How long will it take to transfer or sell a house?
- How long will it take to raise the money needed to pay a lump sum?
- What interest provisions are fair if the paying party fails to make the payment on time?
- Should the payment of the lump sum be simultaneous with the transfer of the property to avoid any issues about the payment of interest arising?
- How will any periodical payments orders be timed? Quantum is an obvious concern but an order's term and whether it should be extendable or non-extendable are also important factors.
- Do the parties understand the tax consequences of each order and do they have the money to pay the tax that will become due? If not, does that money need to be paid from joint funds, if there are any available?
- In relation to pensions, is the receiving party able to choose between internal or external pension sharing? If there is an option, has the recipient taken financial advice about it? How will the parties pay the pension sharing implementation costs? Does this matter need to be provided for during the negotiations?

Finally, the offer should be time limited. An offer which isn't time limited – for example, for a period of 28 days after which it is withdrawn – then remains open for acceptance unless rejected. This can be problematic if the negotiations are ongoing for a long period during which the parties' fortunes suffer a loss.

## 8.3 CONSENT ORDERS

### 8.3.1 Procedural matters

The standard order precedents should be used to draft the consent order once a negotiated agreement is reached. A draft precedent order can be found in the *Matrimonial Finance Toolkit* (M. Ruparel, Law Society Publishing, 2017).

FPR 2010, rule 9.26 sets out the procedural matters that parties must attend to when sending a consent order to the court:

- An application on Form A should be sent to the court. The court may require the other party to send a Form A which is marked for dismissal purposes only – this requirement is court-specific.
- Two copies of the draft order must be sent.
- One copy must be endorsed with a statement signed by the respondent confirming that they agree to the application.
- If both parties have given undertakings, they must sign the order to indicate that they have read and understood the warnings about undertakings and the order itself. In practice, both parties and their solicitors sign the order.
- It is sensible, but not mandatory, to send a 'net effect calculation' which clearly sets out what each party will exit the marriage with once the orders are implemented. This helps the judge to understand the financial impact of the order on each party. Simply put, this is a calculation which sets out how much capital, income, property and pensions each party will exit with once the terms of the order have been put into effect.
- The parties must submit the Form D81 (statement of information in support of the consent order), either as one document prepared and signed jointly, or one form for each party. Each must sign the form to indicate they have seen the other's Form D81 and sign a statement of truth regarding their own disclosure. If the parties attend a hearing at which a consent order is submitted, the court may dispense with the filing of the D81 form (this is usual but often not properly documented at court).
- Where the parties agree an order which contains a pension provision, the FPR 2010, rules 9.40–9.44 should be consulted to ensure that proper notice has been served on the person responsible for the pension arrangement (PRPA). The PAG report details those matters that parties must observe to ensure that pension orders will be implemented by the pension company.
- The appropriate pension annex should be sent with the consent order (Annex P1/P2/PPF1/PPF2) in duplicate.
- If the agreement was reached following an arbitration award, that award should be sent to the court. This complies with *Arbitration in the Family Court: Practice Guidance issued on 23 November 2015 by Sir James Munby, President of the Family Division*, para.7 (**www.judiciary.uk/wp-content/uploads/2015/11/arbitration_pguidance_nov_15.pdf**).
- The court fee or help with fees form should also be sent.

The consent order and supplemental documents may be sent to the court dealing with the financial remedy application, or the divorce centre if no financial remedy application had been issued. In the alternative, the consent order and documents may be e-filed with the digitised consent order system. This system has become mandatory for solicitors to use from 24 August 2020. After this date, paper applications may no longer be sent to the regional divorce centres by a solicitor who represents the applicant in financial proceedings. Solicitors must first register for a Payment by Account with HM Courts and Tribunals Service (HMCTS) and then register for a 'My HMCTS account' to be able to use the digitised consent order system. FPR 2010, PD 41B sets out the process of submitting a digital consent order.

### 8.3.2 Implementation

Once an order has been sealed by the court, solicitors should ensure that the terms are implemented by the parties. The transfers of property and payment of lump sums (if any) are usually straightforward, if all proper enquiries are made before the order is sealed regarding mortgage transfer etc. It should be relatively straightforward for maintenance orders to be put into effect by the payment of maintenance by direct debit to a nominated bank account.

The implementation of pension orders is complex as they take several months to implement. The practitioner will need to check that the consent order and annex have been properly sealed by the court – this is often overlooked; the order cannot be implemented unless the annex is sealed. Although the court should serve the pension sharing order on the pension trustees, it is sensible for the person receiving the pension share to send the order to the pension scheme.

The practitioner is advised not to apply for the decree absolute or final order if there is a pension sharing order made in the financial order without consulting the guidance in the PAG report at appendix F, para.7. The earliest a pension sharing order can take effect is 28 days after the consent order is approved by the court (unless that time is changed in the order). In the normal case, no application for decree absolute should be made in the 28-day period as this could have serious negative consequences for the party expecting to receive the pension share if the pension member were to die in that 28-day period. As long as the parties remain married or in a civil partnership for 28 days after the date of the financial order, the spouse receiving the pension share is protected in the event the pension member dies. As a widow or widower they would be entitled to claim following the death of the member instead of receiving the pension sharing order which would fail if their spouse died within the 28-day period. This is a relevant consideration in every case where a pension sharing order is made and the decree absolute has not been pronounced up to that point.

The solicitor should not close their file until the pension sharing order has been implemented or any issues that arise with implementation have been dealt with. The implementation of orders is just as important as finalising an order – many potential implementation issues can be headed off by careful drafting of the consent order. More detail about post-implementation issues concerning pensions can be found at appendix F of the PAG report.

If issues arise regarding implementation of any clause in the order, particularly with reference to timing, either party can apply to the court under the liberty to apply provision which can be found in every order. The application is made using form D11 together with a statement and the appropriate fee or help with fees form. This is a different process to dealing with the enforcement of orders, where one party simply refuses to comply with a provision contained in the consent order. The proper use of standard order precedents should ensure that enforcement applications are much more straightforward as there should be no problems with regard to drafting issues.

## 8.4 ENFORCEMENT PROCEEDINGS

Undertakings and orders are enforceable in the same way. FPR 2010, PD 33A gives further guidance on the enforcement of undertakings. Enforcement is an extremely complicated subject and the detail is beyond the scope of this book, particularly as the enforcement procedures in the Family Court are rapidly changing following divergent approaches between the county court and Family Court. Enforcement procedures differ in the High Court and in the family division.

The main methods of enforcement are:

(a) sale of property (MCA 1973, s.24A, which can be used where a property transfer has not been made or a lump sum order has not been paid);

(b) a third party debt order (which can be used where a third party owes money to the debtor and that money can be diverted to the creditor to satisfy a debt);

(c) an attachment of earnings order (which can readily be used to secure the payment of regular maintenance) governed by FPR 2010, Part 39;

(d) a charging order (which may be used to secure maintenance arrears or an unpaid lump sum against a property or securities) governed by FPR 2010, Part 40;

(e) contempt proceedings (which may be used to imprison the debtor in appropriate circumstances but fails to recover funds unless the debtor purges their contempt) governed by FPR 2010, Part 37;

(f) a writ or warrant of possession of land (which will assist in recovering possession of property from one of the parties who refuses to vacate);

(g) a writ or warrant control (which allows a creditor to take action against a debtor's goods or chattels; this may or may not result in sufficient funds to pay the debt owed);

(h) judgment summons proceedings (FPR 2010, rule 33.11).

It is often cheaper for a client to engage in enforcement proceedings without the assistance of a solicitor. Most clients do not feel comfortable doing this, but the solicitor must consider the costs proportionality in acting for a client to recover a debt as against the value of the money to be recovered and any costs orders available. Often only fixed costs are recoverable in Family Court enforcement proceedings.

FPR 2010, Part 33 sets out the main factors that need to be taken into account regarding enforcement. The easiest way for a person to apply to enforce an order in the Family Court is set out in FPR 2010, rule 33.3(2)(b), which says that an application for enforcement may be made by filing an application notice which states how much money is outstanding under the terms of the order and how that sum is arrived at. The notice of application may apply for an order 'for such method of enforcement as the court may consider appropriate' (FPR 2010, rule 33.3(2)(a)). This allows the creditor to complete Form D80K (**https://assets.publishing. service.gov.uk/government/uploads/system/uploads/attachment_data/file/ 688044/d50k-eng.pdf**) to ask the court to decide which method of enforcement is best in that particular case. This leaves the heavy lifting to the court rather than placing the onus on the creditor. The difficulty is that the court is slow in dealing with these matters and often will not deal with them in the manner set out by the rules.

In the alternative, FPR 2010, rule 33.3(2)(a) allows the creditor to notify the court of the specific method of enforcement that they hope to pursue. This is much more complicated as the creditor needs to choose a method, complete the right form, pay the right fee and hope that the method of enforcement results in recovery of the debt. Enforcement proceedings are so complicated that a litigant in person is highly unlikely to be able to effectively enforce using this method. Each method of enforcement is governed by a different statute and each has its own quirks – for this reason the solicitor should consult specialist reference books or counsel if embarking upon enforcement proceedings in the Family Court or the High Court.

APPENDIX A

# Disclosure

# APPENDIX A1

# Pre-application protocol

### NOTES OF GUIDANCE

**Scope of the Protocol**

1. This protocol is intended to apply to all applications for a financial remedy as defined by rule 2.3. It is designed to cover all classes of case, ranging from a simple application for periodical payments to an application for a substantial lump sum and property adjustment order. The protocol is designed to facilitate the operation of the procedure for financial remedy applications.
2. In considering the options of pre-application disclosure and negotiation, solicitors should bear in mind the advantage of having a court timetable and court managed process. There is sometimes an advantage in preparing disclosure before proceedings are commenced. However, solicitors should bear in mind the objective of controlling costs and in particular the costs of discovery and that the option of pre-application disclosure and negotiation has risks of excessive and uncontrolled expenditure and delay. This option should only be encouraged where both parties agree to follow this route and disclosure is not likely to be an issue or has been adequately dealt with in mediation or otherwise.
3. Solicitors should consider at an early stage and keep under review whether it would be appropriate to suggest mediation and/or collaborative law to the clients as an alternative to solicitor negotiation or court based litigation.
4. Making an application to the court should not be regarded as a hostile step or a last resort, rather as a way of starting the court timetable, controlling disclosure and endeavouring to avoid the costly final hearing and the preparation for it.

**First letter**

5. The circumstances of parties to an application for a financial remedy are so various that it would be difficult to prepare a specimen first letter. The request for information will be different in every case. However, the tone of the initial letter is important and the guidelines in paragraphs 14 and 15 should be followed. It should be approved in advance by the client. Solicitors writing to an unrepresented party should always recommend that he seeks independent legal advice and enclose a second copy of the letter to be passed to any solicitor instructed. A reasonable time limit for an answer may be 14 days.

APPENDIX A1

**Negotiation and Settlement**

6. In the event of pre-application disclosure and negotiation, as envisaged in paragraph 12 an application should not be issued when a settlement is a reasonable prospect.

**Disclosure**

7. The protocol underlines the obligation of parties to make full and frank disclosure of all material facts, documents and other information relevant to the issues. Solicitors owe their clients a duty to tell them in clear terms of this duty and of the possible consequences of breach of the duty, which may include criminal sanctions under the Fraud Act 2006. This duty of disclosure is an ongoing obligation and includes the duty to disclose any material changes after initial disclosure has been given. Solicitors are referred to the Good Practice Guides available to Resolution members at www.resolution.org.uk and can also contact the Law Society's Practice Advice Service on 0870 606 2522.

# THE PROTOCOL

**General principles**

8. All parties must always bear in mind the overriding objective set out at rules 1.1 to 1.4 and try to ensure that applications should be resolved and a just outcome achieved as speedily as possible without costs being unreasonably incurred. The needs of any children should be addressed and safeguarded. The procedures which it is appropriate to follow should be conducted with minimum distress to the parties and in a manner designed to promote as good a continuing relationship between the parties and any children affected as is possible in the circumstances.
9. The principle of proportionality must be borne in mind at all times. It is unacceptable for the costs of any case to be disproportionate to the financial value of the subject matter of the dispute.
10. Parties should be informed that where a court is considering whether to make an order requiring one party to pay the costs of another party, it will take into account pre-application offers to settle and conduct of disclosure.

**Identifying the issues**

11. Parties must seek to clarify their claims and identify the issues between them as soon as possible. So that this can be achieved, they must provide full, frank and clear disclosure of facts, information and documents, which are material and sufficiently accurate to enable proper negotiations to take place to settle their differences. Openness in all dealings is essential.

**Disclosure**

12. If parties carry out voluntary disclosure before the issue of proceedings the parties should exchange schedules of assets, income, liabilities and other material facts, using the financial statement as a guide to the format of the disclosure. Documents should only be disclosed to the extent that they are required by the financial statement. Excessive or disproportionate costs should not be incurred.

## Correspondence

13. Any first letter and subsequent correspondence must focus on the clarification of claims and identification of issues and their resolution. Protracted and unnecessary correspondence and 'trial by correspondence' must be avoided.
14. The impact of any correspondence upon the reader and in particular the parties must always be considered. Any correspondence which raises irrelevant issues or which might cause the other party to adopt an entrenched, polarised or hostile position is to be discouraged.

## Summary

15. The aim of all pre-application proceedings steps must be to assist the parties to resolve their differences speedily and fairly or at least narrow the issues and, should that not be possible, to assist the court to do so.

## APPENDIX A2

# What to do when your client gives you a document belonging to a third party

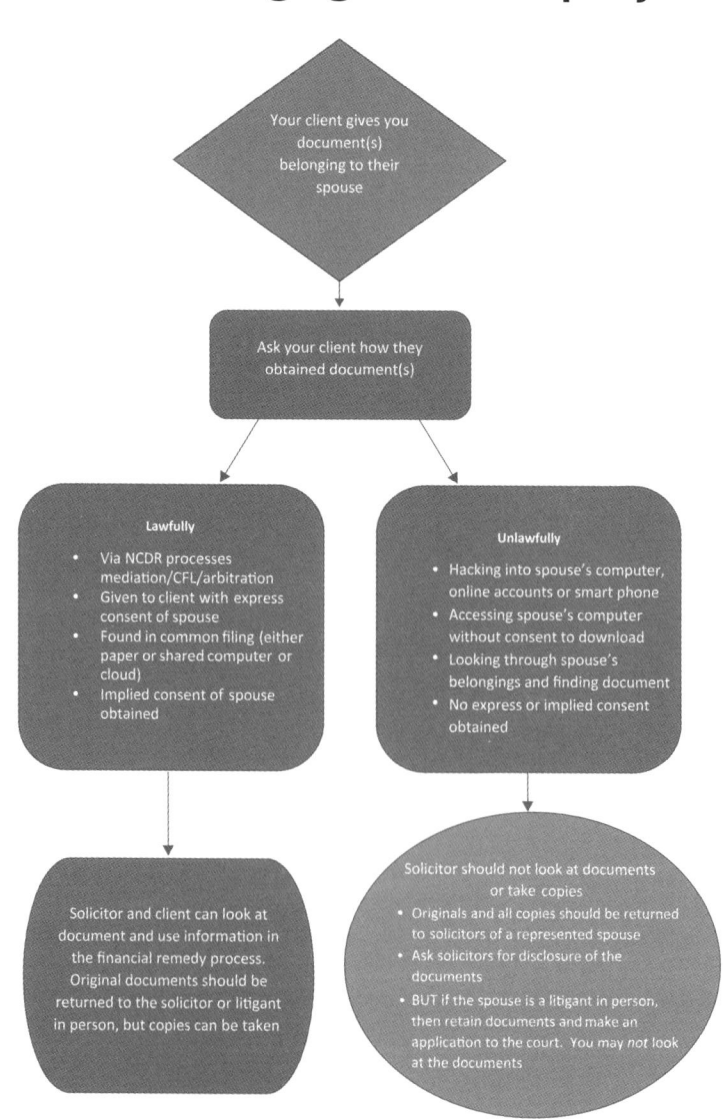

**Your client gives you document(s) belonging to their spouse**

↓

**Ask your client how they obtained document(s)**

↓

### Lawfully

- Via NCDR processes mediation/CFL/arbitration
- Given to client with express consent of spouse
- Found in common filing (either paper or shared computer or cloud)
- Implied consent of spouse obtained

↓

Solicitor and client can look at document and use information in the financial remedy process. Original documents should be returned to the solicitor or litigant in person, but copies can be taken

### Unlawfully

- Hacking into spouse's computer, online accounts or smart phone
- Accessing spouse's computer without consent to download
- Looking through spouse's belongings and finding document
- No express or implied consent obtained

↓

Solicitor should not look at documents or take copies

- Originals and all copies should be returned to solicitors of a represented spouse
- Ask solicitors for disclosure of the documents
- BUT if the spouse is a litigant in person, then retain documents and make an application to the court. You may *not* look at the documents

APPENDIX B

# Available orders

APPENDIX B1

# Table of spousal/civil partnership orders available

Order 2.1 of standard precedent references unless other orders are specified.

| Section | Order | From when/until when | Standard orders precedent | Notes |
|---|---|---|---|---|
| MCA 1973, s.21A / CPA 2004, Sched.5, Part 4, para.16. | Pension sharing. | Only available for petitions issued after 1 December 2000. | Paragraph 92. This precedent will need to be amended to reference a pension sharing order made in CPA 2004 proceedings as it currently only references MCA 1973 applications. | The pension sharing annex (P1) must also be completed and sealed by the court. |
| MCA 1973, s.21B / CPA 2004, Sched.5, Part 4A, para.19A | Pension compensation sharing. | Only available for petitions issued after 6 April 2011. | No dedicated precedent. Paragraph 90 would need to be adapted. | The Pension Protection Fund (PPF) sharing annex (PPF 1) must also be completed and sealed by the court. |

173

# APPENDIX B1

| Section | Order | From when/until when | Standard orders precedent | Notes |
|---|---|---|---|---|
| MCA 1973, s.22 CPA 2004, Sched.5, Part 8, para.38 | Maintenance pending suit (MPS). Maintenance pending the outcome of proceedings (MPOP). | From date of the petition to decree absolute. From date of the petition to final dissolution order. | Paragraph 71 is the main provision for MPS and interim maintenance orders. Also referred to in paragraphs 72-74. Slight amendments may need to be made to the precedents to allow for CPA 2004 MPOP. | An application can be made either using Form A or a Part 18 application. Legal fees can't be met using this application. |
| MCA 1973, s.22ZA / CPA 2004, Sched.5, Part 8, para.38A | Order for payment of legal services. | Introduced on 1 April 2013. | Dedicated precedent at standard order 1.1 para.28. | See **1.6.3.6**. |
| MCA 1973, s.23 / CPA 2004, Sched.5, para.38A–38B. | Financial provision (secured) periodical payment order (PPO); for spouse or civil partner. Lump sum for spouse/civil partner or a child. | Not enforceable until decree absolute or final order. | Declaration para.28 regarding lump sum. Declaration paras.31/32 regarding intention to vary PPO. Undertaking at paras.44/45 to take out or assign a policy to cover PPO in the event of payer's death. Paras.53-55 lump sum orders. Para.72 – PPO no term. Para.73 – PPO with either extendable/non-extendable term. Para.74 – secured PPO. Para.81 – global maintenance order (Segal order). | See **Appendix C2** for references to orders available for children. |

## SPOUSAL/CIVIL PARTNERSHIP ORDERS AVAILABLE

| Section | Order | From when/until when | Standard orders precedent | Notes |
|---|---|---|---|---|
| MCA 1973, s.24 / CPA 2004, Sched.5, Part 2, para.7. | Property adjustment orders. Includes transfer of property, settlement of property, variation of ante-/post-nuptial settlement. | Not enforceable until decree absolute or final order. | Para.56 – transfer of property. Para.58 – trust of land (Mesher order). Para.59 – transfer with charge back. Paras.60–62 payments associated with property. Para.63 – capital gains tax and indemnity. | Consider an order to transfer followed by a default order for sale where appropriate. |
| MCA 1973, s.24A / CPA 2004, Sched.5, Part 3, para.11. | Orders for sale of property. | Not enforceable until decree absolute or final order. | Para.57 – order for sale. Paras.61/62 – payments associated with property until sale. Para.63 – capital gains tax and indemnity. | An order for sale can only be made if an order under MCA 1973, s.23 / CPA 2004, Sched.5, para.2; or MCA 1973, s.24 / CPA 2004, Sched.5, Part 2, para.7 is made first. |
| MCA 1973, s.25A / CPA 2004, Sched.5, Part 5, para.23. | Exercise of the court's powers. | The duty to consider a clean break as soon as possible after the grant of decree absolute or final order. | Clean break clauses are found at paras.96/97. | A clean break can only be achieved where 'just and reasonable'. |
| MCA 1973, s.25(B)–(D) CPA 2004, Sched.5, Part 6, para.24. | Pension attachment orders. | Only available for petitions filed after 1 July 1996. | Para.94. This precedent will need to be amended to reference a pension attachment order made in CPA 2004 proceedings as it currently only references MCA 1973 applications. | Pension attachment orders are available for judicial separation petitions. P2 annex must also be completed and sealed by the court. |

APPENDIX B1

| Section | Order | From when/until when | Standard orders precedent | Notes |
|---|---|---|---|---|
| MCA 1973, s.25(2)(e)/(f) / CPA 2004, Sched.5, Part 7. | PPF and attachment of pension compensation. | Only available for petitions filed after 6 April 2011. | No dedicated precedent available. Para.94 can be amended. | Annex PPF 2 must also be completed and sealed by the court. |
| MCA 1973, s.28(1) / CPA 2004, Sched.5, Part 10, para.47(6). | Duration of financial provision orders. | The effect of remarriage or formation of civil partnership. | Forms part of the precedents in connection with (secured) PPO or (secured) MPOP orders. Para.72 – PPO no term (the classic joint lives order). Para.73 – PPO with either extendable/non-extendable term. Para.74 – secured PPO. Para.81 – global maintenance order (Segal order). | This represents the statutory termination of (secured) PPO or (secured) MPOP orders on remarriage or civil partnership or death of either party. |
| MCA 1973 s.28(1A), (1), (2) / CPA 2004, Sched.5, para.47(5). | No extension to the term of a PPO. | After making the financial remedy order, enforceable after decree absolute or final order made. | A non-extendable term PPO – para.73. | |
| MCA 1973, s.28(3) / CPA 2004, Sched.5, para.48. | Effect of subsequent remarriage or civil partnership. | If a party to a marriage or civil partnership remarries without making an application for financial provision or property adjustment, they are barred from doing so. | No standard orders precedent. | Very important to remember. |

176

APPENDIX B2

# Remarriage trap flowchart

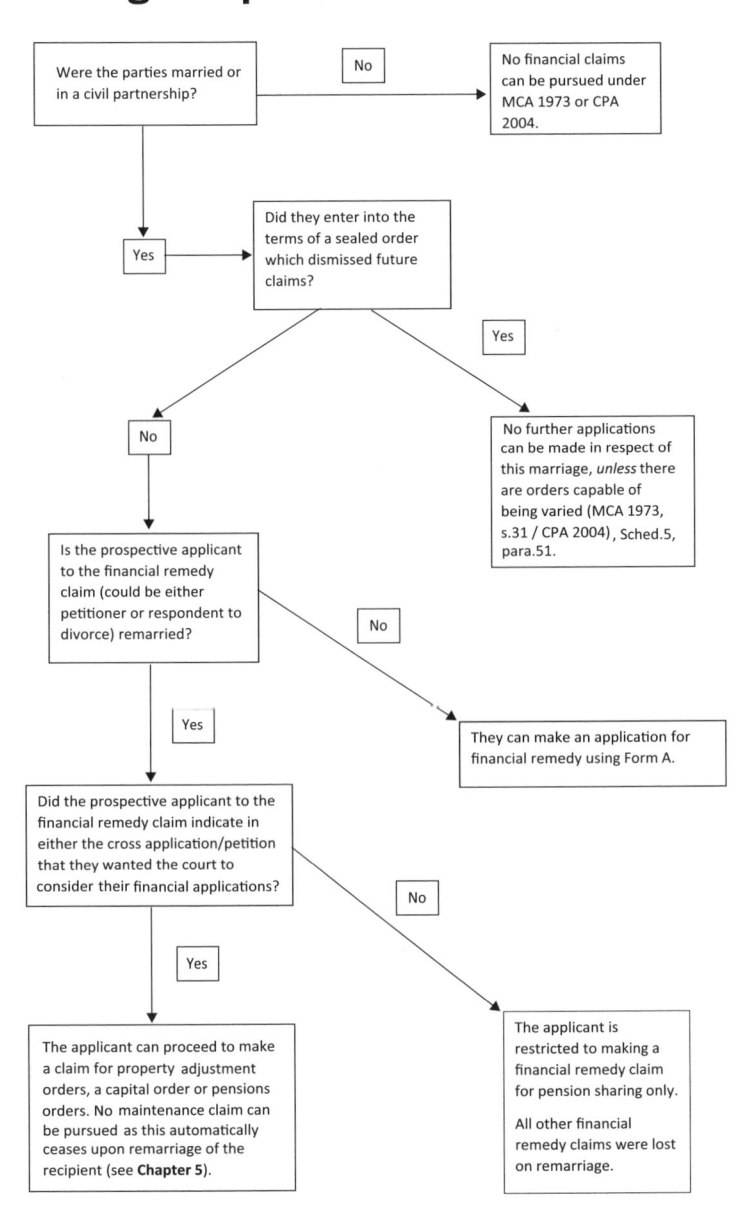

```
┌─────────────────────┐    No    ┌──────────────────────┐
│ Were the parties    │─────────▶│ No financial claims  │
│ married or in a     │          │ can be pursued under │
│ civil partnership?  │          │ MCA 1973 or CPA 2004.│
└──────────┬──────────┘          └──────────────────────┘
           │ Yes
           ▼
┌─────────────────────────────┐
│ Did they enter into the     │
│ terms of a sealed order     │
│ which dismissed future      │
│ claims?                     │
└──────┬──────────────┬───────┘
   No  │              │ Yes
       ▼              ▼
                ┌──────────────────────────┐
                │ No further applications  │
                │ can be made in respect   │
                │ of this marriage, unless │
                │ there are orders capable │
                │ of being varied (MCA     │
                │ 1973, s.31 / CPA 2004),  │
                │ Sched.5, para.51.        │
                └──────────────────────────┘
```

**Is the prospective applicant to the financial remedy claim (could be either petitioner or respondent to divorce) remarried?**

- **No** → They can make an application for financial remedy using Form A.
- **Yes** → Did the prospective applicant to the financial remedy claim indicate in either the cross application/petition that they wanted the court to consider their financial applications?
  - **Yes** → The applicant can proceed to make a claim for property adjustment orders, a capital order or pensions orders. No maintenance claim can be pursued as this automatically ceases upon remarriage of the recipient (see **Chapter 5**).
  - **No** → The applicant is restricted to making a financial remedy claim for pension sharing only. All other financial remedy claims were lost on remarriage.

177

APPENDIX C

# Financial remedies for children

## APPENDIX C1

# Income options for children flowchart

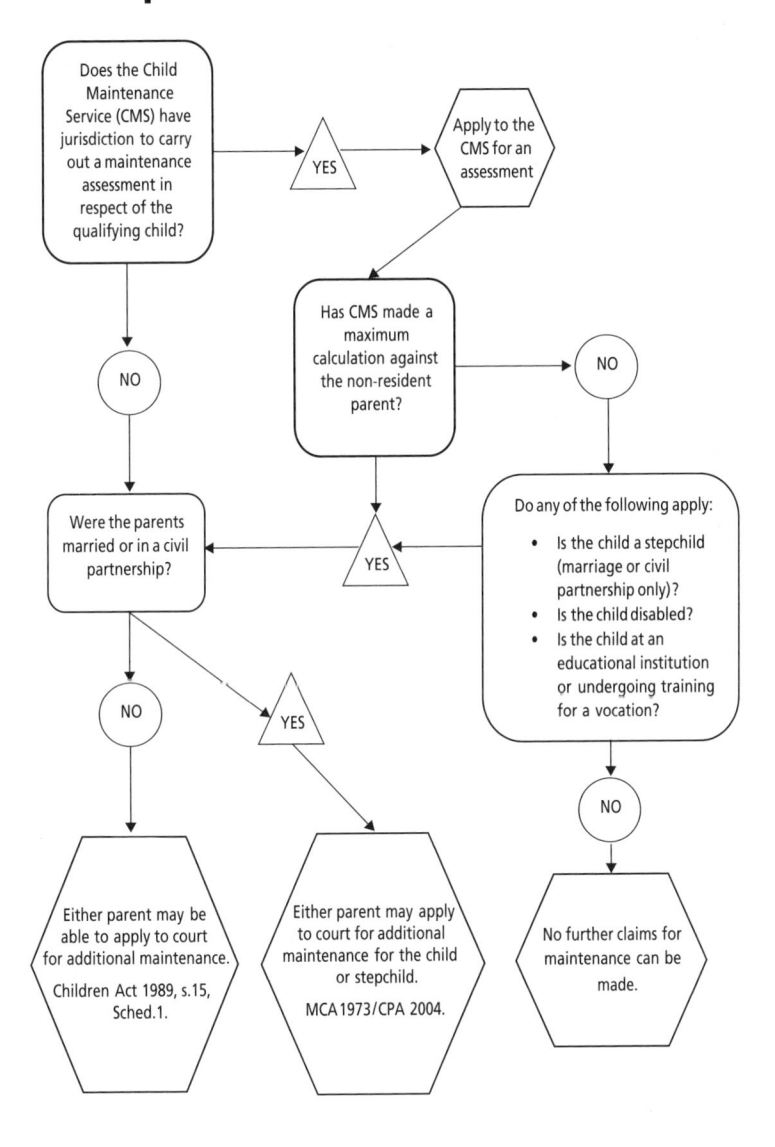

**Does the Child Maintenance Service (CMS) have jurisdiction to carry out a maintenance assessment in respect of the qualifying child?**

- YES → **Apply to the CMS for an assessment**
  - **Has CMS made a maximum calculation against the non-resident parent?**
    - YES → (see below: Were the parents married or in a civil partnership?)
    - NO → **Do any of the following apply:**
      - Is the child a stepchild (marriage or civil partnership only)?
      - Is the child disabled?
      - Is the child at an educational institution or undergoing training for a vocation?
      - YES → (see below: Were the parents married or in a civil partnership?)
      - NO → **No further claims for maintenance can be made.**
- NO → **Were the parents married or in a civil partnership?**
  - NO → **Either parent may be able to apply to court for additional maintenance.** Children Act 1989, s.15, Sched.1.
  - YES → **Either parent may apply to court for additional maintenance for the child or stepchild.** MCA 1973/CPA 2004.

APPENDIX C2

# Orders for children that can be made in divorce or dissolution proceedings

| Section | Order | From when/until when | Standard orders precedent | Notes |
|---|---|---|---|---|
| MCA 1973, s.23 / CPA 2004, Sched.5, Part 2. | Financial provision (secured) child periodical payments order (CPPO) for a child. Lump sum for a child. | Not enforceable until decree absolute or final order. The order shouldn't extend beyond the child's compulsory school age, unless the court considers that the welfare of the child requires that it should extend beyond that date. It shall not extend beyond the child's 18th birthday unless the child is undergoing education, training, or there are special circumstances. | Precedent 75 – CPPO pending Child Maintenance Service (CMS) calculation. Precedent 76 – CPPO. Precedent 77 – CPPO while child in tertiary education. Precedent 78 – CPPO for costs of disability. Precedent 79 – CPPO top-up order. School fees orders at precedents 81/82/83/84. No precedents for lump sum orders for children. However, standard order precedent 2.2 has provision at paras.50/51/52 that can be adapted. | Restriction in MCA 1973, s.29(1) should be observed, no orders can be made in favour of a child who has attained the age of 18. When the payer of a CPPO dies, the order terminates. |
| MCA 1973, s.24 / CPA 2004, Sched.5, Part 2, para.7. | Property adjustment orders. Includes transfer of property, settlement of property, variation of ante-/post-nuptial settlement. | Not enforceable until decree absolute or final order. | No precedents for transfers of property to children. However, standard order precedent 2.2 has provisions at paras.55 and 56 which could be adapted where a property is being provided for the benefit of children on trust. | Property transfers to children are extremely rare in divorce or dissolution proceedings. They are much more common in Children Act 1989 applications. |

APPENDIX D

# Negotiations and consent orders

# APPENDIX D1

# Negotiations and consent orders checklist

| Standard order number | Clause | Yes/No |
|---|---|---|
| 28 | Declaration regarding lump sum order(s) | |
| 31/32 | Declaration of intention not to seek a variation of a periodical payments order (receiving party or paying party) | |
| 33 | Declaration of intention to limit claims under the Inheritance (Provision for Family and Dependants) Act 1975 | |
| 34/35 | Declarations regarding Child Maintenance Service (CMS) involvement | |
| 36 | Undertaking to stand as guarantor | |
| 37 | Undertaking to discharge liabilities | |
| 38 | Undertaking to discharge arrears | |
| 39 | Undertaking to use best endeavours to secure release from liabilities | |
| 40 | Undertaking to mitigate capital gains tax liability | |
| 41/42/43/47 | Medical insurance cover provisions | |
| 44/45/46/48/49 | Life assurance policy provisions to consider | |
| 50 | Undertaking to leave by will / make financial arrangements on death | |
| 51 | Undertaking to obtain a get | |
| 52 | Undertaking not to disclose information | |
| 53/54/55 | Lump sum orders | |
| 56/57/58/59/64/65/66 | Property orders/transfer of tenancy/leasehold property indemnity and variation of settlement | |
| 60/61/62/63 | Property payment orders | |
| 67/68 | Company resignation and transfer of shares/company non-disclosure | |
| 69 | Transfer of car | |
| 70 | Transfer of life policy | |
| 71–74/87/88 | Periodical payments orders | |
| 75–79 | Child periodical payments | |
| 81 | Global maintenance order | |
| 82/84 | School fees orders | |
| 89 | Permission to disclose order to CMS | |

APPENDIX D1

| Standard order number | Clause | Yes/No |
|---|---|---|
| 90 | Variation: periodical payments | |
| 91 | Variation: lump sum or pension sharing in lieu of periodical payments | |
| 92 | Pension sharing order | |
| 93 | Nomination of death in service benefit | |
| 94 | Pension attachment order | |
| 95 | Declaration under the EU Maintenance Regulation | |
| 96/97 | Clean break provisions | |
| 98–102 | Costs orders | |

# Index

**Accreditations** 1.1
**Arbitration**
    after mediation 2.4.11
    arbitrator 2.6.1
    barristers 2.6.5
    cost of 2.6.7
    duration 2.6.6
    failure 2.6.11
    financial input 2.6.13
    guaranteed outcome 2.6.9
    nature of 2.6.1
    no legal aid 2.6.8
    non-disclosure in 3.5.2
    number of parties 2.6.3
    solicitors and 2.6.4
    success 2.6.12
    as voluntary process 2.6.2
    walking away 2.6.10
**Audio recordings of meetings** 1.4
**Available orders** 5.1
    clean break 5.2
    CPA 2004, Sched.5, Part 5 5.8
    MCA 1973, s.25 5.8
    remarriage/civil partnership trap 5.3.1
        application procedure 5.3.2
        flowchart App.B2
        pension-sharing applications post-remarriage 5.3.3
        table of App.B1
    *see also* Income claims; Lump sum orders; Pension orders; Property adjustment orders

**Charging models** 1.5
    billing weekly 1.5
    fixed-fee service 1.5
    hourly rate 1.5
    limited retainer 1.5
    retainer basis 1.5
    unbundled services 1.5

    *see also* Client payment methods; Payment
**Chatbots** 1.1
**Child Maintenance Service** 6.2.1
    absent parent 6.2.2
    applicants 6.2.4
    calculation 6.2.6
        child maintenance rates 6.2.6.1
    fee 6.2.4
    jurisdiction to make 6.2.3
    maximum CMS assessment 6.2.6.3
    shared care arrangements 6.2.6.2
    variation of 6.2.8
    child maintenance rates
        basic rate/basic rate plus 6.2.6.1
        flat rate 6.2.6.1
        nil rate 6.2.6.1
        reduced rate 6.2.6.1
    definitions 6.2.2
    paying party 6.2.5
    payment
        collect and pay 6.2.7.2
        direct pay 6.2.7.1
        enforcement of 6.2.9
    person with care 6.2.2
    qualifying child 6.2.2
    who can apply 6.2.4
**Children**
    applications following divorce/ dissolution proceedings 6.3.1, App.C2
    available orders 6.3.1
    costs 6.3.4
    factors for court consideration 6.3.2
    Form A 6.3.3
    global maintenance order 6.3.1
    procedure 6.3.3
    applications under Children Act 6.4.1
        applicants 6.4.2

**Children** – *continued*
   applications under Children
      Act – *continued*
     available orders 6.4.1
     costs orders 6.4.7
     duration of orders 6.4.4
     factors for court consideration
       6.4.5
     procedure 6.4.6
     respondent 6.4.3
     TLATA 1996 applications 6.5
     who can apply 6.4.2
   income options flowchart App.C1

**Civil partnership trap** *see*
Remarriage/civil partnership trap

**Clean break order** 5.2
   dismissal purposes only 5.2

**Client payment methods** 1.6.1, 1.6.3
   application to fund legal services
     1.6.3.6
   credit cards 1.6.3.3
   financial advice 1.6.3
   good practice guidance 1.6.2
   joint savings/investments 1.6.3.2
   legal aid 1.6.3.6, 1.6.3.8
   loans 1.6.3.3
     from friend/family member 1.6.3.4
     specialist litigation loan 1.6.3.5
   own capital/investments 1.6.3.1
   own income 1.6.3.1
   Sears Tooth agreement 1.6.3.7

**Collaborative family practice (CFP)**
   barristers 2.5.5
   cost of 2.5.7
   disclosure 3.3.3
     remedy for non-disclosure 3.5.1, 3.5.2
     voluntary 3.3.4
   duration 2.5.6
   failure 2.5.11
   family consultant (FC) 2.5.3
   financial input 2.5.13
   nature of 2.5.1
   no legal aid 2.5.8
   number of parties 2.5.3
   outcome 2.5.9
   solicitors and 2.5.4
   success 2.5.12
   as voluntary process 2.5.2
   walking away 2.5.10

**Committal applications**
   disclosure 3.7

**Conflicts of interests**
   checks 1.3.3
   personal conflict 1.3.3

**Consent orders** 8.1
   approval by judge 2.6.12, 8.1
   arbitration 2.6.12
   checklist App.D1
   drafted by mediators 2.4.12
   drafting services 8.1
   enforcement proceedings 8.4
   implementation 8.3.2
   procedural matters 8.3.1

**Costs estimates** 4.4.5.5, 4.5.3

**Costs orders**
   applications under Children Act
     6.4.7
   financial remedy procedure 4.11
   legal aid and 1.6.3.8
   negotiations 8.2.2.5

**Costs rules** 4.8

**Disclosure**
   between first appointment and FDR
     appointment 3.5.3, 4.5.5.2
   client helps themselves to spouse's
     documents 3.4
   civil consequences 3.4.5.1
   cloud storage folders 3.4.5.1
   confidential documents 3.4.2
   criminal consequences 3.4.5.1
   flowchart App.A2
   *Imerman* 3.4.2
   implied consent 3.4.3, 3.4.5.1
   lawful accessing of documents
     3.4.3
   obtained unlawfully 3.4.2
   in practice 3.4.4
   regulatory issues 3.4.5.2
   risks 3.4.5
   self-help approach 3.4.2
   unlawful accessing of documents
     3.4.3
   evidence from third parties 3.9
   Form C 3.3.2
   Form D81 3.3.1
   Form E
     contempt of court 3.3.2
     disclosure 3.3.2
     documentary evidence 3.3.2
     Form C 3.3.2
     large money cases 3.3.4
     NCDR disclosure 3.3.3
     statement of truth 3.3.2

# INDEX

voluntary disclosure 3.3.4
warnings 3.3.2
full, frank and clear 3.2
inspection 3.2
joining parties 3.10
NCDR disclosure 3.3.3
  remedy for non-disclosure 3.5.1
  voluntary 2.8.2, 3.3.4
non-disclosure
  adverse inferences 3.8
  in arbitration 3.5.2
  between first appointment and FDR appointment 3.5.3, 4.5.5.2
  committal applications 3.7
  evidence from third parties 3.9
  financial remedy proceedings 3.5.3
  NCDR non-disclosure 3.5.1
  penal notice 3.6
  remedy for 3.5
in practice 3.3
principle of 3.2
voluntary disclosure 3.3.4
  pre-application protocol 3.3.4, App.A1
  solicitors' negotiation 2.8.2

**Early neutral evaluation/private financial dispute resolution (ENE/private FDR)**
barristers 2.4.5, 2.7.5
cost of 2.7.7
disclosure 3.3.3
  remedy for non-disclosure 3.5.1, 3.5.2
  voluntary 3.3.4
duration 2.7.6
failure 2.7.11
financial input 2.7.13
nature of 2.7.1
no legal aid 2.7.8
number of parties 2.7.3
outcome 2.7.9
solicitors and 2.7.4
success 2.7.12
as voluntary process 2.7.2
walking away 2.7.10

**Experts** 7.1
after the final hearing 7.7
choosing 7.2
costs 7.6
court's consideration 7.3
duties 7.5
instructing 7.2

letter of instruction 7.4
pension on divorce expert (PODE) 5.7.5
shadow expert 7.1

**Financial dispute resolution appointment (FDR appointment)**
advocates 4.6.3
the appointment 4.6.3
consent order 4.6.4.2
directions for the future progress of case 4.6.5.1
FA used as 4.5.4
filing and serving requirements 4.6.2
heads of agreement 4.6.4.1
litigants in person 4.6.3
no deal 4.6.5
purpose 4.6.1
reaching an agreement 4.6.4
requirement to file open offers 4.6.5.2

**Financial remedy procedure** 4.1
after the first appointment 4.5.5
  delay 4.5.5.1
  further disclosure 3.5.3, 4.5.5.2
  housing particulars 4.5.5.5
  mortgage capacity evidence 4.5.5.5
  other directions 4.5.5.5
  schedule of assets 4.5.5.4
  schedule of deficiencies (SOD) 4.5.5.3
applications
  Family Court 4.3.1
  High Court 4.3.1
  standard procedure 4.2
costs estimates 4.4.5.5, 4.5.3
costs orders 4.11
costs rules 4.8
cross-applications
  possibility of 4.3.3.1
  when needed 4.3.3.2
dealing with delay 4.5.5.1
documents to be filed
  before FA hearing 4.4.5
  chronology 4.4.5.2
  estimate of costs 4.4.5.5
  questionnaire 4.4.5.3
  request for further documents 4.4.5.3
  statement of issues 4.4.5.1
evidence of suitable housing 4.5.5.5
FA hearing *see* First appointment hearing

**Financial remedy procedure** – *continued*
    fast-track procedure applications 4.10.1
      before first hearing 4.10.2
      at first hearing 4.10.3
    final hearing
      filing of open statement 4.7.3
      general rules 4.7.1
      trial bundle 4.7.2
    Form A
      cross-applications 4.3.3
      general rules 4.3.2.1
      service of 4.3.2
      service on third parties 4.3.2.2
    Form E 4.4.1
      documents missing from 4.4.4
      local court variations on filing 4.4.3
      use post-NCDR disclosure 4.4.2
    further disclosure after FA 3.5.3, 4.5.5.2
    housing particulars 4.5.5.5
    judgment orders 4.9
    mortgage capacity evidence 4.5.5.5
    schedule of assets 4.5.5.4
    schedule of deficiencies (SOD) 4.5.5.3
    statement of issues 4.4.5.1

**First appointment hearing (FA hearing)** 4.5.1
    costs estimates 4.4.5.5, 4.5.3
    documents to be filed before 4.4.5
      chronology 4.4.5.2
      costs estimate 4.4.5.5
      other requirements 4.4.5.4
      questionnaire 4.4.5.3
      request for further documents 4.4.5.3
      statement of issues 4.4.5.1
    FA order 4.5.2
    further disclosure after 3.5.3, 4.5.5.2
    objectives 4.5.1
    standard order templates 4.5.2
    use as FDR appointment 4.5.4

**First meeting with client** *see* Pre-instruction stage

**Fixed-fee service** 1.5

**Freelance solicitors** 1.2.1

**Housing**
    evidence of suitable housing 4.5.5.5
    file/exchange of particulars 4.5.5.5
    negotiations 8.2.2.1

**Income claims**
    capitalisation of an income stream 5.4.4.1
    maintenance order 5.4.4.3
    variation of applications 5.4.4.2
    duration
      extendable term 5.4.2.3
      general rules 5.4.2.1
      MCA 1973, s.28(1A) bar 5.4.2.2
      nominal order 5.4.2.1
      non-extendable term 5.4.2.2
    interim maintenance 5.4.1
      duration 5.4.2.1
    maintenance pending suit 5.4.1
      duration 5.4.2.1
    maintenance protection insurance 5.4.3.3
    negotiations 8.2.2.4
    nominal order 5.4.2.1, 5.4.3.1
    periodical payments 5.4.1
      death of paying party 5.4.3.3
      duration 5.4.2.1
      extendable term 5.4.2.3
      MCA 1973, s.28(1A) bar 5.4.2.2
      non-extendable term 5.4.2.2
    quantum
      death of paying party 5.4.3.3
      general rules 5.4.3.1
      maintenance protection insurance 5.4.3.3
      practice points 5.4.3.2
      security of parties 5.4.3.3
      universal credit 5.4.3.3
    secured periodical payments 5.4.1
      duration 5.4.2.1
    substantive maintenance order 5.4.3.1, 5.4.4.1, 5.4.4.3
    types of 5.4.1

**Judgment orders** 4.9

**Know your client checks (KYC checks)** 1.3.1

**Law Society accreditations** 1.1

**Legal aid** 1.6.3.6, 1.6.3.8
    arbitration 2.6.8
    collaborative family practice 2.5.8
    costs orders and 1.6.3.8
    ENE/private FDR 2.7.8
    mediation 1.6.3.8, 2.4.8
    MIAM 1.6.3.8, 2.3.8
    solicitors' negotiation 2.8.8

# INDEX

**Limited retainer** 1.5
**Litigant in person**
    enforcement proceedings 8.4
    FDR appointment 4.6.3
    McKenzie friends 1.2.2
    mediation 2.4.4
**Litigation loan specialists** 1.6.3.5
**Lump sum orders** 5.5.1
    adjourned application 5.5.3
    children 6.3.1
    instalments 5.5.1
    interest payable 5.5.2
      start date 5.5.2.1
    interim orders 5.5.4
    negotiations 8.2.2.2
    series of payments 5.5.1
    variation 5.5.1

**McKenzie friends** 1.2.2
**Maintenance protection insurance** 5.4.3.3
**Martin order** 5.6.5.4
**Mediation** 2.4
    barristers 2.4.5
    costs of 2.4.7
    disclosure 3.3.3
      remedy for non-disclosure 3.5.1, 3.5.2
      voluntary 3.3.4
    draft consent orders 2.4.12
    duration 2.4.6
    failure 2.4.11
    family mediation model 2.4.1
    financial input 2.4.13
    hybrid mediation 2.4.4
    legal aid 1.6.3.8, 2.4.8
    memorandum of understanding (MOU) 2.4.12
    nature of 2.4.1
    number of parties 2.4.3
    outcome 2.4.9
    screening 2.4.1
    solicitors 2.4.4
    success 2.4.12
    as voluntary process 2.4.2
    walking away 2.4.10
**Mediation information and assessment meeting (MIAM)** 2.3
    applicant referred to 2.3.2.2
    applicant's exemption to attend 2.3.2.1
    barristers 2.3.5
    cost of attending 2.3.7

    duration 2.3.6
    legal aid 1.6.3.8, 2.3.8
    mandatory attendance 2.3.2
    mediator's exemption 2.3.2.3
    number of parties 2.3.3
    outcome 2.3.9
    solicitors and 2.3.4
    walking away 2.3.10
**Mesher order** 5.6.5.3
**Money laundering** 1.3.1
    client identification 1.3.1
    number of reports 1.3.1
**Mortgage capacity evidence** 4.5.5.5

**Negotiations** 8.1
    checklist App.D1
    costs orders 8.2.2.5
    housing 8.2.2.1
    income orders 8.2.2.4
    lump sum 8.2.2.2
    offers without disclosure 8.1
    open offers 8.2
    pensions 8.2.2.3
    practical matters 8.2.3
    structure of offer to settle 8.2.2
    unachievable offers 8.1
    without prejudice 8.2
    without prejudice save as to costs 8.2
**Non-court dispute resolution (NCDR)** 1.7, 2.1, 2.9
    *see also* Arbitration; Collaborative family practice; Early neutral evaluation; Mediation; Mediation information and assessment meeting; Solicitors' negotiation

**Orders available** *see* Available orders

**Payment**
    information pre-instruction 1.3.2
    *see also* Charging models; Client payment methods
**Penal notice**
    disclosure order 3.6
**Pension orders**
    *A Guide to the Treatment of Pensions on Divorce* 5.7.2
    defined benefit (DB) pension 5.7.3
    defined contribution (DC) pension 5.7.3
    negotiations 8.2.2.3
    offsetting 5.7.1

# INDEX

**Pension orders** – *continued*
    PAG report 5.7.2
    pension attachment order (PAO) 5.7.1
    pension compensation attachment order (PCAO) 5.7.1
    pension compensation sharing order (PCSO) 5.7.1
    pension on divorce expert (PODE) 5.7.5
    pension sharing order (PSO) 5.7.1
      application post-remarriage 5.3.3
    type of pension 5.7.3
    types of 5.7.1
    value of pension 5.7.4
**Pre-instruction stage**
    charging models 1.5
    chatbot options 1.1
    conflicts of interests 1.3.3
    end of 1.8
    first meeting with client 1.1
      audio recording 1.4
    follow-up letter 1.8
    matters to consider 1.4
    money laundering 1.3.1
    NCDR options 1.7
    notes 1.8
    payment *see* Client payment methods; Payment
    pre-meeting information 1.1
    regulatory matters 1.3
**Private financial dispute resolution** *see* Early neutral evaluation
**Property adjustment orders**
    children 6.3.1
    home rights 5.6.4
    property sale 5.6.5.1
      Martin order 5.6.5.4
      Mesher order 5.6.5.3
      trigger events 5.6.5.2
    property transfers 5.6.2
    sole ownership 5.6.3
    types of 5.6.1

**Qualifications** 1.1
    unregulated services 1.2.2

**Remarriage/civil partnership trap** 5.3.1
    application procedure 5.3.2
    flowchart App.B2
    issue of Form A 4.3.2
    pension-sharing applications post-remarriage 5.3.3
**Resolution**
    accreditations 1.1
    Code of Practice 1.6.2

**Schedule of assets** 4.5.5.4
**Schedule of deficiencies (SOD)** 4.5.5.3
**Sears Tooth agreement** 1.6.3.7
**Shadow expert** 7.1
**Solicitors' negotiation**
    barristers 2.8.5
    cost of 2.8.7
    as delaying tactic 2.8.1, 2.8.10
    disclosure 3.3.3
      remedy for non-disclosure 3.5.1, 3.5.2
      voluntary 2.8.2, 3.3.4
    duration 2.8.6, 2.8.10
    failure 2.8.11
    financial input 2.8.13
    legal aid 2.8.8
    nature of 2.8.1
    number of parties 2.8.3
    outcome 2.8.9
    solicitors 2.8.4
    success 2.8.12
    as voluntary process 2.8.2
    walking away 2.8.10
**Specialist litigation loan** 1.6.3.5
**Statement of issues** 4.4.5.1

**Unbundled services** 1.5, 1.6.3.1
**Unregulated services**
    McKenzie friends 1.2.2